Pyrrho's Way

The Ancient Greek Version of Buddhism

Douglas C. Bates

Pyrrho's Way: The Ancient Greek Version of Buddhism
Douglas C. Bates

Text © Douglas C. Bates, 2020
All rights reserved

Editing and book design by John Negru
Cover illustration by Serge Stegloff

Published by
The Sumeru Press Inc.
Ottawa, ON, Canada

ISBN 978-1-896559-56-8

LIBRARY AND ARCHIVES CANADA CATALOGUING IN PUBLICATION

Title: Pyrrho's way : the ancient Greek version of Buddhism / Douglas C. Bates.
Names: Bates, Douglas C., 1959- author.
Identifiers: Canadiana 20200153781 | ISBN 9781896559568 (softcover)
Subjects: LCSH: Pyrrhon, of Elis. | LCSH: Buddhism—History—
To ca.100 A.D. | LCSH: Buddhism—
   Influence. | LCSH: Buddhism and philosophy.
Classification: LCC B613 .B38 2020 | DDC 186/.1—dc23

For more information about The Sumeru Press
visit us at *sumeru-books.com*

Contents

Preface

In Western Europe and North America, adherence to Christianity is collapsing. This collapse started in the Renaissance, in large part due to the rediscovery and publishing of ancient Greco-Roman texts, particularly philosophy texts, and most particularly the philosophy text that inspired this book: *Outlines of Pyrrhonism* by Sextus Empiricus (c. 160 - c. 210 CE, dates uncertain). As in any kind of process that follows exponential growth from a small beginning, the signs of this collapse were small and easy to disregard for a long time. This has now changed. For various reasons, the generations born since WWII have felt decreasing attraction to the Christian worldview. These people are now identifying as atheists, agnostics, nones (i.e., having no religious views), humanists, and spiritual but not religious. Some have adopted Eastern worldviews, most particularly with the spread of Buddhism, yoga, and Advaita Vedanta. Now, in small but increasing numbers, people are turning to pre-Christian Western philosophies of life. Some have turned to Stoicism, others to Epicureanism, and yet others to Aristotelianism. I have turned to Pyrrhonism.

Among the Hellenistic philosophies, medicine and surgery were standard analogies for the function of philosophy. Many of the great Pyrrhonist teachers in antiquity were physicians – so many that Pyrrhonism and the ancient Empiric school of medicine were almost synonymous. Like these other philosophies, Pyrrhonism can be understood as a health maintenance program for the mind. The central element in the Pyrrhonist mental health program is about distinguishing what constitutes knowledge. Pyrrhonism is mental hygiene about what to believe so that the mind is not infected with harmful thoughts, much like physical hygiene prevents the body from being infected with parasites and bacteria.

Most readers of this book will be encountering Pyrrhonism as a novel self-help approach. By "self-help," I am referring to psychological issues: how not to be depressed, angry, unhappy, and so on. Self-help about getting rich, or getting a lover, or other non-inner world matters are beyond the scope of this book, but not beyond Pyrrhonism. Peter Thiel[1] and Nassim Nicholas Taleb[2] describe Pyrrhonist thinking as important to their success.

---

1   https://www.nytimes.com/2017/01/11/fashion/peter-thiel-donald-trump-silicon-valley-technology-gawker.html

2   Nassim Nicholas Taleb, *The Black Swan: Second Edition: The Impact of the Highly Improbable*. 2010

Pyrrhonism is an ability to look at the issues of life in a particular way. Its practice entails a gestalt shift. It's like the ambiguous image that looked at one way is two faces, and another way is a vase. Many other examples of such ambiguous images are available, such as the one viewed one way shows a rabbit and another way a duck, or the one that viewed one way shows an old woman and another way a young woman. Upon encountering such images, some people have great difficulty seeing anything other than their first interpretation of the image. So it is with Pyrrhonism. In

this book you will encounter an alternative way of looking at reality that is difficult for some people to see. The aim of this book is to help the reader make this shift in perception, and this shift will relieve you of mental anguish.

A vase or two faces?

In the ancient era, books were written on scrolls. A longer work, such as this book, would require several scrolls, with each scroll traditionally being called a "book." Usually there would be some change of theme between books, but in many cases the limitation was simply how much text could fit on a scroll. In the era of scrolls there were no page numbers. Without page numbers there can be no index pages; there can only be tables of contents. Consequently, chapters were often short and focused on narrow subjects. This method of organization allowed some ability for looking things up. The work you have in your hands follows this ancient format. It is divided into six books, and each chapter is about a narrow topic.

The first book is the introduction. The second book outlines the basics of Pyrrhonism. The third book contrasts Pyrrhonism with other philosophies, to help clarify what Pyrrhonism is and is not. The fourth book provides extended discussions on aspects of Pyrrhonist practice, addressing common questions and confusions people have about Pyrrhonism. The fifth and final book discusses some historical confusion about Sextus Empiricus, whose surviving works are our best testament of ancient Pyrrhonism, and how the Roman Emperor Marcus Aurelius was influenced by Sextus.

Each chapter of the book begins with two introductory quotes. I urge readers to linger on these as a meditation. Most of these quotes foreshadow what is about to be said.

Outlines of Pyrrhonism, our best surviving account of ancient Pyrrhonism, says in its conclusion: "Because of his love of humanity the Pyrrhonist wishes to cure by argument, so far as he can, the conceit and precipitancy of the Dogmatists." If you should find the cure by argument presented in this book helpful to you, for your love of humanity, please consider how you can best share the cure with others.

Timeline

Note: Most of these dates are known only approximately. Particularly uncertain dates are noted with question marks.

570 – 475 BCE	Xenophanes	155 – 130 BCE	Milinda (Menander)
535 – 475 BCE	Heraclitus	106 – 43 BCE	Cicero
490 – 420 BCE	Protagoras	Circa 50 BCE	Aenesidemus
483 – 375 BCE	Gorgias	46 – 120 CE	Plutarch
480 – 400 BCE?	Buddha	55 – 135 CE	Epictetus
460 – 370 BCE	Democritus	Circa 50 CE	Aristocles
470 – 399 BCE	Socrates		of Messene
424 – 348 BCE	Plato	Circa 80 CE	Agrippa
384 – 322 BCE	Aristotle	80 – 160 CE	Favorinus
360 – 270 BCE	Pyrrho	121 – 180 CE	Marcus Aurelius
356 – 323 BCE	Alexander	Circa 170 CE	Sextus Empiricus
	the Great	150 – 250 CE	Nagarjuna
334 – 262 BCE	Zeno	Circa 250 CE?	Diogenes Laertius
	of Citium	265 – 340 CE	Eusebius
320 – 235 BCE	Timon	Circa 500 CE	Jianzhi Sengcan
	of Philius	Circa 800 CE	Huang Po
316 – 241 BCE	Arcesilaus	1533 – 1592 CE	Montaigne
327 – 325 BCE	**Pyrrho in India**		

....

To study Pyrrhonism is to study belief.
To study belief is to cease to believe.
To cease to believe is eudaimonia.

....

Book I
Introduction

1
Pyrrho's Journey to the East

...[Pyrrho] even went as far as the Gymnosophists, in India, and the Magi. Owing to which circumstance, he seems to have taken a noble line in philosophy....

Diogenes Laertius,
Life of Pyrrho

...whatever Greeks acquire from foreigners is finally turned by them into something nobler....

Plato (or more likely his student, Philip of Opus),
Epinomis

Even in antiquity Westerners looked to India for wisdom. We know the Neoplatonist philosopher, Plotinus, tried to go to there but had to turn back. Some people even claim – on scant evidence – that Jesus went there. But there's only one Westerner from antiquity whom we know not only went to India, but who brought back something that profoundly influences Western thought to this day. His name was Pyrrho. He was a priest at the Temple of Zeus at Olympia, and a philosopher in the tradition of Democritus. Pyrrho successfully made the trip because he was a member of Alexander the Great's court during Alexander's conquest of everything from Greece to India. Alexander had assigned the several philosophers in his court to learn everything they could about the philosophies of his newly conquered lands. Pyrrho spent a year and a half in India (327 – 325 BCE) doing exactly that.

Pyrrho carried with him to India two problems. In the decades following Democritus' death (circa 370 BCE), two key elements of Democritean philosophy had come under attack, first by Plato, and then forcefully and persuasively by Aristotle.

Democritus had outlined a philosophical system for achieving a happy and fulfilling life, based on strategies for eliminating unpleasant and unhelpful mental states and cultivating positive ones such that the resulting peace of mind would lead to a life of virtue. Aristotle countered with a detailed system based on the virtue ethics conceived of by Socrates: that acting in accordance with virtue leads to peace of mind – the inverse of Democritus' formula.

The other problem was worse. Aristotle had persuasively argued that Democritus was wrong about the fundamental nature of knowledge, again starting with ideas conceived of by Socrates. Since the validity of any philosophical system rests upon its epistemology, Aristotle's attack was an existential threat to the entirety of Democritean philosophy.

The Greeks had for long noted a distinction between appearance and reality, based on observations such as how when an oar is put into water it appears bent, and how square towers seen from a distance look round. As appearances were known to deceive, the great epistemological question was about how much they could be relied upon to lead us to the truth about reality. Democritus built upon the views of earlier Greek philosophers, particularly Heraclitus, Xenophanes, and Parmenides, all of whom argued that obtaining the truth about reality was either impossible or highly limited. Aristotle rejected this. In his Metaphysics he declared that Democritus and these earlier philosophers were wrong, and he laid out his theory about how truth was accessible.

In India Pyrrho found a unified solution to both of these problems. He brought it back to Greece and built a new school of philosophy on it: Pyrrhonism, which flourished along with other schools of pagan philosophy until they were exterminated as part of the Christianization of the Roman Empire.

In the 19th Century, when Buddhist texts were starting to become available in European languages, scholars began noticing uncanny similarities between Pyrrhonism and Buddhism. Nietzsche even called Pyrrho "a Buddha." But it would not be until the early 21st Century that it was finally proven by Christopher I. Beckwith, a philologist specializing in the ancient languages used on the Silk Road connecting trade between the ancient civilizations of the East and the West that the solution Pyrrho found involved repurposing key ideas from Buddhism.

Among the Buddhist ideas that identifiably influenced Pyrrho were nirvana, enlightenment, the Three Marks of Existence, the Three Poisons and their Antidotes, and the idea that the root cause of our mental suffering is delusion – all of which he reshaped to make them compatible with Greek thought and useful against Aristotle. On top of this Buddhist philosophical foundation, Pyrrho built an innovative technology. For reasons we can only speculate about, he did not bring back to Greece the Buddhist technology of meditation. Instead he took techniques that already existed in Greek thought – principally from Democritus, Protagoras, Gorgias, and the Megarians – synthesizing them and repurposing them to achieve ends that meditation achieves, all the way to the point of there being a Pyrrhonist version of kensho (enlightenment experience).

Around all of this – due to the fact that the schools of philosophy of ancient Greece criticized each other – subsequent Pyrrhonists built a thick shell of philosophical armor around Pyrrho's nucleus of Buddhist ideas. They repositioned Pyrrhonism as an anti-philosophy philosophy, much as how some people view Zen Buddhism to be.

Nearly all of Western philosophy serves the end of building up of the ego. Look at how clever we humans are for figuring all this stuff out! We are like gods! Pyrrhonism, like Buddhism, is an assault on the ego. To be successful in that assault, Pyrrhonism was built to breach the philosophical conceits of the Western ego. Pyrrhonism turns rationality onto itself, using the same tools we use to build up our sense of who we are and what our world is to dismantle those constructions, leaving each of us with what is known in the metaphorical language of Zen as our original face: the face we had before our parents were born. As a consequence, Pyrrhonism has induced viscerally negative reactions from other philosophers, from antiquity to modernity. Pyrrhonists so riled the Stoic philosopher Epictetus that he thought they should be tortured. One modern so-called "expert" in Pyrrhonism, Professor Jonathan Barnes, called them "quacks" and advertisers of falsehoods. Between these two are countless more who have misunderstood, mischaracterized, and maligned Pyrrhonism.

Unlike Buddhism, Pyrrhonism doesn't come in a warm and fuzzy wrapper. It's not a religion. Its approach isn't mystical. Meditation is not one of its techniques. It's not joined at the hip with an ethics of compassion. Pyrrhonism is a philosophy. Its approach for producing peace of mind is as coldly technical as the assembly instructions for a Japanese bicycle. Its message about the nature of ethics acts like an acid, not a balm.

These are features, not bugs. Pyrrho did something wise and innovative. He reformulated the active ingredients of Buddhism for improved effectiveness in the conditions of the rationalistic Western mind. Pyrrhonism works on minds that are as fully conditioned to adhering to the law of non-contradiction as they are to the law of gravity. Instead of using meditation to launch the mind beyond the sphere of the mundane, producing an experience that grants a new perspective, Pyrrhonism pours rationality onto the ground we think we're standing upon, dissolving it until the ground beneath us disappears, producing a similar experience.

But how do you say "enlightenment" in ancient Greek?

2
Eudaimonia

...philosophy begins in wonder.   *Socrates,*
                                                   Theaetetus

Philosophy does not begin in wonder. It begins in anxiety, with the disquieting suspicion that things are not
how they should be and are not what they seem.
                                            Hans Abendroth,
                                     The Zero and the One

To make Buddhist ideas fit into Greek thinking, one of the first things
Pyrrho had to address was the issue of religion. In India the roles of
philosopher and saint were merged, philosophy and religion were fused,
and innovations in both were tolerated. While the situation in Greece had
once been similar, this had since changed. Three hundred years earlier the
philosopher Thales helped formulate the Delphic Maxims. These maxims functioned as a simple philosophy of life. They were promulgated as
the dictates of the god Apollo and spread throughout the Greek-speaking
world. Two hundred years earlier the Pythagoreans also mixed religion
and philosophy, innovating in both. Then an event happened that would
cleave forever religion and philosophy in Greek and subsequent Western
thought: the sentencing of Socrates to death on charges of introducing
new gods.

Pyrrho knew he could not make Pyrrhonism religious in the way
Buddhism was. Perhaps this was one of the motivations behind his innovations. He knew that any talk of holiness or mystical states or any implications of his philosophy on the gods was a non-starter. This constraint
likely spurred him to employ what in Buddhism is called *upaya* – praise-
worthy application of skillful means – for enlightening his fellow Greeks
using tools he had at hand.

The first thing where Pyrrho would have had to apply upaya was the
Buddhist concept of enlightenment. As the Greeks didn't have a concept
quite like enlightenment, Pyrrho would have to use a concept they would
understand. In Greek the most similar concept is "eudaimonia." Like how
the Buddha saw greed, anger, and delusion as the barriers to enlightenment, the Greeks saw unpleasant and unhealthy emotions, such as anger,
envy, and anxiety as the barriers to eudaimonia. "Eudaimonia" is typically

translated into English as "happiness." This is an unsatisfactory translation, but English has no single word that encompasses the idea. Perhaps
better translations would be "flourishing" or "blessedness." Eudaimonia is
about a happy, flourishing, meaningful life achieved through wisdom. It
is a practical concept, devoid of the spiritual attributes of enlightenment.
For Pyrrho's purposes, this made the term well-suited for his objectives.

Besides this, eudaimonia was nearly universally agreed upon as the
goal of life. Aristotle had claimed that it was self-evidently the goal. All of
the Hellenistic philosophies of life share this goal, giving them a vibrancy
and relevancy to human existence that religions have. They are not philosophy as dry, academic hair-splitting about things normal people are not
interested in. Their chief concerns are wisdom, character development,
and the best way to live. They are philosophies one practices, much like
how one practices Buddhism.

Religion and philosophy were not the only things intertwined in antiquity and the era that came before it. Medicine was mixed in as well. In
pre-literate tribal societies the role of holy man, wise man, and medicine
man were wound together in the person of the shaman. This connection
would continue more loosely with the Hellenistic philosophies. Doctors
commonly studied philosophy and philosophical schools would have
connections with schools of medicine. People saw philosophy as a cure
for the ills of the soul, and medical metaphors were commonly used to
describe how a philosophy helped practitioners attain eudaimonia. For
example, Epictetus described Stoicism as "a surgery. You are not to go out
of it with pleasure, but with pain; for you do not come there in health."
Remember, ancient surgery was without anesthesia. The Stoic cure was
advertised as a painful but heroic intervention to induce eudaimonia. The
Epicurean approach, on the other hand, was the *tetrapharmakos* – literally
the "four-part remedy." It's a collection of recommendations for achieving
eudaimonia described as a recipe for a drug.

Pyrrhonism also uses a medical metaphor. This is particularly appropriate because, of all of the Hellenistic philosophies, Pyrrhonism was the
one most closely associated with medicine. Many of the great Pyrrhonist
teachers were doctors, and Pyrrhonism was so closely allied with the Empiric school of medicine that for all practical purposes Pyrrhonism served
as the theoretical branch and the Empirics as the applied branch of the
same school of thought.

The good news is that Pyrrhonism's prescription for eudaimonia is
not nearly so unpleasant as surgery without anesthesia. The recovery is
much faster, and it comes without scars or possible surgical errors. Like
the tetrapharmakos, it's a drug, which makes it easier to take.

But let's not forget about efficacy. Consider whether the tetrapharmakos will be effective for your condition. Its ingredients are:

1. Don't fear god.
2. Don't worry about death.
3. What is good is easy to get.
4. What is terrible is easy to endure.

If this concoction produces eudaimonia for you – and historically a large number of people claim it did for them – that's wonderful. But I suspect that few readers of this book will find these ingredients impressive; although in its defense I need to point out that it gives useful advice that many people need to hear, particularly with ingredient #3. Most people profoundly misunderstand what will make them happy. They go chasing after hard-to-get things that won't make them happy and ignore easy-to-get things that will. I've sampled a range of lifestyles from living in the austere conditions of a Japanese Rinzai Zen monastery to being a C-level executive at a publicly traded company. I was happier in the monastery.[3]

The Pyrrhonist prescription is not a typical kind of drug. It's a purgative. It works like how one treats food poisoning, by inducing vomiting to get rid of the poison. The poison Pyrrhonism purges is delusion – the delusion that causes suffering. The experience of this purgative is like that of other purgatives. When the effect kicks in, it's not pleasant, but you soon rid yourself of what is ailing you and you recover.

---

3   Eshin Nishimura gives a lovely account about how the happiest days of his life were at the same monastery, in *Unsui: A Diary of Zen Monastic Life*.

....

3

The Allegory of the Cave

Science and mathematics were to be removed from the hands of the merchants and the artisans. This tendency found its most effective advocate in a follower of Pythagoras named Plato. ... He (Plato) believed that ideas were far more real than the natural world. He advised the astronomers not to waste their time observing the stars and planets. It was better, he believed, just to think about them. Plato expressed hostility to observation and experiment. He taught contempt for the real world and disdain for the practical application of scientific knowledge. Plato's followers succeeded in extinguishing the light of science and experiment that had been kindled by Democritus and the other Ionians.   *Carl Sagan*

The mythos is insane. That's what he believed. The mythos that says the forms of this world are real but the Quality of this world is unreal, that is insane! And in Aristotle and the ancient Greeks he believed he had found the villains who had so shaped the mythos as to cause us to accept this insanity as reality.   *Robert M. Pirsig,*
Zen and the Art of
Motorcycle Maintenance

One of the founding myths of Western thinking is Plato's Allegory of the Cave, which appears in his famous book, *Republic*. Plato has his character, Socrates, describe a group of prisoners who have lived all of their lives chained to the wall of a cave, facing a blank wall. The prisoners watch shadows projected on the wall from objects passing in front of a fire behind them. The standards of knowledge that prevail in the cave are based on the abilities to describe what passes by, to remember and record the images, and to predict what images would come next. One day a prisoner breaks his bonds and leaves the cave. By seeing the sun and the natural world above the ground he discovers that reality was not what he thought it was. He feels elation. A wonderful thing has happened to him. He has discovered true knowledge. Socrates says that if the prisoner returns to the cave to tell his fellow prisoners about his discovery, his eyes would have become accustomed to the sunlight, impairing his ability to see in the dark light of the cave. If that prisoner then were to describe his observations of the world above and his opinions of the shadows, the other prisoners would ridicule him.

This myth appears to be deeply imbedded in how people think, not only about knowledge, but also what gets called "enlightenment." Pyrrhonism aims to disabuse people of this myth.

The myth stands on a foundation of common experience. We've all had ah-ha moments where we have come to understand something we did not previously understand. This myth exploits that experience, but it moves the goalposts in both directions. In this myth, Plato creates the idea that what we experience through our senses is not real. Reality is something else, something behind the appearances: the world outside the cave. Plato proposes that the purpose of philosophy (or spiritual training) is to release the human mind from the bonds of the illusory appearances to get to the reality that lies beyond. The result of getting to that reality will be eudaimonia.

Plato, ever the aristocrat that he was, uses the allegory of the cave to divide people into the elite who know – the philosophers – and the ignorant masses. Yet we have no proof that anyone has ever left the cave. The only ways we could have such a proof is if we were to leave the caves ourselves. Plato is perpetrating a con. What we see in the cave is as real as things get for us – which is not to affirm that they are accurate representations of reality. The claims of knowledge that come from beyond the cave cannot be tested for accuracy and are at least as likely to be delusions as truth. Plato, however, paints a flattering picture for this inverted view. It is inverted, because it is not the people in the cave who are held in bondage, but those who think they have left the cave. They think they see things that are not there, and they lose the ability to see things that are there. Even in Plato's story, Socrates has to concede that leaving the cave causes vision impairment in the cave, as the effects of thinking you know things from outside the cave produced obvious impairments.

Pyrrhonism transforms the experience of living in the cave similarly to how Buddhism does it. In Buddhism *samsara* (the common mundane view of existence) and *nirvana* (the enlightened view of existence) are recognized as being the same thing. What changes is the interpretation. With this change in interpretation, the person is changed. Hakuin's *Song of Zazen* puts it this way:

All beings by nature are Buddha,
As ice by nature is water.
Apart from water there is no ice;
Apart from beings, no Buddha.
How sad that people ignore the near
And search for truth afar:
Like someone in the midst of water
Crying out in thirst...

The mind flows like water until it gets frozen with delusion. People think they have to search for truth outside the cave to attain eudaimonia, yet what they desire is at hand. They search like someone in the midst of water, crying out in thirst. All they need to do is melt the ice.

Pyrrhonism seeks to disabuse people of delusive thinking about what is beyond the cave, and to reorient their attention back to what is going on in the cave. In Buddhism this can be described as a process of bringing attention to the present moment and letting go of attachments. Pyrrhonism uses a different technique for achieving similar ends. Instead of orienting mind to the present moment it restores the standards of wisdom of the cave. Instead of training the mind to let go of attachments it trains the mind to dissolve the rationale for attachments.

" let go of the rationale for attachments
gaze within to the source of the
attachment... nowhere to be found "

4
Dukkha

I discovered that when I believed my thoughts, I suffered, but that when I didn't believe them, I didn't suffer, and that this is true for every human being. Freedom is as simple as that. I found that suffering is optional. I found a joy within me that has never disappeared, not for a single moment. That joy is in everyone, always.

Byron Katie

If with a pure mind a person speaks or acts happiness follows him like his never-departing shadow.

Shakyamuni Buddha[4]

The Buddha famously declared "life entails *dukkha*." The term "dukkha" is typically translated into English as "suffering," "stress," or "unsatisfactoriness." No single English word conveys the full meaning of the term. While people disagree about how to translate "dukkha" they don't disagree with the Buddha's proclamation.

Dukkha comes in two varieties. One is the physical pain associated with conditions unfavorable for our bodies, such as hunger, cold, and disease. The other is the mental pain that comes from how we think about things. Great advances have been made in addressing physical suffering, but for mental suffering it appears we have not advanced much – if any – beyond the wisdom of the ancients. In antiquity many approaches were developed for dealing with this second kind of dukkha. Buddhism is just one of those approaches; the Hellenistic philosophies are among the others.

Buddhism is still new to the West. The most recent religion to have converted such a sizable number of Western adherents was Christianity. It took 200 years for Christianity to become a sizable movement, 300 years have sizable areas where it was in the majority, and 600 years to become the majority religion nearly everywhere in the Roman Empire. Buddhism started attracting its first Western converts in the early 20th Century. Organized groups of Western converts first began appearing in the 1960s.

I started practicing Zen in 1991. My observation is that how Buddhism is taught in the West is not working well enough for any but a small minority of people to stick with it. Every long-time member of

---

4 *Dhammapada*, Chapter 1, Verse 2.

a Buddhist practice group has observed that far more people read about Buddhism than ever try to practice it, that few people who try practicing Buddhism stick with it for long, and most of those eventually leave. I've stayed with two practice groups long enough to see 100% turnover of the other participants.

My suggestion in this regard is that Pyrrhonism should be recognized as a previous and successful effort to bring the core message of Buddhism to the West and that Pyrrhonism has upaya to teach the current generation of Western Buddhists. I have immersed myself in Pyrrhonist practice for the past six years. I am writing to testify that it works like the ancient Pyrrhonists claim it does. It works towards the same ends that many Buddhist practices works towards, albeit using a different method. I am also writing to testify that much of what the Western academic literature has to say about Pyrrhonism is about as accurate about Pyrrhonism as descriptions of bicycling would be if they were written by someone who has never ridden a bicycle, never seen one being ridden, never spoken to someone who has ridden one, and who has decided that they can figure it out based on the analyzing the contents of a bicycle assembly manual. As the Zen teacher Taisen Deshimaru said, "If you have a glass full of liquid you can discourse forever on its qualities, discuss whether it is cold, warm, whether it is really and truly composed of H_2O, or even mineral water, or sake. Meditation is drinking it!" No modern Westerner has ever published a report of drinking Pyrrhonism. I suspect that in a few decades some of the existing academic descriptions of Pyrrhonism will look as misguided as some 19th Century Western texts describing Buddhism look now, with their odd interpretation of *sunyata* as being worshiping of "The Void."

My story about drinking Pyrrhonism begins at a time when I felt my Zen practice was stuck. This is not unusual. While I cannot say I've conducted a poll about the matter, based on the things I've heard from others over the years I'm sure this is not only common, but it may well be ubiquitous among long-term practitioners. What I did while feeling stuck was – without abandoning Zen – to explore the Hellenistic philosophies starting with Stoicism. Beginning in the 2000s a revival movement began forming for Stoicism. Already innumerable new books are now on the market about how to practice Stoicism. These and the many articles about the movement drew my attention. After reading several of the first modern books on Stoicism I switched to reading the ancient texts. There's not that much to read. Almost everything we know about Stoicism comes from a modest number of surviving ancient texts, mostly from the Stoic authors Epictetus, Seneca, Marcus Aurelius, and Musonius Rufus, plus a few fragments from other Stoics. This can be fleshed out some more with a few other ancient authors who were not Stoics but who wrote about Stoicism, mostly Cicero, Diogenes Laertius, and Plutarch.

Interestingly, some of the better-known modern Stoic authors such as William Irvine and Massimo Pigliucci report that they seriously considered Buddhism before deciding to follow Stoicism. These days Stoicism and Buddhism are frequently compared. There's even now an entire book devoted to this subject. I predict that in the coming years Stoicism will increasingly become a serious competitor to Buddhism. For Westerners, Stoicism feels both readily graspable, due to its emphasis on rationality, and culturally familiar, due to the fact that many key thinkers of the early Christian church were influenced by Stoicism and built upon Stoic ideas to interpret Christian doctrine.

While I found Stoicism to be interesting and useful, and I would recommend to anyone that they should learn about Stoicism, I found myself coming to the conclusion that its cure for dukkha was partial at best and brought with it a new set of problems. Epictetus was right to compare Stoicism with surgery. I've had several surgeries in my life. While most of them worked, some produced new problems and all of them left scars. And that's with modern techniques, not the ancient techniques the Stoics used as a basis of comparison.

Cicero, Diogenes Laertius, and Plutarch wrote about other Hellenistic philosophies, too. To some degree an interest in any Hellenistic philosophy entails an interest in them all because they all tend to criticize each other and to define themselves in contrast with one another. Any substantial interest in one of them leads to them all. So, I read on to the others until I finally came to Pyrrhonism, which is best known to us in the writings of the ancient Pyrrhonist philosopher, Sextus Empiricus, and for which no modern how-to guide existed.

I was barely into Sextus' most important surviving work, *Outlines of Pyrrhonism*, when I felt an epiphany: I was reading the works of a Western Zen Master who was expressing Buddhist ideas in the rational and precise language of Greek philosophy instead of the metaphorical and paradoxical language of the Buddhists. At the time I had no idea that there was a connection between Pyrrhonism and Buddhism. The publication of the proof of that connection was still years in the future. Despite Sextus' cautious, complex, and legalistic writing style, and the obscurity of the antiquarian examples he provided as illustrations, for me it was the clearest "Buddhist" text I'd ever encountered. Even more interesting was the fact that Sextus offered a set of practices wholly unlike those of Buddhism. Maybe those would work better for me than mediation did. Maybe they would get me unstuck. As I started practicing the Pyrrhonist methods for relieving dukkha, I found that they worked better, faster, and more reliably than anything I ever learned from Buddhism. Without this suffering, I became not only happier, I became a clearer thinker.

After some time of practicing Pyrrhonism, I started noticing correspondences between what I understood from Pyrrhonism and issues brought up by the writer who first aroused my curiosity about Zen: Robert Pirsig. I noticed that the Pyrrhonists criticized Aristotle for much of the same reasons Pirsig had. Instead of importing Buddhist meditation into Greece, Pyrrho substituted techniques created by the Sophists – the same Sophists that Pirsig suspected were the real teachers of wisdom. I recalled a passage in *Zen and the Art of Motorcycle Maintenance* where Pirsig – or more specifically "Phaedrus," his name for his personality before he was subjected to the electroconvulsive therapy that wiped out most of his memory – described what caused him to give up on Eastern philosophy:

> …Phaedrus never got involved in meditation because it made no sense to him. In his entire time in India "sense" was always logical consistency and he couldn't find any honest way to abandon this belief. That, I think, was creditable on his part.
>
> But one day in the classroom the professor of philosophy was blithely expounding on the illusory nature of the world for what seemed the fiftieth time and Phaedrus raised his hand and asked coldly if it was believed that the atomic bombs that had dropped on Hiroshima and Nagasaki were illusory. The professor smiled and said yes. That was the end of the exchange.
>
> Within the traditions of Indian philosophy that answer may have been correct, but for Phaedrus and for anyone else who reads newspapers regularly and is concerned with such things as mass destruction of human beings that answer was hopelessly inadequate. He left the classroom, left India and gave up.

Half a century has passed since Pirsig gave up, but every day in Buddhist centers across the West other people give up too, and for much the same reasons – reasons which Pyrrhonism can address.

When Pirsig was writing *Zen and the Art of Motorcycle Maintenance*, few scholars had written anything about Pyrrhonism. Unless Pirsig had chosen the approach that I had – to read across all of the Hellenistic philosophies directly from ancient sources – he would have had little chance to encounter Pyrrhonism. The approach Pirsig chose was to look for criticisms of Aristotle. While it's true that Pyrrho criticized Aristotle, at the time Pirsig was writing, Pyrrho's criticism was shrouded in obscurity, surviving only as a quote buried in a 4th Century Christian text. It took until the early 21st Century for anyone with enough understanding of both ancient Greek and Pali to detect that the three Greek words Pyrrho used in that criticism were the best equivalents available in his language for expressing the three Pali words that describe the Buddhist Three Marks of Existence: *anatta, anicca, dukkha.*

No wonder I had that reaction to reading Sextus Empiricus! Sextus really was expressing Buddhist ideas! And if Sextus could express those ideas clearly using the vocabulary of Pyrrhonism, perhaps that vocabulary could be substituted for confusing Buddhist ways of saying things.

From my earliest days of Zen practice I have had an instinctive attraction to the *Xinxin Ming,* a poem attributed to the Third Zen Patriarch, Jianzhi Sengcan – not that I particularly understood it, but I had a gut sense that it addressed the dukkha that ailed me. My attraction to this poem was so strong that I even had it recited at my Zen Buddhist wedding. When I emailed it to my non-Buddhist friend, Cliff, who was to recite it, Cliff responded that he thought the text I had sent him must have gotten corrupted because it made no sense. Cliff has a Ph.D. in English from Yale. The text is that hard to understand.

Even the title of the poem perplexes translators. "Xin" has a variety of meanings, and using the term twice in a row adds to the confusion. The result has been large variations on how to translate it, with different translations implying such different understandings that at least some of them must be terribly misleading.

- Inscribed on the Believing Mind
- Verses on the Faith Mind
- Inscription on Faith in Mind
- Inscription on Trust in the Mind
- Have Faith in Your Mind
- The Mind of Absolute Trust
- Trusting in Mind
- Affirming Faith in Mind
- Faith in Mind
- Trust in Mind
- Faith in Heart-and-Mind
- Faith Mind Sutra

You may be familiar with the most popular translation of its often-quoted first lines:

> The Great Way is not difficult
> for those who do not pick and choose.
>
> When preferences are cast aside
> the Way stands clear and undisguised.
>
> But even slight distinctions made
> set earth and heaven far apart.

With my knowledge of Pyrrhonism I started seeing parts of the *Xinxin Ming* where words could be swapped out with Pyrrhonist terms. Each time I did that, the poem made more sense, and as it made more sense I saw more words that could be replaced, until the entire poem could be restated as Pyrrhonist. I found that this trick worked not only with the *Xinxin Ming*, but with many other Buddhist texts. Some Zen koans also became less enigmatic to me when I reconsidered them as Pyrrhonist case studies.

Classical Chinese is not nearly as precise as ancient Greek or modern English, as its small number of ideographs must convey a wide range of meanings which are differentiated among several words in languages such as ancient Greek and modern English, and even more differentiated within the technical philosophical vocabularies of those languages. You've already seen one example of how the ambiguity of Classical Chinese makes it difficult to translate just the three words of "xin xin ming" into English. The most outstanding example of this difficulty I've encountered can be found in *The Zen Teachings of Huang Po*, a Zen text that has much in common with Pyrrhonism. Expressing what I see as Pyrrhonist ideas in Classical Chinese produces baffling statements such as this one from that text, whose ideographs are literally rendered as:

> Dharma original Dharma not Dharma, not Dharma
> Dharma also Dharma, now transmit Dharma not Dhar-
> ma Dharma, Dharma Dharma how can be Dharma.

One translator, John Blofeld,[5] gives that sentence this meaning: "the fundamental doctrine of the Dharma is that there are no Dharmas, yet this doctrine of no-Dharma is in itself a Dharma; and now that the no-Dharma doctrine has been transmitted, how can the doctrine of the Dharma be

---

5   John Blofeld, *The Zen Teachings of Huang Po*, pp 64-65.

a Dharma?" Another translator, John R. McRae,[6] gives it this meaning: "The Dharma is fundamentally the Dharma as non-Dharma; the non-Dharma is the Dharma and still the Dharma. In the present conferral of the non-Dharma, how can the Dharma ever have been the Dharma?"

Huang Po himself acknowledges how difficult it is to understand that statement. Following it he says:

> Whoever understands the meaning of this deserves to be called a monk, one skilled at 'Dharma-practice.' If you do not believe this, you must explain the following story. "The Elder Wei Ming climbed to the summit of the Ta Yu Mountain to visit the Sixth Patriarch. The latter asked him why he had come. Was it for the robe or was it for the Dharma?[7] The Elder Wei Ming answered that he had not come for the robe, only for the Dharma; whereupon the Sixth Patriarch said "Perhaps you will concentrate your thoughts for a moment and avoid thinking in terms of good and evil." Ming did as he was told, and the Sixth Patriarch continued: "While you are not thinking of good and not thinking of evil, just at this very moment, return to what you were before your father and mother were born." Even as these words were spoken, Ming arrived at a sudden tacit understanding.

Since what Huang Po is trying to express is so difficult to do in the words available to him in Classical Chinese, he needs to resort to allegories and other methods of expression so that the reader can achieve the necessary tacit understanding. Such tacit understanding comes onto one as an epiphany, as it did for Wei Ming in this story, and as it did for me. Eastern texts that had perplexed me for years suddenly started making sense by substituting confusing Buddhist wordings with how a Pyrrhonist would say them. It seems to me that this tacit understanding Huang Po refers to is the same as the explicit understanding that Sextus Empiricus conveys using the clearer and more precise terminology of Pyrrhonism.

Looking at what Huang Po said, I see a statement that can be conveyed straightforwardly in English: "The teachings of the original Buddhadharma are not dogmatic. This non-dogmatic doctrine is also the Buddhadharma.

---

6   *Essentials of the Transmission of Mind*, Translated by John R. McRae, In: BDK Tripitaka Translation Series: Zen Texts, 2005, p 40.

7   The transmission from the Fifth to the Sixth Patriarch was disputed. The robe was a symbol of that transmission. Those who disputed the transmission wanted to take the robe away from the Sixth Patriarch.

I now transmit this teaching of non-dogmatic dharma. How can dogmatic doctrines be reality?" For those acculturated, like most Westerners are, to the idea that the law of non-contradiction must be adhered to, Blofeld's and McRae's translations do not make sense, but because the ancient Pyrrhonists figured out how to convey Buddhist ideas without contradictory or paradoxical language, my rendering makes sense.

This same approach can be applied to clear up a great deal of confusing Buddhist texts. For example, let's look at those first two lines of the *Xinxin Ming* again.

> The Great Way is not difficult
> for those who do not pick and choose.

What does it mean to not pick and choose? How can one take any sort of action in life without making any decisions? How could the author even have chosen to write the poem or to have chosen the words to use in it if he did not pick and choose? I've asked Zen teachers these questions and have received answers that made no sense to me. The books about this poem I've read don't make sense either.

That pretty much sums up my feeling of stuckness. I was sick and tired of what I've come to call "zensplaining": the propensity of Buddhist teachings to be packaged with paradoxes and convolutions. This, by the way, is not a criticism of the koan tradition – that method of Zen teaching involving enigmatic questions such as "everyone knows the sound of two hands clapping. What is the sound of one hand?" These are gateways to seeing things differently. My complaint is like Pirsig's complaint about the answer he got when he asked about the bombing of Hiroshima. Apparently in the traditions of Buddhist teaching these kinds of answers are correct, but these answers fail to satisfy modern Western questioners like me. Dissatisfied questioners take their questions elsewhere.

Pyrrhonism, however, has been refined by the fire of centuries of dialog with other Hellenistic philosophies – from around 325 BCE to beyond 200 CE – such that it can offer answers that are free of convolutions and paradoxes. Pyrrhonism makes a distinction between two different types of things that could be called "picking and choosing." It's not an obvious distinction, and it is apparently one impossible to express in Classical Chinese. Even in English it's difficult to express because the grammatical structure of the language drapes the distinction in camouflage. While the distinction takes some effort to understand – like the effort needed for understanding the transformation of equations in algebra – once you see it, the answers become straightforward.

The next section of this book – Book II – outlines the fundamental concepts of Pyrrhonism and the Pyrrhonist methods for addressing dukkha. Book III discusses how Pyrrhonism fits into Hellenistic philosophy and compares Pyrrhonism with a selection of similar philosophies. Its chapter comparing Pyrrhonism with Buddhism details the ideas from Buddhist philosophy Pyrrho borrowed. Its chapter on Taoism demonstrates how the paradoxical Taoist concept of *wu wei* can also be explained non-paradoxically using Pyrrhonist terminology. Book IV expands on topics introduced earlier in the book. Among other topics in that section we will pick up the *Xinxin Ming* again, along with a couple of other famous Buddhist texts, reading them like they were Pyrrhonist texts.

Book II
A Modern Outline of Pyrrhonism

5
When People
Search for Something

In the beginning was the logos,[8] and the logos was with God, and the logos was God.

The Gospel According to John 1:1

The gods did not reveal, from the beginning, all things to us, but in the course of time through seeking we may learn and know things better. But as for certain truth, no man has known it, nor shall he know it, neither of the gods nor yet of all the things of which I speak. For even if by chance he were to utter the final truth, he would himself not know it: for all is but a woven web of guesses.

Xenophanes[9]

When people search for something, the possible outcomes are that they either find what they are searching for, or that they do not find it. Of those who do not find it, some decide to give up searching, perhaps concluding that what they seek cannot be found or it is not worth the effort required. Others simply continue to search. The same is true with the search for truth. Some people have claimed to have found truth. Others say that the task is impossible. A third group reports that they have not found it, but they continue to search.

Those who think they have found truth, we Pyrrhonists call "dogmatists" as they claim to have found principles that are incontrovertibly true. This is slightly different from the way "dogmatism" is typically used in English, as the term entails not only claiming to have found principles that are incontrovertibly true, but doing so without consideration of

---

8   In biblical translations *logos* is usually rendered as "word"; however, "logos" has many other meanings that should also be assumed to have been intended. Heraclitus first used the term in philosophy – and at the time of their writing, texts such as the *Gospel According to John* were considered by Greeks to be philosophy – to represent a principle of order and knowledge. Other definitions include "ground," "account," "reason," "proportion," and "discourse." All of those, too, would appear to have also been meant.

9   Xenophanes was a Greek philosopher who lived about 200 years before Pyrrho. His teachings were a precursor to Pyrrhonism. He was much admired by the Pyrrhonists.

evidence or the opinions of others. In our usage of the term it doesn't matter whether the dogmatist considered evidence or the opinions of others. What matters is that they hold principles as true.

The category of dogmatists appears to include most people. Ask around and you will find not only that most people are full of opinions they are certain of, but also that for any given opinion one is likely to find people who hold the opposite opinion.

The analog to dogma in Buddhism is attachment. Both are forms of conceit. In Buddhism the conceit is about the nature of the self. In Pyrrhonism the conceit is about believing one has found truth when the case is actually uncertain. The concepts of attachment and dogma largely overlap, but with different emphases. An example of dogmatizing would be an attachment to an ideology. An example of attachment would be thinking that one was a better person than others because what they believe is true while others believe in falsehoods. As will be demonstrated later in this book, much of what is firmly believed is without ground to stand upon. Beliefs about the self are just a special case of this, and beliefs about other matters are liable to reinforce the conceit of the self.

Those who claim that truth cannot be found are what we call "nihilists." The nihilists are also a kind of dogmatist, because they are certain that truth cannot be found. They hold this to be incontrovertibly true, and perversely they despise truth. These people are much less common than the regular dogmatists.

The final group takes a middle way and continues to search. This group has been called various things, but here we will call them "Pyrrhonists" after Pyrrho, the first wisdom teacher who made continuing to search the central theme of his teaching, and we call this school of wisdom "Pyrrhonism." What follows is an outline of Pyrrhonist thinking and practice. Put most succinctly, Pyrrhonism is the view that dogmatism is a disease of the mind that causes suffering. Dogmas are like parasites. Pyrrhonist practices remove these parasites and thereby eliminate suffering.

With regard to what is said here about Pyrrhonism, it should be understood that there is nothing in this or any account of Pyrrhonism that Pyrrhonists firmly maintain is absolutely as stated. This and any other Pyrrhonist account should be read as a piece of journalism, where the journalist is just reporting what appears to be the case, based on their limited abilities and perspective of the information available.

6
Overview of Pyrrhonism

...I went to one who had the reputation of wisdom, and observed to him – his name I need not mention; he was a politician whom I selected for examination – and the result was as follows: When I began to talk with him, I could not help thinking that he was not really wise, although he was thought wise by many, and wiser still by himself; and I went and tried to explain to him that he thought himself wise, but was not really wise; and the consequence was that he hated me, and his enmity was shared by several who were present and heard me. So I left him, saying to myself, as I went away: Well, although I do not suppose that either of us knows anything really beautiful and good, I am better off than he is – for he knows nothing, and thinks that he knows. I neither know nor think that I know.
                                                            Socrates,
                                                            Apology

[What learning is most necessary?]
How to get rid of having anything to unlearn.
                                                    Antisthenes[10]

The practice of Pyrrhonism has three main qualities. These qualities are:
- Questioning, due to its focus on questioning and inquiring.
- Suspending, due to its avoidance of firm judgments.
- Puzzlement, due to being at a loss regarding whether to agree or disagree about issues.

The Pyrrhonist way is a process of self-argumentation in which inclinations to accept something as true – and by "true" we mean in the sense that it is an accurate representation of reality – are met with counter arguments until the point where one finds both positions equally plausible. We call this result "equipollence"[11] (pronounced EHK-wuh-POL-ens), the state of being equal in strength, effect, or significance.

---

10   Student of Socrates, founder of the Cynic school of philosophy.

11   "Equipollence" is alternatively rendered as "isothenia" in some translations.

The result of this process is a state of mind we call "epoché" (pronounced E-poh-KAY). The literal translation of the term is "suspension." In this state one neither affirms nor denies any non-evident proposition.[12] Typically this term is translated as "suspend judgment," "withhold assent" or "suspend belief." It is also known as a "standstill of the intellect."

It may be useful to note that the Hellenistic philosophers understood truth in a slightly different way than people commonly do now. Their word for truth was *aletheia*. That word is a negation. The prefix "a" means "not", as in the English words borrowed from Greek such as "atheist" (not a theist), "amnesia" (not remembering), "amoral" (not moral), "asynchronous" (not at the same time), and so on. "Truth" was to them something that wasn't *letheia*, which means covered or hidden. Their word for "truth" thus means something uncovered or revealed. Knowing this, we get an enriched understanding of things the Greeks said, such as "nature loves to hide" (Heraclitus). The key point is that "aletheia" meant an accurate account of reality, a description of a revelation about reality. This is a narrower sense than "true" is commonly used in English.

Pyrrhonists classify things into two categories: "evident" and "non-evident." Evident things are what people directly experience. Non-evident things are things that people do not directly experience. For example, we experience gravity, that's evident, but the theory of how gravity works is non-evident. One may have an evident experience of pleasure eating ice cream, but that does not mean that ice cream is inherently pleasurable. That would be non-evident.

Evident things are those things about reality that have been revealed to us through the appearances, coming with no guarantee that the appearances are accurate representations of reality. Nevertheless, the appearances are forced upon our consciousness. Non-evident things are revealed through the mind alone. They may have little or no relationship with the appearances. Careful inspection of them shows that they are not forced upon us at all like the appearances are. Unlike evident things, which usually, but not always, can be reconciled among people, non-evident things are difficult to reconcile among people. Further, unlike evident things, which in some cases may give pleasure or pain to the person experiencing them, non-evident things can flood the mind with emotional disturbances.

---

12 One complicating factor about this definition for epoché is that Sextus appears to make some small exceptions to it, making his thinking appear to be similar to the fallibilism articulated Karl Popper. In a handful of Sextus' arguments against particular dogmas he says that certain things are absurd or cannot possibly be true, usually because they violate logic. The most obvious examples are in his book *Against the Astrologers*. It would appear that in practice Sextus considers there to be propositions that are so illogical that they may be denied. This will be covered later in the book.

The Greek terms for "evident" and "non-evident" are *délon* and *adélon*. An alternative and perhaps better translation for these terms would be "immediate" and "mediate" in the sense of immediate experience versus one that has been mediated.[13] An analogous term for "evident" used in Zen Buddhism is "intimate," as it is used in this famous Zen story:

> Dizang asked Fayan, "Where are you going?"
> Fayan said, "Around on pilgrimage."
> Dizang said, "What is the purpose of pilgrimage?"
> Fayan said, "I don't know."
> Dizang said, "Not knowing is most intimate."

The world mediated by knowing the non-evident, by "knowledge," is not intimate. The world immediately experienced through the evident is intimate.

Upon learning about this distinction between evident and non-evident, some people think it is a distinction about what does and does not constitute a fact. This is not the case. A "fact" is something that is accepted as true. Just because something is evident doesn't mean it is a fact. If something is evident to everyone, we may all treat it as a fact; but just because something is evident to everyone doesn't necessarily mean that it is true about reality. For example, we may all be unable to perceive the thing correctly, such as in the case of what we see in the night sky. We may agree that what we see are stars, but upon closer inspection those stars may turn out to be different things. Some may be distant suns, others galaxies, planets, comets, or asteroids. So, it's not a fact that the objects are stars, even though they are evident and we might happen to agree that they are stars.

Once a consistent state of epoché is achieved, the Pyrrhonist will eventually experience a state we call *aphasia*. In Greek this term means "non assertion" or "speechlessness." Our surviving ancient accounts of Pyrrhonism give just the briefest mention of aphasia, and with good reason. It is the Pyrrhonist analog to Buddhist kensho. As Pyrrhonism positions itself as a philosophy, the presence of any sort of mystical state as part of its practice is almost an embarrassment.

Aphasia is a temporary stilling of the mind that can have a range of manifestations. For some people it comes as a shock. rendering the person temporarily speechless as if by force, as if they were spitting up a hot iron ball. For others it can be like how a wind-up toy gradually stops moving, gently taking away interest in asserting anything. It is like wakening from a dream, where you have the realization that what you'd been

---

13   Arne Næss, *The Selected Writings of Arne Næss*, Volume II, p 8.

experiencing wasn't real, but you have no words to describe what is happening to you now. It is a thorough recognition of the unverifiability of everything non-evident. This makes one recognize that our mental models of the world built upon those non-evident ideas are similarly unverifiable and, therefore, most everything we formerly said about the world was also unverifiable. It is like seeing yourself and the world you mentally created for yourself drop away, leaving a vacuum. Since you now no longer believe all of these things about you and the world, you're suddenly at a loss about what to say. Hence the description of this state as "non-assertion" or "speechlessness."

No records of Pyrrhonist aphasia experiences from antiquity exist. I know of two people who have reported to me Pyrrhonist aphasia experiences, and I know my own. These are as varied as the reports of Buddhist kensho. Not only do Buddhists describe kensho in a variety of ways, some also describe multiple kenshos, suggesting an experience that can be whole or partial. As more people try the Pyrrhonist path to eudaimonia, we will get more reports. My prediction is that future reports of Pyrrhonist aphasia will be similar to reports of Buddhist kensho. Some differences I suspect will be on the mind/body dimension. Meditation is both a mental and a physical experience whereas Pyrrhonist practice is strictly mental. Hence Buddhists will talk about the falling away of body and mind whereas Pyrrhonists will talk about the falling away of mind. I base this prediction on my own experience. My first kensho I would describe as a falling-off-of-body kensho. It had the classic attributes, but it did not happen in zazen. My aphasia experience (what I consider my second kensho) came from practicing Pyrrhonism. I would describe it as a falling-off-of-mind kensho. It did not happen in zazen either. It came following Pyrrhonist practice.

One of the major issues Buddhist practitioners have to deal with is the conflation of *makyo* (illusion) experiences with kensho experiences. As makyo experiences are usually induced by meditation, it seems unlikely that the Pyrrhonist methodology will induce them. Indeed, such experiences would simply become new targets for the Pyrrhonist methodologies, so that they would also be dispelled along with all other beliefs. We have no ancient Pyrrhonist accounts of this matter.

During the period of aphasia the practitioner reorganizes their understanding of the world on a basis of greater intellectual humility. With continued practice of sustaining epoché, the practitioner goes on to experience *ataraxia* (pronounced at-*uh*-RAK-see-*uh*). Ataraxia is a psychological state of being unperturbed or untroubled by things. It is peace of mind, a state of robust equanimity, free from emotional disturbance and anxiety. Some have described this state as "calm" or "tranquil," but that implies an inactivity that is not inherent to ataraxia. Some translations render ataraxia as "apathy," but ataraxia does not involve a lack of caring. In ancient Greece ataraxia was originally used to describe the ideal mental state for soldiers in battle. This is perhaps where Pyrrho picked up the term, as he developed his philosophy while traveling with Alexander the Great's army on campaign to India. The term is a negation. The prefix "a" is negation in Greek. Thus, it is not a positive state that one achieves by obtaining something. It is a state that is achieved by getting rid of things. It is a state of freedom from things such as confusion, panic, distraction – anything that disturbs, allowing one to focus on the matters at hand, like a well-focused soldier in battle. It is the same state as that of the legendary samurai who had undergone extensive Zen training so that they could be untroubled in life-threatening situations. Ataraxia is the Pyrrhonist analog to the secularized version of the Buddhist nirvana.

It appears that many people would like to achieve ataraxia. They seem to think that what prevents them from achieving ataraxia is what they see as anomalies in the "facts." Some people claim that one thing is true; others claim it is false. If these anomalies could be eliminated, by learning for certain what really is true and what really is false, people reason that they would no longer be troubled, and thus would achieve ataraxia. In the Pyrrhonists' experience, following this process does not achieve the desired result. Indeed, it appears to achieve the opposite result. Further, the more intellectually talented a person is and the more information that they have access to, the more likely it seems that they are to be troubled by the anomalies. Pyrrhonists observe that what is preventing people from experiencing ataraxia is dogmatizing – believing that non-evident things are absolutely true or false. Pyrrhonism proposes a method for achieving ataraxia by ending one's tendencies to dogmatize.

By saying that Pyrrhonists do not dogmatize, we are not using the term "dogma" about things that one merely accepts as part of experience, for we do accept what we experience. For example, if we feel hot, we would accept that we feel hot. We would not go and say that we do not feel hot. If we see a bird flying, we accept that we see what appears to be a bird flying. Typically there is little dispute about how evident things appear; although certainly such disputes occur. What people mostly dispute are ideas and judgments about what appears. We use the term "dogmatize" to refer to asserting for or against propositions that one cannot directly experience. These kinds of propositions Pyrrhonists neither accept nor deny.

Even when Pyrrhonists make arguments that are in opposition to appearances, our intent is not to deny the appearances but to point out how the beliefs held by dogmatists deceive them about appearances. For example, as the Sun rises in the east and sets in the west each day, it appears that the Sun circles the Earth. In the past, dogmatists inferred from this observation that it must be the case that the Sun circles the Earth. A Pyrrhonist might present an argument to this idea that is in opposition to the appearances, such as it may be the case that the Earth circles the Sun. This has now been observed to be the case, moving the matter from something non-evident to something evident, but in the past this matter was non-evident, and many dogmatists held false beliefs about it.

The dogmatists' beliefs enslave them to confirmation bias and cognitive dissonance. Confirmation bias is the tendency to search for, interpret, favor, and recall information in a way that confirms one's preexisting beliefs or hypotheses, while giving disproportionately less consideration to alternative possibilities. Confirmation bias may even be at the root of what disturbs us. It appears that it takes scant evidence for people to form beliefs. Once formed, it seems that in most cases no amount of evidence can un-form them. Therefore what needs to be addressed is the initial belief-forming mechanism. This is the target of Pyrrhonist practice.

Cognitive dissonance is the mental discomfort experienced by a person who simultaneously holds two or more contradictory beliefs. This discomfort arises when the person performs an action that contradicts one or more of those beliefs; or when the person is confronted with new information that contradicts their existing beliefs. If, however, one does not hold any beliefs, there can be no contradiction among beliefs, and consequently no corresponding mental discomfort.

The dogmatists' beliefs cause them to be unable to recognize appearances as what they are. Consequently, why should we trust following the dogmatists' theories about non-evident matters? Our objective is to avoid jumping to conclusions; it is not to deny appearances.

Pyrrhonists use maxims to help them with their Pyrrhonist practice, such as "nothing more" and "I determine nothing." These maxims serve as memory aids. Some people mistake these maxims for dogma. But we do not consider these maxims as being absolutely true, whereas dogmatizers claim that what they are dogmatizing about is certain. For example, we consider the maxim "all things are false" to be just among the many things categorized as false. Similarly "nothing more" is no more the case than its opposite. Dogmatizers say their maxims are true. We say our maxims are self-applicable; therefore, we do not dogmatize in our use of maxims.

The most important thing about Pyrrhonist maxims is that we use them to say what seems to us to be the case. We are just reporting our personal experience, without belief that what we are reporting about our experience actually reflects what is true about reality.

42

People ask whether Pyrrhonism is a system. If one defines a "system" as an attachment to a set of dogmas that fit together coherently with each other and with appearances, and if one defines a "dogma" as an acceptance of something that is non-evident, then it cannot be said that Pyrrhonists have a "system." However, if one defines a "system" as a way of life that follows a rationale and tends to produce a specific outcome, then it can be said that Pyrrhonists have a "system."

The Pyrrhonist system is to follow experience about what is evident. The rationale the Pyrrhonist follows aims towards producing epoché about non-evident matters. This characteristic epoché brings about for the Pyrrhonist a way of life where it is possible to seem to live rightly, where "rightly" should be understood to not only refer to virtue, but just the ordinary sense of making wise judgements.

By "virtue" here, we mean the Greek concept of arete (pronounced ahr-i-TEY), which is more broadly about excellence that what in English is conveyed by "virtue." In English "virtue" strongly connotes correct moral action. As Pyrrhonism has no dogma about what moral action is correct, we hold no absolute sense of moral virtue. By "virtue" here we just refer to what seems most excellent and well-suited for the circumstances as they appear. This is analogous to the Buddhist concept of upaya (skillful means).

Pyrrhonism follows a rationale that leads the practitioner to lead a life in accordance with appearances, one that is in general conformity with local customs, laws, and institutions, and with the practitioner's own experience, temperament, and feelings.

One of the persistent criticisms of Pyrrhonism throughout history is that Pyrrhonists deny appearances. Those who make this claim do not appear to have bothered to understand Pyrrhonism.[14] We do not reject the experience of our senses. What we experience through our senses are the appearances. As the earliest Pyrrhonist writer, Timon, said, "appearance is strong in every way, everywhere." While Pyrrhonists question whether

---

14 These misunderstandings are a long-standing and wide-spread problem and will be discussed in more detail at various points in this book. In Sextus Empiricus' explanation of the Pyrrhonist concepts of appearances, beliefs, evident and non-evident, Sextus himself complains that the critics of Pyrrhonism have failed to comprehend what the Pyrrhonists have said on these matters (Book I, Chapter 10 in *Outlines of Pyrrhonism*). Understanding these concepts is critical for understanding Pyrrhonism. Adrian Kuzminski in his 2008 book, *Pyrrhonism: How the Greeks Reinvented Buddhism*, particularly in the chapter titled "The Evident and the Non-Evident," provides an interpretation of Sextus' explanation of these concepts similar to that provided here. Kuzminski's approach contrasts the concepts as described by Sextus with similar concepts from the writings of the Buddhist philosopher Nagarjuna, writing in India around the same time as Sextus Empiricus, and those of Hume, Wittgenstein, and Berkeley many centuries later in the Western philosophical tradition.

something is as it appears, we grant that it appears. Our questioning isn't about the appearances. It is about what is being said about the appearances. It is about non-evident ideas about those appearances. This is different from questioning the appearances themselves.

This criticism is sometimes put another way: that Pyrrhonists deny the possibility of knowledge. Again, those who make this claim do not appear to have bothered to understand Pyrrhonism. We do not reject what we know from the experience of our own senses. We grant that there is knowledge about the appearances, and we grant that people can report on what they experience, and that these reports are a kind of knowledge. Our criticisms of the dogmatists have always been about their opinions and their beliefs. We do not deny knowledge. Indeed, we argue that denying the possibility of knowledge is a dogmatic position. We just deny belief in the certainty of correspondence between things considered to be knowledge and their match to reality.

Some people claim that Pyrrhonists actually have beliefs, and that we are deceiving ourselves and others by denying that we do so. For example, because a Pyrrhonist will take what appears to be a chair and sit on it, these critics declare that Pyrrhonists believe they are sitting on a chair. From the Pyrrhonist perspective, that's a perverse definition of "belief." The chair is evident. It is as evident to us that we can sit on it as it is to a dog. We use "belief" to refer to things non-evident, such as political ideas.

Another example is that some people will claim that the Pyrrhonist goal of ataraxia represents a belief, such as a belief that it is good. For Pyrrhonists, however, ataraxia is something evident. We experience mental perturbance and we experience the absence of perturbance. Each of us is in a position to prefer one over the other, based on our own experience.

One part of this problem is that the term "belief" in English is vague. For example one can say, "I believe I will have another piece of pie." This usage of "belief" is not about assenting to a non-evident proposition about reality; it's just another way of saying one wants something.

"Belief" is also used to indicate some sort of trust, such as "I believe in you." This is not a statement that you exist – a statement about reality. It is a statement of confidence in you. It's a prediction. This is also not what is meant by "belief" in Pyrrhonism.

Another confusing matter is about what to call non-evident propositions held without being assented to. For example, some people talk about "conjectural beliefs." In the Pyrrhonist view of beliefs, that's an oxymoron. Conjectures are held without belief. If one believes in it, it's not a conjecture anymore.

Other people talk about "provisional beliefs," meaning things that are assented to be true about reality, but not with such strong assent as assert infallibility. In the Pyrrhonist view, this is a kind of self-delusion, as evidenced by how seldom in practice people remove assent from things they claim to have provisionally believed.

This book contains many discussions of non-evident ideas held without assent. The Pyrrhonist admonition against belief is not an admonition against knowing about, thinking about, or talking about non-evident propositions. It is an admonition against thinking those propositions are true.

Another part of the problem is that a large proportion of people subscribe to an intuitively appealing paradigm about belief, and they are consciously or unconsciously imposing it upon the Pyrrhonist account of belief. This causes these people to misunderstand the Pyrrhonist view. The paradigm is known as the Justified True Belief Theory of Knowledge. This theory can be traced as far back as Plato's dialog *Meno*.[15] This theory has three components.

1. The proposition is true.
2. The person believes the proposition.
3. The person can give a rational account (a justification) for their belief.

When all three components are fulfilled, then according to the Justified True Belief Theory of Knowledge one may say one has knowledge.

The term "proposition" here means a statement that can be either true or false. For example:

> Proposition: The Appalachian Trail goes through New Hampshire. This is a true proposition.

> Belief: I believe the Appalachian Trail goes through New Hampshire.

> Justification: I have maps showing that the Appalachian Trail goes through New Hampshire. I can drive to places in New Hampshire where it is marked that the trail crosses the highway. I have hiked many sections of the Appalachian Trail in New Hampshire.

If one looks at Pyrrhonism through the Justified True Belief paradigm, the Pyrrhonist understanding of beliefs and appearances, and the evident and non-evident cannot be properly understood. The Pyrrhonist view of

---

15 Section 98A.

the above example is that the proposition is evident. Evident propositions are not matters of belief. The justification above is a description of the appearances that make the proposition evident. This does not make the proposition true in some ultimate, secure sense about reality, but it does make the proposition something that people can agree upon as being true by convention.

Pyrrhonism reserves "belief" to be about non-evident matters. For example, a central dogma of Stoicism is that virtue is the only good. This cannot be justified by the appearances. We have no criterion to determine whether this is true. Hence, the dogma is in the realm of belief. It is believed to be true by the Stoics and believed to be false by, for example, the Epicureans.

It is evident to me as I write this that I am doing so using a keyboard. The experience of the keyboard is forced upon my consciousness. It is not a matter of choice for me to believe or disbelieve it. From the perspective of the Justified True Belief Theory, however, the keyboard would be considered a matter of belief that I have willed.

With regard to beliefs, Pyrrhonists can give accounts just as well as dogmatists can, and perhaps better, because Pyrrhonist practice requires Pyrrhonists to come up with convincing accounts for and against any belief in order to achieve equipollence. One doesn't have to believe anything to come up with accounts, and one can easily have accounts about things that are not true.

In encountering Pyrrhonism, people who insist on holding the Justified True Belief Theory find Pyrrhonism confusing and frustrating, and they profoundly fail to understand Pyrrhonism. Because they cannot set aside their belief in the Justified True Belief Theory, they insist that things such as chairs, keyboards, the location of the Appalachian Trail, and the experience of ataraxia are all beliefs, whereas for Pyrrhonists such things do not qualify as beliefs.

Some advocates[16] of the Justified True Belief Theory make even more perverse claims about beliefs, claiming that when a Pyrrhonist suspends judgment that they must – get this – believe that they must suspend judgment; therefore suspension of judgment about beliefs is itself a belief.

Thus for those holding the Justified True Belief Theory, Pyrrhonists cannot have any knowledge whatsoever because Pyrrhonists deny beliefs. But in the Pyrrhonist view, Pyrrhonists do have knowledge. We know the appearances. We know what we experience. These are not matters of belief, nor are

---

16 Specifically, Myles Burnyeat. I wish Timon, the great Pyrrhonist writer of parodies of philosophers were here to make a parody of Burnyeat and his ridiculous position. My personal style is too earnest for such things.

they matters of truth with respect to these things being true about reality.

For those who at this point find themselves still unable to put down the Justified True Belief way of looking at the issue, another way to understand Pyrrhonism is to view it as addressing two different kinds of belief. In this way of looking, it must be remembered that this is a word game about the word "belief." This is an attempt to put the idea into a form where it can be understood by those stuck in this perspective. For those stuck in this perspective it can be said that Pyrrhonism allows what one might call "ordinary" beliefs, which are beliefs about evident things, but Pyrrhonism rejects "extraordinary" beliefs, which are beliefs about non-evident things. Most of daily activity is associated with ordinary beliefs, and these beliefs are ordinarily never questioned. No one questions whether I'm justified in my belief that I'm writing this on a keyboard. People do not suffer mental disturbance because of ordinary beliefs. It's the extraordinary beliefs that Pyrrhonism rejects, such as the Stoic belief that virtue is the only good, or the belief that people opposing your preferred political candidate are evil, or that you are forever crippled by your childhood, or that you are not worthy of being loved. These are the kinds of beliefs that are the barrier to ataraxia. These are the kinds of beliefs that Pyrrhonist practice will eradicate in one's self. The absence of these kinds of beliefs is the Pyrrhonist analog to what is called in Buddhism "ordinary mind," which James Ford Roshi describes as "It is the mind when we are, just for a moment, letting go of having to be right, of knowing. It is the ordinary mind of curiosity, of not knowing. That ordinary mind from before we've settled into our various certainties."[17] This ordinary mind is the way of both Pyrrhonism and Buddhism.

A common misunderstanding of Pyrrhonism comes from one of the names our school has traditionally been called. The ancient Greek word Pyrrhonists used to describe themselves was *skeptikoi*. This word is the source of the English word "skepticism,"[18] and so in English we have traditionally been called "Skeptics." The problem is that the English word doesn't mean the same thing as the ancient Greek word. This causes people to be instantly confused about Pyrrhonism. The English word refers to doubting the truth of something. The ancient Greek word refers to the act of inquiring, investigating, or researching. We describe ourselves as those who inquire and research, to be contrasted with those who claim to have already found what they sought – the dogmatists. Pyrrhonism is

---

17   https://www.patheos.com/blogs/monkeymind/2019/04/ordinary-mind-is-the-way-comments-on-one-of-the-great-zen-koans.html

18   Americans commonly spell this word as "skepticism" whereas other writers in English tend to spell it as "scepticism."

an investigation similar to the kind of inquiry that takes place in a Chan *hwadu* (Zen koan), as in the question "what is this?"

Further, later skeptics such as Descartes proposed a skepticism that doubted the existence of an external world, or the existence of reality. This is not something that the ancient skeptical philosophies of Pyrrhonism, Academic Skepticism, or Cyrenaicism doubted. Indeed, Pyrrhonism is not even about doubt. We do not approach the world with doubt. Pyrrhonism is about approaching life with curiosity and intellectual humility. So, the English term "skepticism" is a misnomer. Better terms would be "inquiryism" or "investigationism." To avoid all confusion, we now refer to our school as "Pyrrhonism," and except in reference to the similar competing school of Academic Skepticism, the term traditionally rendered as "skepticism" will be rendered as "inquiryism."

Some people infer that because Pyrrhonists lack beliefs we must therefore be inactive, based on their belief that one must have beliefs to engage in any actions. A related inference is that because Pyrrhonists lack beliefs we must therefore not care about anything and must therefore be inactive, because caring is required for action. If such people would bother to observe us, they would see that this is not so. Pyrrhonists stick to directing their attention towards the appearances, and we act depending on those appearances.

It seems to us that the dogmatists cannot recognize the philosophical space in which we operate. They see that one must either have beliefs or one must exist as some sort of vegetable. Pyrrhonists inhabit a philosophical space between these two extremes. Dogmatists appear to have difficulty seeing this space because they can only imagine spaces defined by beliefs. We exist in a space they do not see a space defined by absence of beliefs.

Some people think that having no beliefs entails some sort of radical disassociation with one's self or mental states. In as much as one's ego gets wrapped up in dogmatism, and Pyrrhonist practice removes that, then there is a kind of disassociation, in the sense that a Pyrrhonist experience of one's self differs from that of a dogmatist's because the dogmatist's sense of self is defined, in part, by beliefs whereas the Pyrrhonist's sense of self is not. As for a disassociation with mental states, Pyrrhonist practice transforms mental states, but one has no disassociation about them, just a different attitude and way of viewing them. It does produce a kind of distancing, a kind that helps one to be totally engrossed in one's mental states, letting them happen, rather than trying to judge them. As Carl Jung said: "Thinking is difficult, that's why most people judge." A judgment is a belief. By avoiding dogmatic judgments, the Pyrrhonist stays in the thinking and inquiring modes.

All experiences encompass the opposite of what we experience.

Pyrrhonism is the recognition that we can know only what we experience. Experience is ever-changing. We can know the clear blue sky, a sky that changes with clouds and with nightfall. Definitions depend not only on what is present, but what is absent. Incompleteness and absence are inherent to experience. Anything that can be present can be absent, and is therefore unstable. Humans instinctively dislike instability. We dislike it in the physical world; we dislike it in the conceptual world. Just as on a rocking ship we want to grab onto something fixed, to steady ourselves, in this unsteady vehicle we call "mind" we want to grab onto dogmas to steady our thinking. While this behavior generally works well in the physical world, in the mental realm this grasping to fixed ideas doesn't work because the ideas themselves are not firmly attached to reality. What we first think solves our instability problem ends up just compounding it.

Like other philosophies of life, such as Stoicism, Pyrrhonism has a criterion for making decisions. However, the term "criterion" has two different meanings. By "criterion" here we mean only one of the two. The meaning we are not using for "criterion" here is about what line of judgment we should use to determine whether one should have a belief. As Pyrrhonists aim to divest themselves of all beliefs, this use of "criterion" is not applicable. The meaning we use here for "criterion" is about action, namely whether to do one thing rather than another. Pyrrhonists use the appearances – what our senses tell us and what we internally experience – as our criterion for action.

Ordinary life is the way of Pyrrhonism. We accept things in life as they appear to us, living without beliefs, and acting in accordance with the ordinary regimen of life. Living without beliefs does not make us inactive. On the basis of appearances we can and do act and make choices about what to do.

The ordinary regimen of life seems to us to have four elements:

1. The guidance of nature, through what our senses tell us.
2. What we experience with our internal drives, such as hunger and thirst.
3. The laws, customs, and social norms of the society we live in, such that we accept that following these is generally regarded as good and rejection of them is generally regarded as bad.
4. Practical education with regard to developing life and vocational skills, and putting these skills into practice.

All of these aspects of the ordinary regimen of life, it seems to us, can be engaged in without beliefs.

7
The Goal of Pyrrhonism

> ...I have a suspicion that you (as you think yourself)
> are pregnant [with an idea] and in labor. So I want you
> to come to me as to one who is both the son of a mid-
> wife and himself skilled in the art; and try to answer
> the questions I shall ask you as well as you can. And
> when I examine what you say, I may perhaps think it
> is a phantom and not truth, and proceed to take it qui-
> etly from you and abandon it.[19] Now if this happens,
> you mustn't get savage with me, like a mother over her
> first-born child. Do you know, people have often be-
> fore now got into such a state with me as to be literally
> ready to bite when I take away some nonsense or other
> from them. They never believe that I am doing this in
> all good-will....
> _Socrates,_
> _Theaetetus_[20]

> Enlightenment is an accident. Practice makes us accident
> prone. _Robert Aitken Roshi_[21]

The goal of Pyrrhonist practice is the mental state of ataraxia, and
for what we experience physically, it is to have moderation in our
feelings. Ataraxia can be viewed as a secular analog to Buddhist nirvana.

Pyrrhonists achieve ataraxia through a process of assessing our own
experiences to determine what to believe. In this assessment, we give attention to all sides of controversies about non-evident matters such that
each of those sides seems to be equally plausible. Due to equal plausibility,
we suspend judgment. What we find is that following this epoché we
experience ataraxia.

⌊ The person who believes that something is inherently good or bad
is constantly upset.⌋ When people do not experience the conditions or
possess the things that they believe are good, they think they are being
tormented by things that are inherently bad. This causes them to chase

---

19 Infanticide of defective children was customary in antiquity.

20 Section 151.

21 Robert Aitken was one of the first Westerners to become a Zen master. A large
    proportion of Western Zen teachers are lineage descendants from Aitken.

after things they believe are good, but when they get them, they fall into new torments. These torments are caused by irrational and immoderate happiness about obtaining what they believe is good, followed by fear of change. Then people do everything they can to avoid losing these things that they believe to be good.

In contrast, the person who has no belief as to what is inherently good or bad doesn't put much emotional energy into pursuing what seems to them to be good or avoiding what seems to them to be bad. As a result, this person achieves ataraxia.

This may be best understood through two anecdotes. The first anecdote comes from how Pyrrhonists have traditionally illustrated this point. It's a story that likely came from Pyrrho himself, as it is about a person Pyrrho almost surely knew, Apelles. In Pyrrho's era, Apelles was the most renowned painter in ancient Greece. Like Pyrrho, Apelles served in Alexander the Great's court, and like Apelles, Pyrrho had worked as a painter before Pyrrho became a philosopher.

> Once when Apelles was painting a horse he wanted to depict the froth on the horse's mouth. He tried and tried to do so, but failed every time. Eventually he became frustrated. He then took the sponge he used for wiping paint off of his brushes and he threw it in anger against the painting. In striking the painting, the sponge hit the horse's mouth and, by accident, the desired froth effect was achieved.

People who have become Pyrrhonists once hoped to achieve ataraxia by figuring out what they could and could not believe. Just as Apelles tried to paint the froth, we found that no matter how hard we tried, we came no closer to ataraxia. Indeed, our goal seemed to become increasingly distant. As it seemed that the task was impossible, we gave up and suspended judgement. But then, as if by chance, the ataraxia we were seeking followed, like a shadow.

The second anecdote comes from a traditional story used by Taoists to illustrate their thinking about having beliefs about good and bad. Coincidentally, it is also about a horse.

> Among the people who lived close to the border, there was an old farmer who led a righteous life. One day, for no apparent reason, his mare ran off, and was lost. Everyone pitied him, but the old man said, "what makes

you think this is a bad thing?"

Several months later, his mare returned, accompanied by a superb wild stallion. Everyone congratulated the old man, but he said, "what makes you think this is a good thing?"

The old man's son enjoyed riding the stallion, but one day he was tossed from the horse and broke his leg. Everyone pitied the old man, but he said, "what makes you think this is a bad thing?"

Shortly thereafter, a barbarian army crossed the border. All of the young men were called up to fight. The first troops to face the barbarians were those from close to the border. Outnumbered, nine out of ten died holding off the barbarians before reinforcements from more distant regions arrived. But because the son's leg was broken and he was unable to fight, the son survived.

People think that by settling matters of good and bad and right and wrong that they can achieve ataraxia. The old farmer understands that this is mistaken. He has learned to suspend judgment. His mind is in a state of epoché. His neighbors, who suffer from dogmatism, have wild emotional swings. They are perturbed by the news; whereas the old man enjoys ataraxia.

These two anecdotes are usefully contrasted with the story given in the *Book of Genesis* about Eve being tempted by the serpent to eat the forbidden fruit from the tree of knowledge of good and evil. Eve gets Adam to eat the fruit too. After doing so, it occurs to them that there's something wrong with being naked. Following that, God expels them from paradise. A Pyrrhonist interpretation of this parable is that the fruit represents taking on beliefs in non-evident propositions, such as the belief that there's something wrong with being naked. Once one brings those beliefs into one's self, by eating the fruit, the world is no longer a paradise. This is the problem of mankind that Pyrrhonism is the cure for, and the cure is to vomit up the forbidden fruit.

We are not saying that Pyrrhonists are wholly untroubled. We are troubled by certain unavoidable feelings. The old farmer's son felt the pain of a broken leg, for example. We feel pain, hunger, thirst, cold, and so on. We do not deny that these are troubling. But even in such cases we see that dogmatists are perturbed by two things whereas we are perturbed by only one. While we are both affected by unpleasant physical sensations, dogmatists are also affected by the judgements they make that these things are inherently bad. Hence, Pyrrhonists are less troubled by unavoidable feelings than dogmatists are.

In the *Sallatha Sutta*, known in English as "The Arrow Sutra," the Buddha explains how this works. The Buddha begins the discourse by saying that both ordinary people and well-taught noble disciples feel pleasure and pain, and asks his monks what is the difference between these people? They don't have an answer, so the Buddha has to provide it. The Buddha says it is like being struck with an arrow. Both people feel the physical pain of the arrow. For the well-taught noble disciple, that is the end of the matter, but for the ordinary person there comes another arrow, an arrow that causes mental pain. That person sorrows, grieves, laments, beats his breast, and becomes distraught – all expressions of mental anguish that comes about through a psychological identification with the pain. They do everything they can to escape the pain, causing them to chase after physical pleasures, because that is the only path of escape that they know. The well-taught noble disciple, however, does not psychologically resist the pain. They have no "resistance-obsession;" they do not psychologically identify with the pain.

Consequently, we say that regarding beliefs, the goal of Pyrrhonism is ataraxia, and with regard to unavoidable experiences, the goal is moderation of feeling.

....

8
The Pyrrhonist Concept of Signs

The God whose oracle is at Delphi neither speaks plainly
nor conceals, but indicates by signs.   *Heraclitus*

We should have a great fewer disputes in the world if
words were taken for what they are, the signs of our ideas
only, and not for things themselves.   *John Locke*

Some things come into awareness directly. For example, that there is a
book in front of you is something that comes directly into your awareness. Such things are evident. They don't need what we call "signs."

Some things are non-evident. These often entail what we call "signs."
These things can be divided into three categories.

1. Things that are permanently non-evident. For example, there's no reason to expect we'll ever learn how many stars there are, simply because
   we lack the ability to see them all.
2. Things that are temporarily non-evident. These are things that are evident under some circumstances, but are at the moment not evident.
   For example, the city of Athens is at the moment not evident to me.
   Correspondingly, when I was in Athens, the city was evident to me.
3. Things that are inherently non-evident. These are things we cannot
   directly perceive, such as things that have been hypothesized to exist
   based on inference, but are incapable of being observed directly.

For the first category, the permanently non-evident, signs are unnecessary because these things are permanently closed off to us and we have
little need to talk about them. The other two categories, the temporarily
non-evident and the inherently non-evident, are closed off to our direct
experience yet we need to talk about them. These things, instead of being
experienced, are understood via "signs."

A temporarily non-evident thing is understood via what we call a
"mnemonic" sign – a sign that remind us of what it is. The original Greek
term is a bit difficult to translate. Other translations include: "recollec-
tive," "suggestive," "commemorative," and "admonitive." The key idea
here is that one starts with something that is evident, then one uses some
sort of symbol (usually words but other methods, such as pictures can be
used) as a way of recalling something evident to memory. For example, the

word "Athens" is a sign for that city in Greece that can be directly experienced if one were to go there.

Mnemonic signs also apply to evident things that have a relationship with each other. For example, smoke is a mnemonic sign of fire, and a scar is a mnemonic sign of a wound. The two go together. When smoke is evident while fire is temporarily non-evident, we say that the smoke is a mnemonic sign for fire. When a scar is evident, we associate it with a past wound. The wound itself is no longer evident.

Recall the Allegory of the Cave. In the cave, the standards of knowledge are about accurately recalling and describing the shadows seen on the wall, and accurately predicting what shadows will come next based on those that preceded it. These are the tasks that mnemonic signs are used for.

An inherently non-evident thing is understood via what we call an "indicative" sign – a sign that indicates something non-evident. Inherently non-evident things are things which are all conceptual, such as the immortality of the soul, that virtue is the only good, that adopting some 'ism will solve all of our problems, and so on. We do not have direct experience of these things. These are just concepts. Dealing in indicative signs puts one at great risk of falling into the reification fallacy, which is treating something abstract or hypothetical as if it were something concrete or real. Or worse – true. All dogmas depend on indicative signs, as it is only through indicative signs that we can acquire knowledge of the dogmas.

For example, I once saw a black cat cross my path. I can recall it to myself and relate this story to you using mnemonic signs, such as "cat" as representative of the animal I saw. But there also happens to be a superstition about this situation being a harbinger of bad luck. I can recall and relate these as mnemonic signs, too, of the stories I was told, but the content of the superstition itself – that a black cat crossing one's path is bad luck – is an indicative sign. It's something non-evident; so, it's something about which belief must be suspended. Superstitions are easy dogmas to criticize, but the same ideas apply to tougher targets, such as philosophical and political dogmas.

Pyrrhonism accepts concepts that are conveyed by mnemonic signs and rejects concepts that are conveyed by indicative signs. In the normal course of life people rely on mnemonic signs. Pyrrhonism embraces following the normal course of life. Pyrrhonists assent to making the kinds of associations used with mnemonic signs, and we rely on them undogmatically. This seems to be difficult for some people to grasp. The academic literature is full of philosophy Ph.D.s insisting that the ancient Pyrrhonists had beliefs. For example, they would argue that in the above example a Pyrrhonist would have a belief that the thing that crossed their path was an animal, and that animal was a cat. This is not what Pyrrhonists mean by "beliefs." We use the term to refer to dogmas about the non-evident, not about mnemonic signs. We do not consider mnemonic signs to be beliefs; we consider them to be recollections of evident matters, and we do not classify evident matters as "beliefs."

9

The Modes of Epoché

> Almost every wise saying has an opposite one, no less wise, to balance it.
> *George Santayana*

> And so this doctrine of withholding judgements ... is no idle tale, as Colotes[22] thinks; it is a settled state and attitude of grown men that preserves from error and refuses to abandon judgement to anything so discredited and incoherent as the senses or to be deluded as these people are deluded who call the seen the evidence of things unseen although they observe that appearances are so untrustworthy and ambiguous.
> *Plutarch*[23]

Epoché may be achieved through the opposition of arguments. Opposition of arguments is the foundational practice of Pyrrhonism. This is the cure by argument that produces inner peace.

The arguments used may be about what is observed, or they may be about ideas. For example, an argument about what is observed would be created when we say that a particular tower looks round when viewed from a distance but appears to be square when viewed from nearby. An argument about ideas could be a response to someone who infers that divine providence must exist due to the order of the heavenly bodies. In opposing this idea, it could be pointed out that bad things often happen to good people and that bad people often have good things happen to them. From these facts one may deduce that divine providence does not exist.

For these arguments we sometimes shift time frames. For example, we might argue that before the founder of this belief system one follows was born, the arguments they have for supporting that system had not yet

---

22 Colotes was a student of Epicurus who wrote a treatise entitled *That it is impossible even to live according to the doctrines of the other philosophers*, which contained Epicurean arguments against the other schools of philosophy. While this treatise is now lost, Plutarch's refutation of it survives.

23 *Against Colotes* 1124. Historians of philosophy generally classify Plutarch as a Middle Platonist. However, Plutarch routinely speaks, as he does here, as an Academic Skeptic, a philosophy closely related to Pyrrhonism. Sextus Empiricus tells us that in its earliest form Academic Skepticism, as taught by Arcesilaus, was nearly indistinguishable from Pyrrhonism, but after Arcesilaus the two philosophies diverged. This will be covered in more detail later.

appeared. While these arguments may be sound, they were not previously known to exist. Isn't it then possible that in the future someone will find arguments that soundly contradict those which they now support? As the past has demonstrated that this is possible, why should we assent to these current arguments that presently seem so strong?

Pyrrhonists use a collection of argumentation methods for achieving epoché. We traditionally call these methods "modes." They may also be called "arguments" or "points" or "tropes." Whenever one is experiencing falling into a belief about something non-evident, the modes may be reviewed and called upon for creating arguments that will lead to epoché.

We use two sets of modes. The older set will be referred to here as the Ten Modes of Aenesidemus. There's some disagreement about the origin of these modes. Diogenes Laertius and Plutarch say they are from Pyrrho. Sextus and Eusebius say they're from Aenesidemus. Sextus also says that they are from the early Pyrrhonists. My guess is that the ten modes appear in Timon's writings about Pyrrho, not in a systematized way but as part of discourses with Pyrrho. Aenesidemus later systematized and expanded these modes. This might explain why different writers about the modes, such as Favorinus, Aenesidemus, and Sextus, put them in slightly different orders and say slightly different things about them.

The newer set is the Five Modes of Agrippa. Agrippa, who lived around 100 CE, devised a second set of five modes of epoché. These modes do not replace the earlier ten modes. They are simply an alternative or supplementary set. They are all tools in our toolbox for developing arguments.

We make no case here about how strong these modes are, or whether this is an exhaustive list of all possible modes. They may even be unsound. Remember, our goal is ataraxia. It is not about having justified true beliefs. That's the goal of the dogmatists.

....

10
The Ten Modes of Aenesidemus

I already am eating from the trashcan all the time. The
name of this trashcan is ideology. The material force of
ideology makes me not see what I am effectively eating.

Slavoj Žižek

You can tell when you are talking to someone [who is
ideologically possessed]...because you can predict absolutely everything they are going to say. Once you know
the algorithmic substructure of their political ideology,
which is usually predicated on about five or six axioms,
you can use the axioms to automatically generate speech
content. You don't even have to hear the person. You can
predict what they are going to say. So that alleviates any
responsibility they have whatsoever for thinking, and it
also allows them to believe that they have full control and
full knowledge not only about the entire world, but also
the capacity to distinguish without a moment's thought
between those who are on the side of the good and those
who are not. And that's where the danger really comes.

Jordan B. Peterson[24]

The early Pyrrhonists developed a set of ten modes, each of which is
based on a single concept, as follows:
1. Variations among animals
2. Differences among human beings
3. Differences among the sense organs
4. Differences in circumstances
5. Differences in position, distance, and location
6. Effects due to mixing
7. The number and quality of external objects
8. Issues of relativity
9. Differences in frequency of occurrence

---

24 At the time of this writing, Jordan B. Peterson is a controversial and polarizing figure.
If you find yourself being happy or angry that he is being quoted here, consider that
there's nothing good or bad by nature. He's not inherently good or bad. He presumably sees himself as an agent of good. If you find yourself having strong feelings about
just quoting him here, consider whether you are suffering from dogmatism.

10. Differences in customs, laws, ways of life, mythic and religious beliefs, and dogmatic opinions

One can look at these ten modes and see a higher-level three-mode structure as follows:
1. Differences in what does the judging
2. Differences on what is being judged
3. A combination of both

The first four of the ten modes are about what does the judging. The seventh and tenth modes are about what is being judged. The fifth, sixth, eighth, and ninth modes are based on both.

Mode 1 – Variation Among Animals

Different species of animals experience the world differently. Dogs have a keen sense of smell. Bats use echolocation to fly. Some animals can see parts of the light spectrum we cannot see. Migratory birds have a sense organ to identify the direction of magnetic north. Insects have eyes that are constructed very differently from those of mammals. Dogs can hear high frequencies that humans cannot hear.

Animals also have different likes and dislikes. Seawater is unpleasant to drink, and in sufficient quantities it is poisonous for humans, but fish in the ocean like it. Pigs enjoy wallowing in stinking mud rather than going into clear water. Some animals can only eat meat. Others can only eat grass. Dogs like to eat things humans think are disgusting.

At our home we have a glass-topped dinner table. Our dog, Maggie, also known as "our Labrador of perpetual hunger," always watches us intently as we eat. If food falls off of someone's fork, she acts as if she is convinced that it will fall through the see-through table, quickly going to the spot where she predicts the food will land, when instead the food lands on the table. This has been happening for years, but she has never figured it out.

How do we know that we are not like Maggie?

When we consider what appears to us humans, given what we know about how other animals perceive things, how can we say that our way of perceiving things is right and that our perceptions are right? Other animals have different ways of perceiving things, and these different ways lead them to different perceptions. How can we say that some of those might not be better and more accurate than our own? Bats can fly in the dark without running into things. Can we (unaided by technology) do the same?

If things appear differently to animals than they do to us, how can we have confidence that the appearance of the external object is inherently as we perceive it and not as another species perceives it?

Thus, we must suspend judgement about the appearances of external objects as representing what they are truly like.

Mode 2 – Differences Among Human Beings

Just as different species experience the world differently, so too do different humans. Some people feel hot while other people in the same place feel cold. Some people find certain foods agreeable, while those same foods are disagreeable to or even sicken others. Some people enjoy one thing, while other people despise it.

These differences among people have been often mentioned by the ancient poets. For example:

> The crowns and trophies of his storm-foot steeds
> Give joy to one; yet others find it joy
> To dwell in gorgeous chambers gold-bedecked;
> Some even take delight in voyaging
> O'er ocean's billows in a speeding barque.
> Pindar

> One person delights in one activity, another in another.
> Homer, The Odyssey 14.228

> Tragedy, too, is full of such things:
> If the same things were beautiful and wise for everybody,
> There would be no disputatious strife among mankind.
> Euripides, Phoenissae 499-500

Since choosing and avoiding are based on pleasure and displeasure, and since pleasure and displeasure arise from what appears, when the same things are chosen by some people and avoided by others, it is logical for us to infer that these people are not affected in the same way by the same appearances, for if they were, they would all have the same preferences. Because of these differences among people, we cannot rely on human experience to tell us what things are by nature.

Not only are there differences among people, there are differences within single individuals. Think about yourself when you were a child. Aren't your likes and dislikes now much different from what they were then?

Time differences do not need to be involved in this. I experience simultaneous differences within myself. If I look at things with only my left eye, everything becomes slightly yellower, whereas looking with only my right eye, everything becomes slightly bluer. You do not need to see things with my weird eyes to have such an experience. To experience a difference within yourself, get three bowls. Fill one with warm water, one with cold water, and one with water at room temperature. Put one hand in the cold water and the other in the warm water for a few minutes. Then put both hands in the bowl with water at room temperature. The hand that was in the cold water will experience the water as warm, and the hand that was in warm water will experience the water as cold.

Anyone who says that we ought to give assent to the majority view is making a foolish proposal. No one is able to collect the opinions of the whole of humanity and find out what pleases the majority. Besides, what pleased people in the past is different from what pleases them today. Because of that we should suspect what pleases people in the future will likewise be different. We cannot go to the past and the future to find out what those people think.

Dogmatists egoistically claim that, in deciding the facts, preference should be given to themselves above all other people. This is not fair, as these dogmatists are part of the dispute. They cannot fairly judge.

Our experience of life is inherently subjective. We cannot expect the subjective experiences of others to conform to our subjective experiences.

Mode 3 – Differences Among the Sense Organs

Further, the senses differ from each other. To the eye it seems that paintings have hollows and prominences, but to the touch, the painting seems flat. For some people honey is pleasant when placed on the tongue, but unpleasant when placed on the eye. Perfumes please the sense of smell, but not the sense of taste. Hence, we aren't able to say how each of these things is inherently, but only how they appear to be in each instance.

Each thing that appears to us via our senses seems to affect us as a complex of things. For example, an apple seems smooth, fragrant, sweet, and red. But it is not evident whether the apple really has these and only these qualities, or whether it has more qualities than are apparent, but some of them do not affect us. Consider the experience of someone who can neither hear nor see. This person won't be able to see the apple, nor hear the sound an apple makes when one bites into it. It is possible that apples have qualities that we are not able to sense, due to our lacking sense organs for those qualities.

Technology has allowed us to perceive many things that, unaided by technology, we could not experience. We now perceive things such as radio waves, sounds at pitches higher than our ears can hear, and actions going on at the microscopic level. We should not assume that everything has been discovered and that we have a full picture.

Mode 4 – Differences in Circumstances

Things appear differently based on circumstances. Examples of circumstances include awake versus asleep, young versus old, being in motion or being at rest, being in need or being satisfied, drunk versus sober, healthy versus sick, being predisposed to courage or fear, distressed or cheerful. Thus things affect us in dissimilar ways depending on conditions.

In sleep we sense things that are different from what we sense when we are awake. Old people experience things differently from those in their prime. Children like toys, but people in their prime prefer different things, and the elderly still others.

Objects appear differently depending on whether one is stationary or in motion. Things that we see as stationary when we are at rest seem to be moving when we are in motion.

Many people who have ugly spouses think them beautiful. Depending on hunger and satiety, food that seems pleasant to the hungry can be perceived as unpleasant to the sated. Actions one would consider shameful when one is sober appear not to be shameful when one is drunk.

Food tastes differently depending on what one has eaten immediately before. Someone who has just eaten sweets will find the same wine sour that tastes sweet to them when not consumed after sweets.

Some things are annoying to those who are depressed, but when the same people are cheerful the same thing may be pleasant.

Since therefore perceptions vary so much depending on conditions, and human beings are in one condition at one time and in another condition at another time, how each external object appears to each person can be said, but they cannot say how that object actually is, for anyone making the assessment is in one condition or another, and those conditions continuously vary.

Mode 5 – Differences in Positions, Distances, and Locations

The fifth mode is about positions, distances, and locations. Depending on these, the same things appear different. For example, from afar a boat may appear stationary, but the same boat when viewed up close may be seen to be in motion. From afar a tower may appear to be round, but viewed close up it appears square. The light of a lamp appears dim in the sunshine, but bright in the dark. An oar appears broken when it is in the water, but straight when it is out of water. The necks of pigeons appear to be different colors depending on the angle from which they are viewed.

Everything apparent must be sensed from some location, from some distance, and in some position, each of which produces variation in the appearances. Therefore we cannot conclude from appearances how things inherently are because we cannot view things from all positions, distances, and locations.

Mode 6 – Effects Due to Mixing

The sixth mode is about admixtures. None of the external objects affect us by themselves alone, as they are always in combination with other things. It is perhaps possible to say what the mixture of the external object and that together with which it is observed is like, but we cannot do the same for the external object considered just by itself. For example, the same sound produced in an open space sounds different when produced in a narrow space. It is also different between dry air and humid air. Because of admixtures, the senses do not perceive precisely how the external objects are.

Perhaps the biggest admixture of all is our own minds. Our minds supply an admixture to the report of the senses. If we expect to see X, we tend to see X, even when we are looking at Y. Even more so, if we are not looking for X, X may be there and we do not notice it.

Modern psychology has given good examples of this. Here's one about how we interpret images. Does it appear as a duck or a rabbit?[25] Maybe you can see both a duck and a rabbit, but you cannot do so at the exact same time, because your mind can only supply one interpretation at a time.

Another interesting example was an experiment where subjects were asked to count passes of a basketball among players on a basketball court, as shown in a video. During the experiment, a person in a gorilla costume walks from one side of the screen to the other. Midway they stop and beat

---

25   https://commons.wikimedia.org/wiki/File:Duck-Rabbit_illusion.jpg

their chest. Most viewers of the video didn't notice the gorilla, as they were so focused on counting ball passes.[26]

Mode 7 – The Number and Quality of External Objects

The seventh mode is about quantities. Things affect us differently depending on the quantity we encounter. A little wine often invigorates; a lot will put one in a stupor. The same goes with medicines. The right dose will help; too much is toxic. Small amounts of water look clear. Dive deep into the ocean, look up, and the water is opaque. Small amounts of ice look nearly clear. Large amounts look white, or sometimes blue.

Because of this, we should suspend judgment about the true nature of objects.

Mode 8 – Issues of Relativity

The eighth mode is about how all observations are relative.

In casual use people say something "is" when what they really mean is that something "appears to be." To a large degree, this is a function of language. This book was composed in English. English is one of the languages in which sentences require verbs. Other languages, such as the Chinese languages, do not require verbs to form a sentence. Usually the differences between such languages boils down to whether the verb "to be" is needed in sentences. I suspect that these differences in language structures are a factor in how easy it is to intuitively grasp or practice Pyrrhonism.

Some languages have multiple forms for the verb "to be." When I studied Spanish, I had to learn the difference in usage between the two forms of "to be": *ser* and *estar*. *Ser* was for the permanent form of being; *estar* was for the impermanent form of being. For example, the sentence "I am in Madrid" means different things depending on which verb "to be" is chosen. *Ser* means I live there. *Estar* says I happen to be there now but will not remain there. Having to make such a distinction turns out to have some interesting cultural ramifications, such as discussions of death and marriage. References to death are always *estar* because according to Catholic dogma – Catholicism was the state religion in Spain – everyone was going to be brought back to life on Judgement Day. References to marriage are always *ser*, because divorce was prohibited.

How I wish English had such an easy way of distinguishing between whether the speaker intended to just say how things appeared to them versus making a dogmatic claim. English speakers, like speakers of ancient Greek, must break from conventional word usage and apply alternative

---

26   Christopher Chabris and Daniel Simons, *The Invisible Gorilla: How Our Intuitions Deceive Us*, 2011.

verbiage to convey their Pyrrhonist perspectives. I have found taking this up as a habit is useful in helping me to suspend judgment. I pay attention to whether the verb should be "to be," or should it be "seems to be" or "appears to be" or "perhaps is."

All appearances involve a relationship between the perceiver and what is perceived. One part of that relationship is which one is the perceiver and which one is the perceived. Another part is their relationship to each other, for example, one is on the left and the other is on the right. Everything is in relation to everything else. There is no place to get a god's eye view of everything at once.

As all things are relative, the obvious consequence regarding each external object is that one cannot say how it really is, but only how it appears to be in relation to something else, particularly the perceiver. Because of this, one should suspend judgment about the true nature of the objects.

Mode 9 – Differences in Frequency of Occurrence

The ninth mode is about how our attention is drawn towards that which is unusual and away from that which is commonplace. Things that are rare seem precious, but things that are commonplace do not. This effect distorts our ability to evaluate things.

The sun is a far more important thing to us than a comet, but as we see the sun all the time, and comets only infrequently, we marvel at the comet, but not the sun. Earthquakes are less disturbing to those who have experienced them previously than they are to those who have not. The sea is marvelous to people the first time they see it, and not so for those who see it regularly.

We typically think of water as cheap, but should it become sufficiently scarce we would value it more than gold. And if gold were as common as stones on the ground, would we think it worth hording?

At the time of this writing, several books popularizing Stoicism and countless books on Buddhism have been recently published, but right now this is the only book aiming to popularize Pyrrhonism. So, in how people evaluate whether this is a good book or not, they will not have other books on Pyrrhonism to compare it with. The book is rare. And rare is considered precious. Of course, from your perspective it may not be rare. You may view it as just another self-help book. From that perspective, it's just one of thousands among the current self-help titles. In that case, you will just evaluate it on how interesting you find it and whether your attempt to practice Pyrrhonism works for you.

In your evaluation you will just have to go by what seems to you to be the case on this matter. It will seem different to other people. But what it actually is, well, it's best to suspend judgment on that.

Mode 10 – Differences in Customs, Laws, Beliefs, and Opinions

The tenth mode is principally concerned with ethics – what is morally good and bad. Ethics depend on one's way of life, and on customs, laws, mythic beliefs, and dogmatic suppositions.

A way of life is about how one chooses to live life. It may be adopted by one person or many. Pyrrhonism, Stoicism, Buddhism, and Christianity are all examples of ways of life. It's also possible for a single person to have their own way of life. In antiquity Diogenes the Cynic was an example of this. In recent years, the Unabomber would be an example of someone who pursued a way of life unique to themselves. Each of these ways of life have views about what is good and bad.

A law is a written decree to which the citizens are held accountable. Violators of the law are subject to punishment. Laws indicate what is considered good and bad.

Customs reflect a collective acceptance by a people about how one should act. This may or may not include punishment for violations, but public awareness of a violation of a custom likely entails some cost of some sort to the violator. Customs also indicate what is good and bad.

Mythic belief is the acceptance of things that are demonstrably not the case, such as that Zeus can be found living on Mount Olympus, or that Noah put two of every creature in his ark when the entire world flooded. Some mythic beliefs indicate what is good and bad.

A dogmatic supposition is something that seems established by analogy or some kind of non-evident proof, such as the effectiveness of homeopathy, or that people have auras, or that the universe is filled with dark matter. These suppositions can indicate what is good and bad.

Upon considering any one of these items, a Pyrrhonist contrasts it with something contrary to it to demonstrate that there is nothing inherently good or bad. For example, it is legal for male Egyptians to have up to four wives, but it is illegal for a French man to have more than one wife.

It is legal for American homosexuals to get married, but just being homosexual in Saudi Arabia is punishable by death.

In Japan it is customary to slurp noodles and drink directly from the soup bowl. In Europe this would be considered bad table manners.

In America, some people fly the Confederate battle flag considering it a symbol of Southern pride. Other people consider that flag a symbol of hate.

Mormons abstain from alcohol, as being contrary to their religion. Catholics use wine in the Eucharist to represent the blood of Christ.

It is against the law to strike someone, yet this is the object of contact sports such as boxing, judo, and American football.

Among the Mosuo (an ethnic group in Southwestern China) women have multiple sexual partners and raise their children relying on help from their siblings, not the fathers of the children. Some societies in the Amazon believe that one child comes from multiple fathers, believing that a fetus is literally made of accumulated semen.[27] Americans believe that each child has one biological father, who under traditional circumstances should ideally be closely involved in raising the child.

In America owning guns is a legal right. In some other countries, it is legally prohibited.

East Asians eat with chopsticks and consider knives on the table to be rude. Westerners eat with knives, forks, and spoons.

The list of possible examples is immense, but these should suffice to convey the idea. What the Tenth Mode does is to demonstrate anomalies in moral "facts." For these kinds of issues, it appears impossible to be able to say how any of these should be by nature. We can only say how they appear in relation to a given way of life, or law, or custom. Consequently, we must suspend judgment about these kinds of "facts."

Mode 11 – Differences in Language

Astute readers will notice that this chapter is about the 10 Modes of Aenesidemus. How can there be 11?

It seems to me that there's another mode that should be included in this list. Modern research on bilingualism has identified that people focus on different things, think differently, and understand differently as a function of what language they are speaking. For example, one study found that English-German bilingual speakers seemed to switch perspectives based on the language context they were given the task in. In German they were more goal focused whereas in English they were more action focused.[28]

I once attended a lecture by Keido Fukushima Roshi, abbot of the Tofuku-ji Rinzai Zen monastery in Kyoto, where I later did a brief residency. In his talk, Fukushima Roshi pointed out that the dialog of the famous encounter between Bodhidharma and Emperor Wu cannot be

---

27   These are drawn from the book *Sex at Dawn*. This book is a wonderful deep history of all of the different social arrangements for sex in primates, including humans, since the early hominids. It's a recommended read for helping dispel one's beliefs about correct and incorrect social arrangements.

28   Panos Athanasopoulos, Emanuel Bylund, Guillermo Montero-Melis, Ljubica Damjanovic, Alina Schartner, Alexandra Kibbe, Nick Riches, Guillaume Thierry, "Two Languages, Two Minds Flexible Cognitive Processing Driven by Language of Operation", *Psychological Science*, March 2015.

readily rendered into English because the Chinese is so ambiguous relative to the structure of English. The relevant part of the conversation is this:

> Emperor: "What is the first principle of the holy
>   teachings?"
> Bodhidharma: "Vast emptiness, nothing holy."
> Emperor: "Who is standing before me?"
> Bodhidharma: "I don't know."

Fukushima Roshi said that in the original Chinese, what is translated as "vast emptiness" is actually "clear blue sky," but more importantly, what is translated as "I don't know" is actually just a negation of the verb "to know." Bodhidharma could have meant any, or even all of the following: I don't know; There's no knowledge; Do not know; I, the one who doesn't know; Not knowing; Unknown; Know not.

In Chinese one gets a kind of indeterminacy around Bodhidharma's "not-know" that cannot be rendered into English without it being an explanation.

So, even the language we use changes what we think about the appearances. How can we be sure that the language we speak accurately captures them?

11
The Five Modes of Agrippa

There is no truth. There is only perception.
Gustave Flaubert

A belief is not merely an idea the mind possesses; it is an idea that possesses the mind.   *Robert Oxton Bolton*

The Five Modes of Agrippa are based on the following concepts:

1. Disagreement
Among people – be they ordinary, proclaimed as experts, or proclaimed as wise – there are disagreements. If people disagree, then how can one know with any confidence which position is right?

2. Infinite Regress
When giving support for their propositions, dogmatists will give supporting arguments that are themselves in need of support. The arguments provided to support the supports are similarly in need of support, and so on to infinity. Consequently, we have no place from which to begin to establish anything.

3. Relativity
As described previously in the Ten Modes, external objects appear differently depending on the perspective of who is making the observation and the thing observed.

4. Assumption
To support their propositions, dogmatists will provide something that they do not establish and that they deem worthy of being accepted without question or demonstration.

5. Circularity
To support their propositions, dogmatists will provide the same thing as that which is being questioned.

All of these cases produce situations where one must suspend judgment, and it can be demonstrated that every issue about which might be disputed is subject to these modes.

Anything that is proposed for consideration is either a sense object or a thought object (i.e., something that is perceived with the mind, e.g., ideas). Regardless of which, there is an ongoing disagreement about which are true. Some people claim that only sense objects are true. Others claim that only thought objects are true. Yet others say that some of each are true. So, even about what could possibly be true, we start from a basis of fundamental disagreement that would cover everything.

Can this disagreement be resolved? If it cannot, one must suspend judgment. On the other hand, if it can be resolved, then we want to know how it will be resolved. If one argues that it is sense objects that are true, then what will support this case? Will it be a sense object or a thought object? If the support is to come from a sense object, then since the truth of sense objects is in question, this sense object will also need to be supported. If that support comes from another sense object, that one too will need support, and so on, over and over, without end.

If one argues that the truth of sense objects is supported by a thought object, and since there is a similar disagreement about thought objects, this thought object will need to be supported. If it is supported by another thought object, then that too will need support.

As there is no firm ground on which to rest any of these arguments, one must suspend judgment.

To get around this, suppose one argues that we should assume something by consent and without demonstration to serve as firm ground on which to rest one's arguments. But if one may assume one thing, then there is nothing to prevent one from assuming the opposite. And if one starts by assuming the opposite, then one will come to a completely different conclusion. Worse, if we allow something to be assumed, why not just skip having to develop an argument to support what is disputed and instead just assume it? So, arguing from assumptions gives no firm ground either.

That all sense objects are relative is evident. They are relative to whoever is doing the sensing. The thought objects are relative too, as they are relative to the individuals who think them, and if they were actually part of nature, as some people claim, then there would be no dispute about them.

In summary, it appears that we are unable to find any ultimate foundation for any claim to truth about non-evident matters.

....

12
The Pyrrhonist Maxims

[Philosophers are] excessively cunning murderers of
many wise proverbs.   *Timon*

A good maxim allows you to have the last word without
even starting a conversation.   *Nassim Nicholas Taleb*

While one or more of the Pyrrhonist modes can show any belief to be
unworthy of assent, thus leading one to suspend judgment, their
use in everyday life can be time-consuming and unwieldy for generating
epoché on matters as they arise. For this purpose, we Pyrrhonists have
developed short maxims that help to call about the Pyrrhonist's temper of
mind and emotions. These are an important tool in Pyrrhonist practice.

The "Not More" Maxim
This maxim is also said as "nothing more" with identical meaning. It is
a shortened form of a longer maxim: "not more this than that, up than
down" that originated with Pyrrho. It can also be said as "why more this
than that?" or "why this and not that?" – stating the maxim as a question
rather than an assertion. It is a refusal to define or assent to a non-evident
proposition.

Another variation of the maxim, one that originates with Pyrrho, is,
"it no more is than it is not or it both is and is not or it neither is nor is
not." By "it" this maxim refers to any non-evident matter. This version of
the maxim is prone to being misunderstood. Some take it as a dogmatic
statement denying the law of non-contradiction. This is not what we take
it to mean. We take it to reflect the practitioner's state of mind, indicating
that the matter at hand cannot be determined, and that one has exhausted
all of the possibilities that appear for doing so.

The maxim "not more this than that" makes our feelings clear about
how we reach equilibrium through equipollence of opposed arguments
and ideas. We use the term "equipollence" with regard to a kind of equality between things that appear persuasive to us, and "equilibrium" to refer
to not assenting to either alternative, as a balance on an old-fashioned
scale would be with equal weights on each side.

More than any other image, such a scale can be considered the symbol of Pyrrhonism. The Pyrrhonist philosopher, Michel de Montaigne,

had this image[29] put on the wall of his study, captioned by the Pyrrhonist maxim he invented, which will be discussed shortly.

It may appear that the maxim "nothing more" looks like it could be a denial, but Pyrrhonists do not use it with that meaning or intent. We take it as an abbreviated way of saying: "I don't know which of these I ought to give assent to and which I should deny assent to." This maxim, like all of the other Pyrrhonist maxims, serves to affect our state of mind. The maxims are not something we say to indicate something entirely true and firm. They just represent what appears to us. The maxims are reminders, not truth claims.

The "Non-Assertion" Maxim

The term "assertion" has two senses: a narrow one and a broad one. In the broader sense an "assertion" indicates affirmation or negation, such as "it is daytime," or "it is not daytime." In the narrower sense it is used just to indicate affirmation only. Pyrrhonists use "non-assertion" in the broader sense, to cover statements of either affirmation or negation.

Pyrrhonists practice non-assertion about the non-evident. We don't affirm or deny anything non-evident. In using the maxim, we are not making an assertion that assertions cannot be made about things. We are just expressing our own feelings about our own abilities to make assertions about non-evident things.

To be clear about what things we're talking about, by "assertions" we mean dogmatic statements about the non-evident — statements of belief about non-evident things. These are what we neither affirm nor deny. We do make assertions about evident matters, such as "the language of this book is English," or "this book is about Pyrrhonism." By "evident" here we are referring to things that affect our senses and our feelings such that they force us to assent to them.

The Greek term for "non-assertion" is *aphasia* (pronounced uh-FAZE-e-uh). In Greek the term also has the meaning of "speechlessness"

---

29 https://commons.wikimedia.org/wiki/File:Montaignes_Motto.png

or "wordlessness." Another way to work with this maxim is to take it to mean "say nothing," "be silent." Voicing opinions makes them stronger than merely thinking about them. Using *aphasia* as the maxim can help with this form of practice.

[handwritten margin note: Silence]

The Maxims: "Perhaps," "Possibly," "Maybe"

These belong to the following set of maxims which are all variations on the same theme:
- Perhaps
- Perhaps not
- Possibly
- Possibly not
- Maybe
- Maybe not

[handwritten margin note: Perhaps]

These maxims represent shorter versions of the following maxims:
- Perhaps it is the case
- Perhaps it is not the case
- Possibly it is the case
- Possibly it is not the case
- Maybe it is the case
- Maybe it is not the case

Again, these maxims are not statements of what one believes, but statements that one doesn't have beliefs. They are expressions that one finds the state of affairs about non-evident matters to be undecided.

The "I Withhold Assent" Maxim

[handwritten margin note: unable to select which to believe or not]

"I withhold assent" is short for "I am unable to say which of the proposed alternatives I ought to believe and which I ought not to believe." By saying this, we mean that the arguments for affirming or denying the matter at hand appear equal in terms of credibility. As to whether they actually are equal, we have no firm opinion. We just state what appears to us to be the case about them.

The "I Determine Nothing" Maxim

By "determine" here we use the word in the sense of assenting to something non-evident. In using this maxim, a Pyrrhonist is saying that they are in a state of mind such that they neither dogmatically affirm nor deny the matter in question. This is not a dogmatic statement about the role of the Pyrrhonist. It is just a description of the Pyrrhonist's state of mind and their feelings.

Everything is in flux

The "Everything Is Indeterminate" Maxim

Indeterminateness is a state of mind in which one takes neither an affirmative nor a negative position.

The use of the word "is" here has the benefit of brevity, but it is not appropriately used. What should be used is "appears to be." The word "everything" is also sloppy. By "everything" we are not referring to all things that exist. We are referring just to all non-evident things. For example, the matter of whether you are reading a book right now is evident, but the matter of whether this is the best book about Pyrrhonism is non-evident. By "indeterminate" we mean that, among the non-evident things that are opposite or mutually inconsistent, none of them are clearly more credible or clearly less credible.

Essentially, this maxim is a short way of saying "all of the non-evident matters that I have considered appear to me to be such that not one of them is of superior credibility or of inferior credibility relative to anything that is inconsistent with it."

The experiences are not to be judge

The "Everything Is Non-Apprehensible" Maxim

This maxim is similar to "everything is indeterminate." The issues with wording and meaning are the same except that the topic is apprehension – whether something can be grasped or understood – rather than determination.

This maxim is a way of saying "all of the non-evident matters that I have considered appear to me to be non-apprehensible." In saying this, we are not saying that those matters are inherently non-apprehensible. We are saying that this is simply our experience about those matters. Dogmatists try to refute what we say by insisting that maxims such as these are dogmatic statements, but their arguments are irrelevant to what we are reporting. We are reporting about our experience of equipollence, which is leading us to find things to be non-apprehensive. We are not making dogmatic assertions about the state of reality.

The Maxims: "I Am Non-Apprehensive" and "I Do Not Apprehend"

Again, each of these maxims expresses our personal experience. This experience causes us to decline to take an affirmative or negative position on non-evident matters.

The "To Every Argument an Equal Argument Is Opposed" Maxim

By "every argument" we mean only the arguments we have considered. We don't mean every argument that has been or could ever be made. By "argument" we mean only the sense of the term that applies to establishing dogmatically something not evident. Further, we don't limit "argument" to meaning putting forth by means of premises and conclusions. We also include any method of persuading one to adopt a belief about the non-evident.

By "equal" we mean with regard to credibility or lack thereof. As before, for "is" we tacitly mean "appears to me." Thus, by this maxim we mean "for every argument I have examined for establishing a belief about something non-evident there appears to me to be another argument in opposition, and that argument appears to me to be equally credible."

Again this maxim is not making a dogmatic statement about the nature of arguments. It is just describing what we experience.

An alternative version of this maxim is: "to every argument an equal argument is to be opposed." This turns the maxim into an admonition meaning "to every argument attempting to establish a belief about the non-evident we are to oppose some conflicting argument that is equally credible." The purpose of stating the maxim this way is to encourage the practitioner to resist being tricked by the arguments of the dogmatists into ceasing to raise questions and to rashly give in. This would cause the practitioner to lose the ataraxia that tends to come following epoché.

The "What Do I Know?" Maxim

This maxim was created by the Pyrrhonist philosopher Michel de Montaigne, which he adopted as his motto. It is perhaps the single statement for which he is most known for. Montaigne's *Essays* were a rambling inquiry into a vast array of subject matters in which Montaigne freely entertained doubt, and, like Plutarch, who was his primary inspiration, endeavored to look at each issue from multiple perspectives, finding great variety, volatility, and fallibility to be the basic features of human nature. The longest and most influential of his essays, *Apology for Raymond Sebond*, marks his adoption of Pyrrhonism and the creation of this maxim that Montaigne used to remind himself that he, like all other humans, was incapable of attaining truth.

Concluding Remarks About the Pyrrhonist Maxims

More maxims than these exist. These are just the most popular and traditional ones. Anything that calls to mind the practice of Pyrrhonism can be used as a maxim, contingent on the personal feelings, thinking, and experience of the practitioner.

It is important to understand that in using these maxims we absolutely are not firmly maintaining anything about whether they are true. On the contrary, we say that they are actually self-refuting, as they themselves are included among all the things to which the maxims apply, just as cathartic drugs not only flush things out of the body but cause themselves to be expelled as well. In this respect, the maxims should be viewed as cathartic ideas that flush things out of the soul, expelling themselves in the process as well.

The maxims reflect what appears to us. They are not firmly maintained assertions about the nature of reality. They are not applied to all things in general. They are only applied to non-evident things. We do not propose these maxims as statements which sharply express the points they make. We see that they are imprecise and not strictly correct. We are not concerned about hair-splitting the precise meanings of the maxims. They are just practice aids. They are not absolute statements.

13
Can Pyrrhonists Question
What Is Said by the Dogmatists?

The most subversive people are those who ask questions.
Jostein Gaarder, Sophie's World

We ought to bring up the question whether it is the sane or the demented who speak at the right moment. For whenever anyone asks this question they answer that the two groups say the same things, but that the wise speak at the right moment and the demented at the wrong one. And in saying this, they appear to be making a small addition, "the right moment" or "the wrong one," so that the situation is no longer the same.   *Anon.,* Dissoi Logoi[30]

One of the principal concepts developed by Arcesilaus and thereby associated with Pyrrhonism goes by the term *acatalepsia* (pronounced a CAT-uh-LEP-see-UH). It means incomprehensibleness, or the impossibility of comprehending or conceiving a thing. It is the incomprehensibility of all things. This word sums up what appears to be the case about human knowledge: that it never amounts to certainty, but only to things that look like they may be true. Acatalepsia is a synonym of a word often used in describing Buddhism: non-apprehension.

Acatalepsia is typically contrasted with the Stoic's counter-argument, the concept of *katalepsis.* The Stoics believe that the mind instinctively discriminates between real and false impressions. However, one ought not to give credit to everything which is perceived, but only to those perceptions which contain some special mark of those things which appeared. In Stoicism such a perception is called a "kataleptic phantasia," meaning a comprehensible perception. The kataleptic phantasia is that which is impressed by an object which exists, which is a copy of that object and can be produced by no other object.

Cicero said that Zeno of Citium, the founder of Stoicism, illustrated katalepsis as follows:

---

30   The *Dissoi Logoi* is a treatise written by an anonymous sophist at some time subsequent to the Peloponnesian War. It was preserved appended to one of the manuscripts of Sextus Empiricus' works.

...he would display his hand in front of one with the fingers stretched out and say "A visual appearance is like this;" next he closed his fingers a little and said, "An act of assent is like this;" then he pressed his fingers closely together and made a fist, and said that that was comprehension (and from this illustration he gave to that process the actual name of katalepsis, which it had not had before); but then he used to apply his left hand to his right fist and squeeze it tightly and forcibly, and then say that such was knowledge, which was within the power of nobody save the wise man.[31]

The Pyrrhonists responded to the Stoics on this matter in the Ten Modes of Aenesidemus, demonstrating that there is no sure katalepsis.

Because Pyrrhonists say that reality seems acataleptic, some of the dogmatists proclaim that Pyrrhonists are not in a position to raise questions about philosophy, claiming on the basis of the Pyrrhonists' own testimony that we cannot even comprehend the issues. They do this by presenting a dilemma: either the Pyrrhonists apprehend what the dogmatists say, or they do not.

1. If Pyrrhonists do apprehend, how is it that the Pyrrhonists can claim to be at a loss about what they claim to apprehend?

2. If the Pyrrhonists don't apprehend, how is it that they even know how to discuss the issues that they have not apprehended?

So, just as a person who is ignorant about particular subjects is unable to discuss them or raise objections about them, the dogmatists say that Pyrrhonists' failure to apprehend the things said by the dogmatists precludes us from raising objections to or questioning the statements of the dogmatists.

This argument can be demonstrated to be sophistry. Let's start with what it means to "apprehend." In one sense it can mean simply to conceive, to understand, to grasp. None of these things require the person doing the apprehending to agree that the thing apprehended actually exists. A person can apprehend the idea of a unicorn, but that doesn't mean they agree that unicorns exist, nor does it preclude them from questioning whether unicorns exist or objecting to the assertion that unicorns exist.

In another sense, the dogmatists may be using the term to "apprehend" as the Stoics and some others use it to mean "to assent to an impression."

---

31   Cicero (1967). *De natura deorum academica*. Transl. H Rackham. Cambridge, MA: Harvard University Press. II.145

In this usage, "impression" means "something that is derived from, and stamped and impressed in accordance with, an existent object or state of affairs, and is such as something that would arise from something non-existent." If that's what the dogmatists mean by the term "apprehend," then it seems that they themselves would want to claim an inability to raise questions about things that they have not apprehended. For example, when a Stoic raises questions in opposition to the Epicurean's statements that Being is divided, or that God lacks foreknowledge of events, or that pleasure is good, has the Stoic apprehended the Epicurean's statements or not? If the Stoic has apprehended the Epicurean's statements in the sense we're talking about here, then this Stoic has completely broken with Stoicism by assenting to these impressions. On the other hand, if they have not apprehended them, they cannot say anything against them. This same situation would similarly apply to people who subscribe to other dogmatic systems, preventing them from raising questions against one another. Alternatively, if one grants that it is impossible to raise questions about what is not in this sense apprehended, then one is granting that all of dogmatic philosophy is wrong and, correspondingly, Pyrrhonist philosophy must therefore be the only correct philosophy.

Someone who makes a dogmatic assertion about a non-evident matter does so either having or not having apprehended that non-evident matter. If they have not apprehended the matter, they won't be worthy of being believed. If they have apprehended the matter, they must either have apprehended it directly, through itself, and with clarity, or else they have apprehended it by means of research and inquiry. If they claim that the non-evident thing has been apprehended immediately through itself and with clarity, then that thing would not be non-evident. Instead, it would be equally apparent to everybody. It would be a matter that everyone would agree on and would not dispute. But endless controversy exists among the dogmatists about every single non-evident matter. Consequently, anyone who firmly maintains and asserts something about the existence of a non-evident thing or state of affairs cannot have apprehended it immediately through itself and with clarity.

On the other hand, if they have apprehended it through research, how were they able to conduct the inquiry before they had accurately apprehended its object? This is what the dogmatists are claiming in this argument that Pyrrhonists are unable to do. For since the inquiry requires the prior accurate apprehension of, and thus an inquiry into, what is going to be inquired about, while in turn the apprehension itself of the object of inquiry certainly requires an inquiry into that object beforehand, it becomes impossible for dogmatists to inquire into and dogmatize about things non-evident. Thus the dogmatists' argument here falls into the problem of circularity. If any of them wish to begin with the apprehension, then they must inquire about the object before apprehending it. If they wish to begin with the inquiry, they must apprehend the object before inquiring about it. Consequently, according to this argument it is impossible to apprehend anything non-evident. This, of course, precludes making any claims about anything non-evident.

If the dogmatists say that it is not this kind of apprehension that they are claiming needs to precede inquiry, but rather simply the conception of the matter, then it is not impossible for those who are suspending judgment to inquire about the existence of non-evident things. Pyrrhonists are not precluded from conceptions that arise during a discussion that produce clear appearances to them that are experienced passively, and that this happens does not at all imply the existence of the apprehended objects since, people conceive not only of things and states of affairs that exist, but also of those that do not. Hence, a person may be suspending judgment when he is inquiring and when he is forming conceptions. He assents to whatever things affect him according to passively received impressions, insofar as those impressions appear to him.

One interesting ramification of this is that it is the dogmatists who are precluded from inquiry. Inquiring about objects and states of affairs is not inconsistent for those who do not know how those things are by nature. But for those who do think they already have accurate knowledge about those things there is no opportunity for further inquiry, because once accurate knowledge is attained the inquiry has already reached its goal. For those who do not think that they know, the supposition on which every inquiry is based still holds – that they have not yet found out the facts. Thus the mind of the Pyrrhonist remains fully open whereas the dogmatist closes off parts of their mind.

14

The Basis of
Pyrrhonist Criticism of Dogmatism

Whoever undertakes to set himself up as a judge of Truth
and Knowledge is shipwrecked by the laughter of the
gods.   *Albert Einstein*

The Intellectual-Yet-Idiot pathologizes others for doing
things he doesn't understand without ever realizing it is
his understanding that may be limited.
                                      Nassim Nicholas Taleb,
                                      The Intellectual Yet Idiot

Pyrrhonism argues against the dogmatists' claims that they have found
any truth that can be held to be certain about anything that people
have meaningful disagreements about. We don't argue against things that
are evident, such as 2+2=4 or that Socrates was a human being. Our arguments are about the disputed, non-evident matters that the dogmatists
claim that they know the truth about.

Any inquiry into the truth must involve a criterion. The word "criterion" has two senses. In one sense it means that by which one may decide
questions about existence or non-existence. In the other sense it means
that with regard to which one may conduct their life. This second sense
of the term and how it applies to Pyrrhonist practice has already been
addressed. We will now examine the first sense of the term: what is called
the "criterion of truth."

The criterion of truth has three senses: the general, the specific, and
the most specific. In the general sense, it is any standard of apprehension.
In this sense even physical features, such as eyesight, are called criteria.
Thus one can use eyesight to look at a printed version of this page and
determine that the words are printed in black ink. In the specific sense,
it is any technical standard for apprehension, such as a measuring stick.
Thus one can use a scale to determine how much the printed version of
this book weighs. These are the criteria not only of ordinary life, but also
of empirical science.

In the most specific case, the criterion of truth represents any technical standard for the apprehension of a non-evident object or state of

affairs. It is this criterion of truth that we find lacking. Without a criterion of truth, there's no way to tell truth from delusion.

15
Does a Criterion of Truth Exist?

Then you were quite right in affirming that knowledge is only perception; and the meaning turns out to be the same, whether with Homer and Heraclitus, and all that company, you say that all is motion and flux, or with the great sage Protagoras, that man is the measure of all things; or with Theaetetus, that, given these premises, perception is knowledge.

Socrates,
Theaetetus

I am glad you do not palter with the truth. But what are your hopes in pursuing philosophy, then? You see that neither your own teacher, nor his, nor his again, and so on to the tenth generation, has been absolutely wise and so attained eudaimonia. It will not serve you to say that it is enough to get near eudaimonia; that is no good; a person on the doorstep is just as much outside and in the air as another a long way off, though with the difference that the former is tantalized by a nearer view. [32]

Lucian of Samosata,
Hermotimus

Some philosophers in antiquity, such as the Stoics and Epicureans, claimed that a criterion of truth exists. Not only that, according to the Stoics, their idea of a sage is a person who possesses an infallible criterion of truth, which makes that person in all respects god-like.[33] Others said one does not exist. These included Xeniades and Xenophanes, who said "opinion holds sway over everything."

Resolving whether a criterion of truth exists represents a circular problem. Those involved in the dispute must declare whether they think this dispute can be decided. If they say it can be decided, then how is it to be decided given that we do not have any agreed-upon criterion of truth to use to decide it and we do not know whether one even exists?

To this day all attempts to demonstrate a criterion of truth have result-ed in criteria that suffer from erroneousness, incompleteness, circularity, or

---

32 Lucian is criticizing Stoic dogma, that sagehood is unattainable.

33 Sextus Empiricus, *Against the Professors* (7.423)

infinite regress. Let's review the things that people use as criteria of truth. None of them is without flaws. Five of these that we will consider appear to have some utility, but they are each seriously insufficient to be a criterion of truth. Even combined, these five still don't form a criterion of truth. At best they are partial criterions of falseness. These five are as follows.

Correspondence

Correspondence is when a claim corresponds with its object. For example, the claim that Athens is in Greece is true if Athens is actually located in Greece. The problem with correspondence is that it doesn't go beyond the appearances. We can see for ourselves that Athens is in Greece, but we cannot directly experience correspondence with non-evident things, such as theories about how gravity works. At best we can just observe that the appearances correspond with the predictions.

Coherence

Coherence refers to a consistent and overarching explanation for all facts. To be coherent, all pertinent facts must be arranged in a consistent and cohesive fashion as an integrated whole. The theory which most effectively reconciles all facts in this fashion may be considered most likely to be true. The problem is that we are unable to acquire all the facts because we are not omniscient. Therefore coherence only works as a criterion of falseness by way of demonstrating incoherence.

Pragmatic

Some people conclude that if an idea works then it must be true. But some myths work for telling farmers when to plant and harvest. So this turns out only to be only a criterion of falseness. If something doesn't work, it is not true.

Mere Consistency

Mere consistency is just that the logical rule of non-contradiction is not violated. Violating that rule is just a criterion of falseness, not truth.

Strict Consistency

Strict consistency is when claims are connected in such a fashion that one statement logically follows from another. Again this ends up merely working as a criterion of falseness, because the proving the premises of a logical argument falls into infinite regress or circularity.

***

Next we will consider other criteria of truth that people use. These have all sorts of problems. The better ones are merely heuristics. The poorer ones are paths that are just as likely to lead to error as to truth.

Authority
The opinions of those with significant experience or training are often considered a form of proof. The problem is that for most things of any interest, different authorities disagree.

Intuition
Intuition is an assumed truth with an unknown, or possibly unexamined, source. It is a judgment that is not dependent on a rational examination of the facts. Intuitions are often erroneous.

Revelation
Revelations are presumed to come from God or some other higher power. Revelation is a mix of intuition and authority, both of which are demonstrably fallible.

General Consent, Majority Rule, Custom, and Tradition
The opinions held by large numbers of other people have been considered a criterion of truth. The problem is that general consent once held the earth was flat and that the sun revolved about the earth. So, this technique is known to fail. Majority rule is just a version of general consent that requires fewer people to consent. Custom and tradition are a type of general consent based on what people consented to in the past. These have the advantage of being tested over time. But of course, customs and traditions change over time, as people determine that they no longer work as well as desired.

Most people employ custom as a guide to action based on the assumption that doing what is customary will help one avoid error. Indeed, we Pyrrhonists recommend that one should follow custom as a guide. We just don't think our customs are truer than the customs of others.

Emotions
Many people allow feelings to determine their judgment, often in the face of contrary evidence, or even without even attempting to gather evidence. This implicitly accepts emotions as a criterion of truth. Acting on emotion is an infamously good way to make bad decisions.

Naïve Realism

Naïve Realism is the idea that only that which is directly observable by the human senses is true. This has been shown not to work because it is easy to demonstrate differences between what is directly observed and the reality of its cause. For example, an oar stuck in the water looks bent, but in reality, it is not bent.

So, except for some limited and usually uninteresting and uncontroversial things for which correspondence works for as a criterion of truth, such as $1 + 1 = 2$ and simple statements such as "this book was written in English" we have no demonstrated criterion of truth.

If we have no criterion of truth by which to go by, shouldn't we take the Pyrrhonist advice to suspend judgment?

16
The Problem of Induction

Make a commitment, delusion is nearby.
The Third Delphic Maxim

Those who believe in the unconditional benefits of past experience should consider this pearl of wisdom allegedly voiced by a famous ship's captain:
"But in all my experience, I have never been in any accident...of any sort worth speaking about. I have seen but one vessel in distress in all my years at sea. I never saw a wreck and never have been wrecked nor was I ever in any predicament that threatened to end in disaster of any sort." *E. J. Smith, 1907, Captain, RMS Titanic*

Captain Smith's ship sank in 1912 in what became the most talked-about shipwreck in history.
Nicholas Nassim Taleb

Induction is the inference of a general principle from particular instances. It is commonly contrasted with deduction, which is the inference of particular instances by reference to a general principle. For example, deduction works as follows:

General principle: All people die.
Particular instance: You are a person.
Inference: You are going to die.

Induction works in the opposite direction.

Particular instance 1: Socrates died.
Particular instance 2: The Buddha died.
Particular instance 3: my grandparents died.
And so on.
Inference: All people die.

The problem of induction is whether inductive reasoning leads to knowledge because it suffers from two problems.

1. Induction requires generalizing about a class of objects based on numerous observations of it. The classic example is that inference that all swans are white, which is the subject of an ancient Roman saying that assumes that black swans do not exist. The saying was used to indicate that something was impossible. Then the Europeans got to Australia and discovered black swans there. This spectacularly showed that what was once a statement of impossibility was itself wrong.

2. Presupposing that a sequence of events in the future will occur as it has in the past. The classic example of this is the turkey who infers that his owner is magnanimous for housing it, keeping it safe, and feeding it every day. Then Thanksgiving comes, and the owner slaughters the turkey.

The problem of induction is a famous problem about the unreliability of what people consider to be knowledge. It's also one of the great successes of Pyrrhonism, as the Pyrrhonists were the first in the West to point it out.[34]

People use induction to find causal relationships. Science is built upon induction. But induction is simply unreliable. It periodically and unexpectedly fails. While induction is useful as a guide in making decisions and developing technologies, it cannot be relied upon to provide truth.

---

34 To be fair, the Indian Charvaka philosophers may have pointed it out earlier that the Pyrrhonists did, and that this may even have been one of the ideas that Pyrrho brought back with him from India. On the other hand, it's also possible that Pyrrho introduced the idea to India, as firmly dateable records of it in Pyrrhonism long predate any such records in India. These issues are much contested and are not relevant to Pyrrhonist practice. It doesn't matter who first pointed out the problem of induction. What matters is understanding that induction is flawed. Readers who are curious about such issues may wish to explore the discussion of them in *Greek Buddha: Pyrrho's Encounter with Early Buddhism in Central Asia* by Christopher I. Beckwith.

17
The Criterion of Action

Pyrrho did not want to make himself a stump or a stone; he wanted to make himself a living, thinking, reasoning man, enjoying all natural pleasures and comforts, employing and using all his bodily and spiritual faculties in regular and upright fashion. The fantastic, imaginary, false privileges that man has arrogated to himself, of regimenting, arranging, and fixing truth, he honestly renounced and gave up.   *Montaigne*

Stepping forward is a mistake; stepping backward is also a mistake, taking one step is a mistake, taking two steps is also a mistake; therefore one mistake after another mistake. Whatever we say is a mistake.

Dogen
Gyobutsu Igi

Pyrrhonists are not only philosophers (the term we use for anyone engaged in seeking wisdom), we are also human beings who have to make everyday decisions. These decisions are critical for any life form. It seems to us that the skill that humans developed for making these decisions somehow got hijacked into making decisions about non-evident things.

One of the dogmatists' arguments against Pyrrhonism is that epoché precludes action. They base this on the premise that motivation involves beliefs; therefore, for there to be action a person must believe that they should perform some action, or believe that some outcome is good. Our argument is that actions do not require beliefs. Indeed, nature provides an abundance of examples of living creatures mentally incapable of having beliefs but fully capable of making decisions and taking action. It appears that the dogmatists refuse to understand our distinctions about appearances, signs, the evident and the non-evident, and to insist that beliefs must be involved. Neuroscience indicates that this is a delusion. In *The Knowledge Illusion: Why We Never Think Alone* the cognitive scientists Steven Sloman and Philip Fernbach describe the problem this way:

Why do we live in an illusion of understanding? To get a better sense of why this illusion is central to how we think, it helps to understand why we think. Thought could have evolved to serve several functions. The function of thought could be to represent the world – to construct a model in our heads that corresponds in critical ways to the way the world is. Or thought could be there to make language possible so we can communicate with others. Or thought could be for problem solving or decision making. Or maybe it evolved for a specific purpose such as building tools or showing off to potential mates. All of these ideas may have something to them, but thought surely evolved to serve a larger purpose, a purpose common to all these proposals: Thought is for action. Thinking evolved as an extension of the ability to act effectively; it evolved to make us better at doing what's necessary to achieve our goals.[35]

This reflects the Pyrrhonist view. Thought is for action. Investing thought into the non-evident, where no action is entailed, is what gives rise to beliefs.

Pyrrhonism is not a technique for stopping thought. It is a technique for preventing thought from getting taken over by beliefs. Thought for supporting action is necessary, as are criteria to use in decision making. We see four criteria for action: nature, our senses, laws and customs, and practical expertise.

The Guidance of Nature
Our own bodies, including our perceptual and cognitive abilities, our reflexes, our instincts, and the experience of being human, show the world to us in a particular way and direct us towards some things and away from others. As Plutarch put it:

> The inductive argument by which we conclude that senses are not accurate or trustworthy does not deny that an object presents to us a certain appearance, but forbids us, though we continue to make use of the senses and take the appearance as our guide in what we do, to trust them as entirely and infallibly true. For we ask no more of them than utilitarian service in the unavoidable essentials, since there is nothing better available; but they do

---

35   Steven Sloman, Philip Fernbach, *The Knowledge Illusion: Why We Never Think Alone.* 2017, pp 10-11.

not provide the perfect knowledge and understanding of a thing that the philosophical soul longs to acquire.[36]

One of the difficulties for modern readers in understanding the guidance of nature is lack of clarity of what is meant by "nature." We have nothing from the ancient Pyrrhonists clarifying what they meant by the term. However, other Hellenistic philosophies also used the term, most notably, one of the Stoics' core prescriptions for life was to live according to nature. It seems that we can infer that the Pyrrhonists and Stoics shared a common understanding of the term, and so we can use the Stoics' literature to illuminate what Sextus meant by the guidance of nature.

The word that is conventionally translated as "nature" is the Greek term *physis*. *Physis* refers to the process of natural growth. Aristotle said that *physis* is its own source of motion. For example, consider the process of an acorn becoming an oak tree. It is a natural process that has its own driving force behind it. No external force pushes this acorn to its final state. Rather, the acorn progressively develops towards the end of becoming a tree. So, the guidance of *physis* would mean the guidance of how organic things, which includes humans, change and grow.

In Seneca's fifth letter to Lucilius he says this about the Stoics:

> Our motto, as you know, is "live according to nature;" but it is quite contrary to nature to torture the body, to hate unlabored elegance, to be dirty on purpose, to eat food that is not only plain, but disgusting and forbidding. Just as it is a sign of luxury to seek out dainties, so it is madness to avoid that which is customary and can be purchased at no great price. Philosophy calls for plain living, but not for penance; and we may perfectly well be plain and neat at the same time. This is the mean of which I approve; our life should observe a happy medium between the ways of a sage and the ways of the world at large; all men should admire it, but they should understand it also.

Seneca appears to be saying that nature guides our choices to align with our physical requirements, and that people should reach for the things which nature has designed humans to desire, such as health, safety, and community. It appears that this is what is meant by the guidance of nature.

---

36 Adv. Col. 1118

The Zen tradition also has pointers to what is meant by the guidance of nature. One example appears in this Zen story:

> When Bankei was preaching at Ryumon temple, a Shin-shu priest, who believed in salvation through repetition of the name of the Buddha of Love, was jealous of his large audience and wanted to debate with him. Bankei was in the midst of a talk when the priest appeared, but the fellow made such a disturbance that Bankei stopped his discourse and asked about the noise. "The founder of our sect," boasted the priest, "had such miraculous powers that he held a brush in his hand on one bank of the river, his attendant held up a paper on the other bank, and the teacher wrote the holy name of Amida through the air. Can you do such a wonderful thing?" Bankei replied lightly: "Perhaps your fox can perform that trick, but that is not the manner of Zen. My miracle is that when I feel hungry I eat, and when I feel thirsty I drink."

Another version of the story goes:

> A student once asked his teacher, "Master, what is enlightenment?" The master replied, "When hungry, eat. When tired, sleep."

This story exemplifies how beliefs are just fanciful things, like writing through the air, but eudaimonia comes from living non-dogmatically, following the guidance of nature.

Physical Sensations
We experience things such as hunger and thirst. These are forced upon us from the circumstances of our bodies.

Laws and Customs
We live in general conformity with the guidance of our society. That doesn't mean we believe in the laws and customs. We just follow them, undogmatically, seeing that going against the laws and customs produces difficulties.

Teaching of Forms and Expertise
It's useful here to differentiate between two kinds of knowing. One is knowing *how*, such as how to ride a bike, how to bake a cake, and how to perform

surgery. This kind of knowing is fully open to Pyrrhonists. Another is a knowing *that*. There are two kinds of knowing *that*. One is of what is evident; the other is of what is non-evident. Knowing the evident, as long as it is done undogmatically, is also fully open to the Pyrrhonist. It is knowing the non-evident that Pyrrhonism recognizes is problematic. For example, one may know how to follow the Christian ritual of the Eucharist, and one may engage in following it. One may know that there is bread and wine involved in it. One may know that some people believe that the bread and wine are transubstantiated into the body and blood of Jesus Christ. But about whether transubstantiation happens, a Pyrrhonist suspends judgment. It is, however, the custom of the ceremony that the transubstantiation does happen; therefore the Pyrrhonist engaged in the ritual follows the custom. Similarly, if a Pyrrhonist is engaged in an activity where it is the custom to believe that certain non-evident propositions are true, the Pyrrhonist follows the custom. For example, a Pyrrhonist in doing work as a biologist would follow the custom that the theory of evolution was true.

In observing a Pyrrhonist, the typical person would see someone who looks pretty much like any ordinary person. The only clues that the person was a Pyrrhonist would likely be their skepticism regarding the various controversies of their day, and their failure to be convinced that they should give up that skepticism. This is not to say that Pyrrhonists cannot make decisions where controversy or abstract issues are involved. The philosopher Favorinus specifically mentioned that Pyrrhonists were fully capable of making legal decisions.

As an aside, Favorinus is a particularly interesting character. He presented himself as an Academic Skeptic, although this was long after the Academy ceased to be inquiryist. He was a student of Plutarch. He wrote a book on the Ten Modes of Pyrrhonism and appears to have drawn little distinction between Pyrrhonism and Academic Skepticism. Diogenes Laertius, in his biography of Pyrrho, cites Favorinus several times, in ways that seem indistinguishable from his citations of Pyrrhonist philosophers. Favorinus was intersex, and quite obviously so. It would seem natural that having such an experience in life would cause one to be interested in the philosophy of indeterminacy. Favorinus also had an Indian slave. There's a modern tendency to think of the Roman Empire as being much too far away from India for there to have been any meaningful contact. This simply was not so. The two civilizations engaged in robust trade, and the journey was not so difficult that people could not make it, including people of such fungible value as slaves.

Does becoming a Pyrrhonist entail believing that nothing really matters? No, because that itself is a belief. Things do seem to matter. There appear to be causes and effects. Some actions seem to be beneficial. Other actions appear to be harmful. The whole point of Pyrrhonism is not to get caught up in believing that they actually do matter, that we actually know that they matter, and that we can accurately predict how our actions will affect things. We are constantly mistaken about things, most particularly about the non-evident things. Pyrrhonism redirects our attention away from non-evident things and towards the evident, our natural sentiments, and what is customary. These are all reasonable, although imperfect guides towards actions that are less likely to be badly wrong. As James Ford Roshi said, paraphrasing Dogen: "life is one mistake after another." Of course it is. We don't know the truth. Therefore every action is in some way a mistake.

It should be evident that Timon, Aenesidemus, Sextus Empiricus, and I all think that Pyrrhonism matters. It mattered enough to us to write books on it. It appears to us that Pyrrhonism is beneficial. I – and I presume the other authors – hoped that writing books on it would have beneficial effects, and that these effects would matter. But as I write this, these effects are unknown to me. Perhaps this book will never get published, and I will have wasted a huge amount of time on it. Perhaps it will get published and become an object of ridicule. Perhaps it will become a best-seller, entailing a transformation of my life that I may not end up liking.

Life is a series of choices. The dogmatist believes their choices are right, based on non-evident ideas that encompass a variety of circumstances beyond what is needed for choice. The Pyrrhonist takes a best guess, on an as-needed basis, without ideological commitment.

Some people argue that for modern people there is no chance of suspension of judgement on all theoretical subjects, particularly in the natural sciences, where we now know too much for suspension of judgement to be an option. Many questions have been settled, and not just at a theoretical level, but in ways that the answers are incorporated into our lives via technology. The ancient Pyrrhonists said that if one saw smoke it was reasonable to conclude that there was fire. Sometime in the far distant past, people who saw smoke didn't know enough to conclude that there was fire. If something is so well worked out that there's no dispute about it anymore, like how smoke indicates fire, then this just becomes something that becomes either a mnemonic sign, or something commonly accepted. Pyrrhonism is not a program for convincing people to reject things that are commonly accepted. Once something becomes commonly accepted, it falls into the area of custom. Pyrrhonists follow customs. Our goal is ataraxia; it is not disputing for the sake of disputing.

Some people express concern that Pyrrhonism involves giving up the search for truth. Consider as an example a Pyrrhonist cancer researcher who is hot on the trail of finding a cure for cancer. It seems to some people that this researcher would become troubled or would lose their enthusiasm by continually subjecting a theory that holds promise to arguments that produce epoché. But the great thing about science is that it is empirical. Each questioning of the non-evident parts of the theory can be subjected to empirical testing. The testing results in appearances. Pyrrhonists accept appearances. There's no reason for the researcher to be disappointed one way or the other. The research is just a kind of game where predictions that turn out right are rewarded. The decisions needed in the ordinary activities of life operate in the same way.

Some people have difficulty understanding the Pyrrhonist criterion of action. I suppose because it is so simple and so broad. It's simple because we use the appearances, laws, customs, and our own feelings in deciding what to do. We don't use beliefs. As dogmatists base their decisions on their beliefs, they don't know what to make of this. Here is a classic example of this reaction. In the Stoic philosopher Epictetus' *Discourses*,[37] Epictetus lays out his argument against the Pyrrhonist criterion of action.

> It is said that there are those who will oppose very evident truths, and yet it is not easy to find a reason which may persuade such a one to alter his opinion. This may arise neither from his own strength nor from the weakness of his teacher; but when a man becomes obstinate in error, reason cannot always reach him.
>
> Now there are two sorts of obstinacy: the one, of the intellect; the other, of the will. A man may obstinately set himself not to assent to evident truths, nor to quit the defense of contradictions. We all dread a bodily paralysis, and would make use of every contrivance to avoid it; but none of us is troubled about a paralysis of the soul. And yet, indeed, even with regard to the soul, when a person is so affected as not to apprehend or understand anything, we think him in a sad condition; but where the emotions of shame and modesty are under an absolute paralysis, we go so far as even to call this strength of mind!
>
> Are you certain that you are awake? "I am not," replies such a person, "for neither am I certain when in dreaming I appear to myself to be awake." Is there no difference, then, between these appearances? "None." Shall I argue with this man any longer? For what steel

---

37   Book 1, Chapter 5.

or what caustic can I apply, to make him sensible of his paralysis? If he is sensible of it, and pretends not to be so, he is even worse than dead. He sees not his inconsistency, or, seeing it, holds to the wrong. He moves not, makes no progress; he rather falls back. His sense of shame is gone; his reasoning faculty is not gone, but brutalized. Shall I call this strength of mind? By no means, - unless we allow it to be such in the vilest debauchees publicly to speak and act out their worse impulses.

Epictetus seems to perversely misunderstand the Pyrrhonist position. We do not oppose "evident truths." We accept what is evident. Suspending judgement so as to avoid belief does not make Pyrrhonists incapable of action. When we need a decision to determine an action, we make the decision. We make the decision based on how things appear to us. We just don't believe that how things appear to us represents how things are. They're just our best efforts to address what the situation requires.

The Enchiridion of Epictetus opens with the following famous words regarding a fundamental aspect of Stoic philosophy, known as the "dichotomy of control."

Of things some are in our power, and others are not. In our power are opinion, movement towards a thing, desire, aversion, turning from a thing; and in a word, whatever are our acts. Not in our power are the body, property, reputation, offices (magisterial power), and in a word, whatever are not our own acts. And the things in our power are by nature free, not subject to restraint or hindrance; but the things not in our power are weak, slavish, subject to restraint, in the power of others. Remember then, that if you think the things which are by nature slavish to be free, and the things which are in the power of others to be your own, you will be hindered, you will lament, you will be disturbed, you will blame both gods and men; but if you think that only which is your own to be your own, and if you think that what is another's, as it really is, belongs to another, no man will ever compel you, no man will hinder you, you will never blame any man, you will accuse no man, you will do nothing involuntarily (against your will), no man will harm you, you will have no enemy, for you will not suffer any harm.

Many ancient Pyrrhonist arguments against fundamental aspects of Stoicism were preserved, yet we have no sign that there was a Pyrrhonist argument against the dichotomy of control. I suspect that's because the Stoic dichotomy of control is so congruent with the Pyrrhonist criterion of action, and as such may provide some insight for those who have trouble understanding the criterion of action. The surviving Pyrrhonist literature says little about the criterion of action. Perhaps it did not need to. It seems apparent enough that we can all agree that some things are in our control and others are not. If it's not in our control, it's not in the realm of our being able to take action on it. If we cannot take action on it, there is no need to make any decision upon it. There's no utility to having a belief about it. Correspondingly, Pyrrhonists avoid getting wrapped up in thinking about things that do not require a decision. Perhaps you've met people who are emotionally wrapped up in all sorts of matters that they can do nothing about, such as politics.

Pyrrho was once on a ship as a storm was approaching. The other passengers became anxious about the storm. Pyrrho pointed out a pig that was being transported on the ship. The pig was eating, untroubled by thoughts of the approaching storm. Pyrrho said that the pig's reaction to the storm was wise and that it should be emulated. This is much like the dichotomy of control. Neither the pig nor the passengers could do anything about the storm. What they could take action on was their attitude towards the storm.

One of the implications of focusing on decisions needed for action and removing attention away from the speculative issues involving the non-evident is that it results in a drastic reduction in what one needs to focus on or worry about. Pyrrhonists do not get caught up in obsessing about the past or the future. Actions cannot be retrospectively made, so the past just becomes information for informing decisions. Yes, Pyrrhonists do think about the future, but as we lack the kind of castles-in-the-sky view of the dogmatists, our thinking about the future is focused on the pragmatic.

Recognizing that nothing is inherently good or bad, Pyrrhonists are freed from insecurity about the material possessions or successes of others. One cannot know whether those things turn out to be good or bad for others. Indeed, one can find plenty of examples of people who won the lottery, and the money caused their lives to be ruined. Focusing the mind away from speculations of the non-evident, and away from speculations about the nature of good and bad frees up a lot of mental capacity. Where does the capacity go to? Where else can it go to? It goes to the present moment, and it does so without any effort or design to put it there.

An anecdote is recorded in which Pyrrho fled for safety upon being attacked by a dog. Pyrrho was later criticized for this on the basis of his own philosophy: that being attacked by the dog should be no different from not being attacked. Pyrrho responded that one "ought to strive with all their power to counteract circumstances with their actions if possible, and at all events with their reason." Pyrrhonism is not inactive. It is not like ensconcing oneself in a monastery and meditating all day, avoiding the world. It deals with ordinary life in the ordinary way. Ordinarily we protect ourselves from being attacked. We should act if possible. If we cannot act, then we should use reason, i.e., Pyrrhonist self-argumentation for dealing with our situation.

What matters for action? Whether it works. Hence Pyrrhonists embrace the pragmatic criterion. We just don't delude ourselves that the pragmatic criterion produces truth. It just works reasonably well in making decisions. It entails mistakes. Some myths worked for telling ancient farmers when to plant and harvest. Then we came up with some better ideas for making those decisions. In the future we will likely come up with even better ideas that invalidate our current ideas just the way our current ideas invalidated the myths.

The life of a Pyrrhonist is filled with a kind of philosophical activity, but one unlike that of the philosophical dogmatists, which is what most people intuitively imagine. It is a life of engaging in philosophical argument on multiple sides of issues, due to the ability the Pyrrhonist develops to assemble arguments and data on any given topic in such a way as to demonstrate equal strength. As a result, the Pyrrhonist is no more inclined towards any position over any other. This results in epoché, which in turn yields ataraxia. Most of the surviving ancient Pyrrhonist writings are at-length examples of this procedure. While its purpose may have included converting others to Pyrrhonism, its chief purpose was as an on-going activity for helping Pyrrhonists maintain epoché. Epoché is unstable and requires maintenance. One is liable to lapse into holding beliefs. Pyrrhonists search for new arguments and new information as part of the maintenance; hence, the traditional names for us as being "inquirers" and "investigators." The process is an ongoing search for truth combined with great intellectual humility with regard to finding truth.

The Pyrrhonists' distinction between the criterion of truth and the criterion of action has an analog in the Buddhists' two-truths doctrine, which distinguishes between "ultimate" truth and "conventional" or "provisional" truth. In this doctrine the phenomenal world (what Pyrrhonists call the "appearances") is accorded a provisional existence. The character of the phenomenal world is declared to be neither real nor unreal, but logically indeterminable. Ultimately, phenomena are empty of an inherent self or essence (a perspective known to Buddhists as *sunyata*), but exist depending on other phenomena.

18
Pyrrhonist Ethics

I distrust those people who know so well what God
wants them to do, because I notice it always coincides
with their own desires.   *Susan B. Anthony*

The road to hell is paved with good intentions. Sometimes doing good to others and even doing good to oneself is amazingly destructive. Because it is full of conceit.
How do you know what's good for other people? How
do you know what's good for you?   *Alan Watts*

People seldom get perturbed about differences of opinion about the
properties of aspects of physical reality. What mostly upsets people are
moral issues. While it can be a bit maddening when one person looks at
a dress and says it is blue and gold, and another person looks at the same
dress and says it is brown and black, these disputes seldom cause people
to lose friends, unless perhaps egos or livelihoods are at stake. In contrast,
differences in moral opinions have a history of upsetting people and de-
stroying relationships. Consequently ethics is the principal focus for most
Pyrrhonist practice.

Ethics concerns itself with things that are good, bad, and indifferent.
The Pyrrhonist position is that these things do not exist in nature, and
therefore lack inherent existence. Dogmatists fall into the error of thinking
that things are inherently bad or evil, and therefore it becomes imperative
that they stay away from them, stop them, or fight them. Similarly, dogmatists think some things are inherently good, and therefore are to be pursued.
The Pyrrhonist view, however, is that nothing is inherently good or bad.

What is "good"? Some people argue that the good is "what benefits"
or "what is choiceworthy for its own sake" or "what contributes to happiness." But these definitions do not actually explain what the good is. They
are just associations with consequences. Not only are they just associations, the associations are so unreliable that they might rightly be called
"accidents." Such consequences are not limited to the good, and therefore
are not definitive of the good.

Someone who has no concept of a horse will not know what neighing
is. They will not be able to obtain a concept of a horse by learning this
sound that horses produce. Similarly, someone who has no concept of the

good will not be able to obtain a concept of the good just by learning of some of the things the good produces. While neighing is a sound unlikely to be produced by anything other than a horse (of course, some people are good at imitating this sound), these claimed outcomes of the good are often produced by things declared bad or indifferent.

That the good is beneficial, choiceworthy, and productive of happiness we do not dispute. Indeed, it seems that all people would agree to this idea. The problem is that there is widespread disagreement as to what causes these outcomes. For example, some argue it is moral virtue, others argue it is pleasure, and others say it is absence of pain. It appears to us, however, that these outcomes are accidents, and the ongoing dispute among those dogmatists who claim to know the good demonstrates that the nature of the good is unknown.

Similarly, the dogmatists also disagree about the concept of the bad. Some say the bad is "hurtful activity, or what is not alien to hurtful activity." Others say it is "what is to be avoided for its own sake," and others say it is "what is productive of unhappiness." Again the dogmatists fall into the problem of defining the bad not on the basis of the substance of the bad, but only on the accidents they claim are produced by the bad.

"Indifferent" with regard to the good and the bad is used in three senses.

1. Something that is the object of neither inclination nor disinclination, such as the answer to whether the number of stars in the sky or the number of hairs on a head is an even or odd number.
2. Something that is an object of inclination or disinclination such as the case of two indistinguishable pieces of pie. You're hungry. You like pie. You have been offered a piece of pie. You are inclined then to accept a piece of pie, but between the two pieces you have no inclination or disinclination for one or the other.
3. Something that contributes neither to happiness nor unhappiness. For example, the Stoics argue that health and wealth are indifferents because these things can sometimes be used for good and other times used for evil.

The first two senses it would seem that no one would disagree with. It is the third sense that is problematic. If there is no clear understanding of what is good and bad, there cannot be a clear understanding of what is indifferent.

This lack of agreement about what is good, bad, and indifferent suggests to us that these things inherently do not exist. Nothing is by nature good, bad, or indifferent.

19

Is Anything Inherently Good, Bad, or Indifferent?

> To enter the Buddha Way is to stop discriminating between good and evil and to cast aside the mind that says this is good and that is bad.
> *Dogen,*
> A Primer of Soto Zen

> The rules of morality are not the conclusion of our reason.
> *David Hume*

It appears that everyone agrees that fire produces heat and that snow cools. In this way we say that fire is inherently, or by nature, hot and that snow is inherently, or by nature, cold. In contrast, none of the so-called "goods" affect everyone as being good. From this we can conclude that nothing is inherently good.

Even the dogmatists agree that it is evident that none of the so-called "goods" affect everyone the same way. For example, many non-philosophers consider mindless entertainment to be good, others sexual intercourse, others gluttony, others drunkenness, others gambling, others greed, and some others even more questionable things, whereas philosophers dispute that these things are good.

Aristotle argued that there were three kinds of goods. One is of the soul, such as the moral virtues. The second is of the body, such as health and fitness. The third is of externals, such as wealth and friends.

The Stoics also argue that there are three kinds of goods. They also say that the moral virtues concern the soul, and that there are some external goods, such as friends. However, they say external things that concern the body are not goods, contrary to what Aristotle says.

Other philosophers, such as the Epicureans, argue that pleasure is a good. Yet, Antisthenes, the student of Socrates and founder of the Cynic school of philosophy, considered pleasure to be not only unnecessary, but actually evil, going so far as to proclaim "I would rather be demented than delighted."

Hence, as we agree that something that has an inherent quality affects everyone in the same way, like heat is inherent to fire, which warms everyone, we must conclude based on the arguments of the dogmatists that since we are not all affected in the same way by the things called "good" that nothing is inherently good.

Some say the good is in the act of choosing rather than what is chosen. This doesn't make sense. If it were, we would be in no hurry to get to that which we are choosing because we would not want to lose the power of continuing to choose it. For example, if seeking something to eat were good, we would act quickly to obtain food, as that would free us from our hunger. Therefore the act of choosing is not choiceworthy in itself. Indeed, it seems disagreeable. The thirsty person has to obtain drink so that they can get rid of the discomfort of being thirsty. Besides, making decisions is mentally laborious.

Similarly, nothing is inherently bad. Some things that seem to some people to be bad seem good to others, such as, intemperance, injustice, money grubbing, and so on. Since the things said to be bad do not affect everybody in the same way, we can conclude that nothing is inherently bad.

The same applies to indifferent things; nothing is inherently indifferent. For instance, the Stoics say that of indifferent things some are preferred, some rejected, and some neither preferred nor rejected. Preferred indifferents are things of value, such as health and wealth. Rejected indifferents are things having negative value, such as poverty and disease. Indifferents that are neither preferred nor rejected are things that seem inconsequential, such as bending one's finger.

Against this view one can see that none of the indifferents are simply preferred or rejected. Every indifferent thing is subject to circumstances. For example, if the wealthy are being rounded up, tortured, and killed by Communists while the poor are being left in peace, everyone would choose to be poor rather than wealthy. So, under these circumstances, wealth becomes a rejected indifferent. Every so-called "indifferent" thing is called "good" by some people in some circumstances and "bad" by others in other circumstances, whereas if there were indeed things that are inherently indifferent there would be no such disagreements. Thus we can conclude that nothing is inherently indifferent.

Some argue that courage is inherently choiceworthy. They point out that lions seem to be naturally bold and courageous, also bulls, roosters, and some human beings. But by that logic it seems that cowardice is also inherently choiceworthy. Deer, rabbits, and many other animals are naturally inclined to it. Furthermore, most human beings are found to be cowardly, for rarely does anyone wish to give themselves up to death for the sake of his country. Almost everyone is averse to such a thing. As George C. Scott playing the courageous George S. Patton in the film *Patton* remarked:

> I want you to remember that no bastard ever won a war
> by dying for his country. He won it by making the other
> poor, dumb bastard die for his country.

The Epicureans think they have shown that pleasure is inherently choice-worthy. They point out that animals right from birth, and when still un-trained, are inclined to pleasure and averse to pain. Against this position one can argue that what produces something bad cannot be inherently good. Pleasure, however, produces bad things, as pain is bound up with pleasure. For example, the drunkard feels pleasure filling himself up with wine, the lecher feels pleasure in risky and inappropriate sexual inter-course. But these activities lead to poverty and disease. Therefore pleasure is not inherently good.

Similarly, things which produce good things cannot be said to be inherently bad. But pains produce pleasures. For example, hard work is painful, but we gain things through hard work, such as knowledge and wealth. Exercise produces health. Therefore hard work is not inherently bad. Medical procedures are often painful, but people submit to them because the procedures so often make people feel better. If pleasure were inherently good and pain inherently bad, everyone would make the same decisions about them, but we see many people choosing hard work and temperance while disdaining pleasure. Therefore pleasure must not be inherently good nor pain inherently bad.

That nothing is inherently good or bad is demonstrated in the variety of assumptions concerning what is shameful, prohibited, legal, customary, pious, and so on. In investigating these we see a great anomaly concerning what various people think is proper.

Some people find certain kinds of sex acts shameful. Other people promote them.

In Japan one can buy beer and sake from vending machines on the street. In the United States, this is illegal, as the government requires each seller to ensure that the purchaser is of legal drinking age.

In many Muslim countries, women must be fully covered, even at the beach. In some European countries, women are topless at the beach.

Until the early twentieth century, some remote tribes practiced canni-balism. Elsewhere most people consider cannibalism abominable.

In East Asia and Eastern Europe it is customary to remove one's shoes upon entering a home. In other places it is customary to wear one's shoes in the home.

About religion there has been endless controversy. Some societies re-quire citizens to conform to the state religion. Other societies are secular.

In some circles, theists are shunned as gullible and superstitious; in other circles atheists are shunned as hateful and immoral.

Jews and Muslims think pigs are unclean and should not be eaten, but among other people, such as the Chinese and people in the southern United States, pork is one of the most popular foods.

Most Americans are horrified at the idea of eating dog meat. In parts of Korea and China eating dog meat is customary.

Protestant Christians and Japanese Buddhists think it is acceptable for priests to marry, but for Catholics and many non-Japanese Buddhists, this is unacceptable.

Some people think of death as something to be feared. Other people think of it as the entry point to a heavenly afterlife. Yet others consider death to be indifferent. Many Romans put on their tombs these words: *non fui fui non sum non curo* – I did not exist. I existed. I do not now exist. I have no cares.

This list could go on and on. We know that our ancestors thought differently than we did. When my grandmother was born, women did not have the right to vote. When I was a child, it was almost impossible for women to get mortgages. For my mother to get a mortgage, the owner of the company where my mother worked had to threaten to change banks if the bank continued to refuse to lend to her. Go back farther and one will see even greater differences. So too should we expect that our descendants will differ from us, perhaps in ways unimaginable to us now.

Thus, we Pyrrhonists, seeing so much variance in the matters of whether things are good or bad and whether certain things should or should not be done, suspend judgment about these matters. In doing so, we avoid the errors and perturbations that the dogmatists fall into. Instead, we follow, without any belief, the ordinary course of life. Through Pyrrhonist practice we have no feelings one way or the other about beliefs. By lacking feelings about whether things are inherently bad, when painful or unpleasant things are forced upon us, our suffering is moderated. As human beings we do experience the unpleasant and painful, but by lacking any belief about whether those experiences are inherently bad, we make them no worse for ourselves. In contrast, people who believe that something is inherently good or bad become upset in all sorts of ways. When they see something they consider to be inherently bad, they seem to think that they are being tormented by demons from hell. When they get something they believe is inherently good, then they fear to lose that thing, becoming continuously anxious in the process. Perhaps this is why the current generation of people in affluent countries is so much more anxious than those of previous, poorer generations, and why it seems that people who all live in meager circumstances seem more content than those who live in societies of abundance.

As for those who say that they concern themselves only with goods – the so-called "virtues" – that cannot be lost, we have already demonstrated their error about anything being inherently good.

From all this we reason that if what is productive of the bad should be considered bad and is to be avoided, and if the belief that certain things are inherently good and others are inherently bad leads to anxiety, anger, fear, and other unpleasant emotions, then the belief that something is inherent good or evil is bad and it should be avoided.

....

20
Is There a Techne of Living?

The fool's standpoint is that all social institutions are games. He sees the whole world as game playing. That's why, when people take their games seriously and take on stern and pious expressions, the fool gets the giggles because he knows that it is all a game.   *Alan Watts*

The shoe that fits one person pinches another; there is no recipe for living that suits all cases.   *Carl Jung*

The Greek term *techne* (pronounced TECH-nee) is commonly translated as "art," but this does not accurately convey the idea. Techne is know-how applied to any goal-directed activity. In English, "art" has strong associations with creativity, aesthetics, and originality that "techne" lacks. "Techne" is closer to "craft" or "skill." It is just as applicable to a mason building a wall, a lawyer arguing a case, or a doctor diagnosing a patient as it is to an artist creating a painting.

The dogmatists propose conflicting technes of living. For example, the Stoics endorse a life of virtue. The Epicureans endorse avoiding pain and seeking pleasure. The Peripatetics say the contemplative life is best. But as nothing is good or bad by nature, how could anyone possibly identify a techne of living so that they could attain the good and avoid the bad? Consequently there can be no such thing as a techne of living.

Every techne is associated with some special activity, such as carpentry, selling, teaching, and so on. But living is no special activity. All aspects of living are as common to ordinary people as they are to those who profess to be skilled in the techne of living. Yet ordinary people – people untrained in philosophy – learn and practice living all the time. Some of these ordinary people appear wiser than many philosophers, and many more appear happier. Therefore how can it be said that there is a techne of living?

Consider the techne of carpentry. One might think it is a techne for ensuring things are level and square. In almost all cases these are desired, yet near my home there is an amusement park for small children, called "Story Land." One of the charms of this park is that the buildings all avoid being square and level, and instead display all sorts of crazy angles. It all looks like it is part of a different world, which is, of course, the intent. It is in part this appearance that has fueled the success of this park for many decades now. Level and square therefore are not inherently good. Anyone who held these as beliefs could not have built this successful amusement park. So too is it with the dogmatists and their various and conflicting technes of living.

Consider people the dogmatists have held up as role models. Many of them had moral behavior or opinions that most people now find reprehensible. For example, in Plato's time many philosophers engaged in pederasty. Zeno, the founder of Stoicism, thought women should be held as communal property, and that it was fine for fathers to beget children with their daughters and mothers with their sons. Why should we believe these people knew a techne for living?

Consider how the ideas of some political philosophers, when put into practice, produced dystopian societies. Who would wish to live in the society prescribed in Plato's Republic? Yet the dogmatists have the audacity to claim they know the techne for living. How can any of them be believed?

In antiquity, Lucian of Samosata satirized the conflicting technes of living in his Book of Necromancy:

> In this perplexity, I determined to go to the people they call philosophers, put myself in their hands, and ask them to make what they would of me and give me a plain reliable map of life. This was my idea in going to them; but the effort only shifted me from the frying-pan into the fire. It was just among these that my inquiry brought the greatest ignorance and bewilderment to light. They very soon convinced me that the real golden life is that of the man in the street. One of them would have me do nothing but seek pleasure and ensue it; according to him, eudaimonia was pleasure. Another recommended the exact contrary – toil and moil, bring the body under, be filthy and squalid, disgusting and abusive – concluding always with the tags from Hesiod about Virtue, or something about indefatigable pursuit of the ideal. Another bade me despise money, and reckon the acquisition of it as a thing indifferent. He too had his contrary, who declared wealth a good in itself.

Lucian's conclusion was to eschew all of these dogmas and to live an ordinary life. In doing so, he presents a beginning and an end that's the same as those of the Ten Ox Herding Pictures, a series of short poems and accompanying pictures illustrating the stages of a Zen practitioner's progress towards enlightenment. The stages of Pyrrhonist practice closely parallel these stages of Zen practice.

1. The Search for the Ox – The search for enlightenment/eudaimonia begins in perplexity.

2. Discovering the Footprints – The Zen poem says "I discover footprints…. These traces can no more be hidden than one's nose, looking heavenward." For the Pyrrhonist, this is the recognition of the anomalies in the appearances, which force themselves upon us.

3. Perceiving the Ox – The poem notes the ox has a "massive head and majestic horns." These symbolize the intellectualization of right and wrong, i.e., dogmatizing. The practitioner now has a clue.

4. Catching the Ox – The poem says "I seize him with a terrific struggle. His great will and power are inexhaustible" This describes the laborious initial process of both Zen practice and of applying the Pyrrhonist modes to achieve equipollence.

5. Taming the Ox – As practice is sustained, the ox is tamed and practice becomes easier.

6. Riding the Ox Home – The practitioner returns to their original condition, which for the Pyrrhonist is epoché – the condition they were in before they started having beliefs.

7. The Ox Transcended and 8. Both Ox and Self Transcended – The poem says "Whip, rope, person, and Ox – all merge in No Thing. This heaven is so vast, no message can stain it." For the Pyrrhonist, this is aphasia. Nothing can be said.

9. Reaching the Source – Nirvana/ataraxia is achieved. The poem says "Better to have been blind and deaf from the beginning! Dwelling in one's true abode, unconcerned with and without – The river flows tranquilly on…." This recognizes that the ability to chase after the non-evident turned out to have been a kind of curse.

10. In the World – The final picture portrays the Zen sage as a common man in the street – the same ordinary life that the Pyrrhonist aims for.

21
Concluding Comments

Love of truth is one of the strongest motives for replacing what really happens by a streamlined account or, to express it in a less polite manner – love of truth is one of the strongest motives for deceiving oneself and others.

Paul Karl Feyerabend,
Conquest of Abundance: A Tale of
Abstraction versus the Richness of Being

We think we can congratulate ourselves on having already reached such a pinnacle of clarity, imagining that we have left all these phantasmal gods far behind. But what we have left behind are only verbal specters, not the psychic facts that were responsible for the birth of the gods. We are still as much possessed today by autonomous psychic contents as if they were Olympians. Today they are called phobias, obsessions, and so forth; in a word, neurotic symptoms. The gods have become diseases; Zeus no longer rules Olympus but rather the solar plexus, and produces curious specimens for the doctor's consulting room, or disorders the brains of politicians and journalists who unwittingly let loose psychic epidemics on the world.   *Carl Jung*[38]

Because of our love of humanity, Pyrrhonists wish to cure by argument the suffering caused by dogmas. Accordingly, just as doctors have remedies that differ in strength, and who prescribe the powerful ones for people with severe illnesses and milder ones for those with minor illnesses, so too do Pyrrhonists create arguments that differ in strength. For those who are severely afflicted with dogmatic precipitancy, Pyrrhonism employs arguments that are weighty and capable of vigorously disposing of the dogmatists' conceit. For others, who have the illness of dogmatism in a more superficial way and are capable of being cured through mild persuasion, we don't hesitate to use weak arguments that may be readily accepted.

Many people seem to fail to comprehend that the objective of Pyrrhonism is not the same as the objective the dogmatists claim for

---

38 "Commentary on 'The Secret of the Golden Flower,'" *Collected Works* 13, para. 54.

themselves. We do not claim that having truth is our objective. With regard to the truth, what we do is search for it. What we find in our search are beliefs which cannot be proven, and so are likely false. These dogmas not only hinder our search for the truth, they cause suffering. Consequently, we remove them. Our objective is eudaimonia, and our experience is that this is achieved not through the methods of the dogmatists, but in being free of dogmas within ourselves. Our technique is suspension of judgment. It is not to replace one belief with another. We don't take positions; we just attack positions. We ask questions that are difficult or uncomfortable to answer. We provide counter evidence.

For those accustomed to the psychological support of having beliefs, giving up beliefs appears to be like falling into an abyss. Except for the negative evaluation of the prospect, this is not wrong. The bad news is there's nothing to stand on, nothing to hold onto, but the good news is, there's also nothing you're going to hit as you fall. Without the impediment of beliefs, the mind is free.

At this point the reader should understand the following key Pyrrhonist concepts:

- Dogma: Belief in a non-evident proposition. The cause of mental perturbation. Delusion.
- Dogmatist: A person who engages in dogma.
- Appearances: The information provided by our senses and our minds.
- Evident: Information that is currently available via the appearances.
- Non-evident: Information that is not available via the appearances. This may be temporary or permanent.
- Acatalepsia: The ungraspability of anything non-evident.
- Ataraxia: A state of being free from anxiety and perturbation that is achieved through the ability and the habit of developing epoché about non-evident matters. Analog to nirvana.
- Aphasia: A temporary psychological effect that appears when one first thoroughly puts Pyrrhonism into practice. It manifests differently in different people, but it can be described as a quieting or a stalling of thought processes. Analog to kensho.
- Epoché: A mental state of suspension. Suspension of judgment or belief, withholding assent.
- Equipollence: The state at which arguments for and against are equally strong, such that judgment must be suspended.
- Belief: Assent to a non-evident proposition.
- Knowledge: In Pyrrhonism knowledge is information about the appearances. In dogmatism knowledge is belief.
- Mnemonic sign: A sign about something temporarily non-evident.

- Indicative sign: A sign about something inherently non-evident.
- Criterion of truth: Except with regard to it being apparent that one thing corresponds with another, there is no criterion of truth. In practice we don't know what truth is. Analog to Buddhist "ultimate" truth.
- Criterion of action: Without believing anything, a Pyrrhonist makes choices on the information available about the appearances to achieved desired outcomes. Analog to Buddhist "conventional" or "provisional" truth.
- Good and evil: Nothing is inherently good or evil.

To further clarify Pyrrhonism, Book III will compare Pyrrhonism with similar philosophies. Book IV will explore a variety of topics associated with better understanding these key concepts and putting them into practice.

....

Book III
Pyrrhonism and Other Philosophies

....

22

Where Pyrrhonism Fits in Hellenistic Philosophy

> Let us not admit discourses by Epicureans or Pyrrhon-
> ists – though indeed the gods have already in their wis-
> dom destroyed their works, so that most of their books
> are no longer available. Nevertheless, there is no reason
> why I should not, by way of example, mention these
> works too, to show what sort of discourses priests must
> especially avoid; and if such discourses, then much more
> must they avoid such thoughts.
>
> *Julian, Emperor of Rome, 361-363 CE*
> *Neoplatonist philosopher and apostate Christian*[39]

> Since we can never know anything for sure, it is simply
> not worth searching for certainty; but it is well worth
> searching for truth; and we do this chiefly by looking for
> mistakes, so that we can correct them.   *Karl Popper*

Of the many writers who have influenced our understanding of how
the schools of ancient Greek philosophy stood in relation to each
other, two have been particularly influential: Aristocles of Athens (427-347
BCE) and Diogenes Laertius (circa 250 CE).

Aristocles was an Athenian aristocrat writing in the period following
the death of Socrates. His philosophical perspective was primarily Pythag-
orean. He held a variety of beliefs that even when he was alive were considered strange, such as there having been an ancient city called "Atlantis"
that had sunk beneath the sea. He was a storyteller who was paradoxically
opposed to art, particularly fiction such as theater and epic poetry. He
claimed to be obsessed with truth, but he plagiarized and lied about what
other people had said. He claimed to be obsessed with justice, but he advo-
cated totalitarianism and a caste system. He had strong beliefs about what
did and did not constitute philosophy. His focus was almost entirely on
non-evident matters, particularly politics. He was disinterested in evident
matters, particularly the study of nature. In his view, the world had three
sorts of people: those who were devoted to wisdom (the philosophers),

---

39   Julian, *Fragmentum Epistulae*, 288a-305d.

those who were promulgating falsehoods (the sophists), and those among the ignorant and foolish masses.

Aristocles was influential because he was a superb storyteller and he had fascinating material to work with. Those with some background in ancient philosophy may be perplexed about why they're unfamiliar with this Aristocles. Those with a bit more background may have caught on to the trick being played here, as the writer whose given name was "Aristocles" is best known by his nickname, "Plato."

Plato played a trick, too. The trick was on posterity. He leveraged the ideas and reputation of Socrates for his own purposes. Socrates had little or no positive doctrine. Mostly he taught method and tried to exemplify a life of virtue. After Socrates' death his students scattered, both geographically and intellectually. There was little agreement among them. The philosophies of Aristippus, the founder of Cyrenaicism, Antisthenes, the founder of Cynicism; and Euclid, founder of the Megarians, had little resemblance to Platonism, or one another. Phaedo, another of Socrates' students, founded the short-lived Elean School, in Elis, about which we don't know enough to draw a conclusion, although we have a report that Phaedo and Plato ended up as enemies. The words and deeds of other students, such as Alcibiades and Critias, hardly seem like they would come about from studying what Plato said Socrates taught.

The only account of Socrates that has survived other than that by Plato comes from Socrates' student Xenophon, who became a historian and a writer on practical matters such as horsemanship. Xenophon's account of Socrates presents him as a much less larger-than-life figure than Plato's does. Until late antiquity, rival and unflattering accounts of Socrates circulated, and Socrates was hardly uniformly venerated as he is now. Indeed, many influential people openly criticized or denounced Socrates, such as Cato the Elder. Here's what Timon said of Socrates:

> From these diverged the sculptor, a prater about laws,
> the enchanter of Greece, inventor of subtle arguments,
> the sneerer who mocked at fine speeches, half-Attic in
> his mock humility.

Since late antiquity, the great philosophical divide has been considered to be the divide between Plato and his student, Aristotle. In contrast with his entertaining teacher, Plato, the imaginative creator of dialogs and utopian ideals, Aristotle (at least with regard to his works that were preserved) is a pedantic and careful observer and detailer of common sense, although his common sense leads him to detail why women are intellectually and morally inferior to men, and why slavery is natural and just.

The tension between these two ways of thinking have represented the greatest divide in the Western intellectual worldview. This divide appears in the most compelling physical image we have of Hellenistic philosophy, that of Raphael's fresco, *The School of Athens*. The painting includes depictions of many of the famous philosophers of Western antiquity, but the images of Plato and Aristotle dominate the center, with Plato pointing to the sky and Aristotle pointing to the earth. Raphael's painting makes vivid how all of philosophy was perceived to be centered upon the differences in how these two philosophers looked at things: Plato the idealist and Aristotle the commonsensical. Tellingly, neither Democritus nor Pyrrho nor Timon nor Sextus Empiricus can be identified in the painting.

Plato's dialogs have Socrates addressing some of the issues raised by the philosophers who came before him: The "pre-Socratics" such as Heraclitus, Parmenides, and Protagoras. Plato had to deal with them, because everybody knew about their philosophies. But there was also a slightly younger contemporary to Socrates, a philosopher who shunned fame, unlike Socrates who was eager to interact with everyone and who accumulated a large number of followers. He lived far away from Athens, in Abdera. Unlike Socrates, who wrote nothing and whose philosophical interests were confined to ethics, he wrote many books on both natural and moral philosophy. Plato despised him and wanted to ensure that no one knew about his philosophy. That philosopher was Democritus, who is also now classified as a "pre-Socratic." Plato would not speak of him, except with regard to wanting all of his books burned.[40]

Our second most influential author regarding how the various schools of philosophy related to each other was Diogenes Laertius, and his book was *Lives and Opinions of the Eminent Philosophers*. This book is in many cases our only surviving biographical source for some of the philosophers of antiquity. It's unclear when Diogenes Laertius wrote his book. The latest philosopher he writes about that we know anything about is – perhaps tellingly – Sextus Empiricus. He lists Sextus' books and names Sextus' successor, Saturninus, about whom nothing else is known. The oldest surviving quote from his book comes from around about 500 CE, leaving a nearly 300-year window during which Diogenes could have written.

Unfortunately, as a writer Diogenes Laertius was a hack. He just repeats what he finds in other sources, showing no concern about their reliability, and at times showing poor understanding of what he is writing

---

40 Diogenes Laertius, *Lives and Opinions of Eminent Philosophers*, ix. 40: "Aristoxenus in his Historical Notes affirms that Plato wished to burn all the writings of Democritus that he could collect."

about. Montaigne, who loved what Diogenes tried to do and was unsatisfied with how he did it, wished there had been a dozen writers like him instead of just one. I recall reading one scholar's mention of Diogenes, "the maddening, frustrating, and indispensable Diogenes Laertius."

Diogenes' chapter on the life of Pyrrho is the longest in his book. In it he once refers to Pyrrhonism as "our school," but he was so sloppy in his copying from other sources that he could have simply forgotten to edit that out. He quotes Timon and Favorinus throughout his book. Writers of philosophy in antiquity tended to be partisans and who distorted the positions of other schools to make them easier to attack. The exception to this was the Pyrrhonists, who tended to avoid distorting the positions of the dogmatic philosophers, as distorting those positions would make the Pyrrhonist arguments less effective. Pyrrhonists also liked to collect the arguments the dogmatic philosophers used against one another so that these arguments could be repurposed towards Pyrrhonist ends. Like a Pyrrhonist, Diogenes frequently cites sources that disagree with each other, and he is generally evenhanded and accurate, within his limited competency. Hence, Diogenes' project was a characteristically Pyrrhonist one in both tone and substance.

On the other hand, Diogenes devotes great attention to Epicurus, whom he defends, and whom he places at the end of his book, in a major section all of its own, immediately following the major section that ends with Pyrrho and Timon. While this placement fits with the logic of how the book is organized, it may also indicate something about Diogenes' sentiments. Consequently many scholars suspect that Diogenes may have been an Epicurean. However, this favorable treatment would not be surprising for a Pyrrhonist. Sextus even refers to Epicurus as a "sage" – a compliment he does not give to any Stoic, Platonist, or Aristotelian. Sextus also finds far less to criticize in Epicureanism than he does in Stoicism.

Whether Diogenes was a Pyrrhonist or an Epicurean doesn't matter here, because the Pyrrhonists and the Epicureans are the two great intellectual descendants of Democritus, and it is Democritus who is of primary concern. It is in part this philosophical family connection that may explain some of the relatively favorable views the Pyrrhonists had of the Epicureans.

What is important here is that Diogenes Laertius gives us an overview of lineages of philosophical thought that is different from what is now the generally received view: that all important Western philosophical thought can be categorized as fundamentally Platonic or Aristotelian. Diogenes is almost certainly a writer in the Democritean line, the line where almost none of the books survived. His view is strikingly different from that which Plato presents.

It's hard to say why Diogenes' book survived when those of his many sources, which he names, did not. Those books were probably more thorough than his. Perhaps Diogenes' book survived because it was such a simplified overview and it contained so many entertaining, albeit implausible, stories about the lives of the various philosophers. It helped that he was a later writer, as later books were more likely to survive than earlier ones. There was also a substantial element of chance with regard to what survived and what did not.

There's no good or bad by nature. The things scholars now disparage about Diogenes may have been reasons his book survived. Would we be better off if his book did not have those flaws? If it did not, maybe his book would have been among the many others that were lost.

Diogenes organizes his biographies into groups representing lineages of thought. One of these groups is especially ancient. It is the thinking of this group that sets the foundation for all of Greek civilization. These include all of the Seven Ancient Sages of Greece (which include Solon, 630-560 BCE, and Tales, 623-545 BCE) and a few other thinkers. Of these, only Thales is conventionally considered a philosopher – the first philosopher. These thinkers are a common heritage to all subsequent philosophers.

In Socrates' intellectual lineage Diogenes lists four philosophers leading up to Socrates: Anaximander, Anaximenes, Anaxagoras, and Archelaus. Socrates personally studied under the last two of these. According to Diogenes' schema, these are the only actual "pre-Socratic" philosophers. Everybody else who now gets called a "pre-Socratic" is in one of two lineages of thought separate from that of Socrates. These lineages are not presented as "pre-Socratic" – they are non-Socratic. They began before Socrates and continued after Socrates.

One of these non-Socratic lines is Pythagoreanism, which Plato tried to fold into Platonism. The other one is the line of philosophers that culminates in Pyrrhonism. This line originates with Heraclitus, and includes Xenophanes, Parmenides, Zeno of Elea, Protagoras, Democritus, and Anaxarchus. It is wrong to position these thinkers as somehow leading up to the thinking of Socrates. They form a competing lineage to that of Socrates, and the Platonic dialogs that deal with them need to be understood as arguments against that lineage. This distinction is an obvious one to a Democritean such as Diogenes, but it is one that neither Plato nor Aristotle want you to see. For Plato and Aristotle it's all just what came before Socrates vanquished them from the field. Sadly, they have been highly successful in getting subsequent generations to accept that view. But they were not vanquished. Their line of philosophy continued. It was alive and well into the third century. It is alive right now.

What, exactly, did Plato and Aristotle think they had vanquished?

The key point of difference the Heraclitean and Socratic lines is with respect to the nature of change and its implications for knowledge. The question of change is a major theme of the Heraclitus-Democritus-Pyrrho line. How can a thing change without losing its identity? Heraclitus says that everything is change. Things are not really objects; they are processes. Things are like fire. While fire has a definite form, it functions as a process, not an object. That's what Heraclitus means by "fire" in this statement:

> The world, an entity out of everything, was created by neither gods nor men, but was, is and will be eternally living fire, regularly becoming ignited and regularly becoming extinguished.

Aristotle calls Heraclitus the "obscure." Perhaps that's because he did not understand Heraclitus, because Heraclitus' view is so fundamentally different from his own. Here's a quote from Aristotle on this matter of fire.

> Really there is no similarity. A flame is a process of becoming, involving a constant interchange of moist and dry. It cannot be said to be nourished since it scarcely persists as one and the same for a moment. This cannot be true of the sun; for if it were nourished like that, as they say it is, we should obviously not only have a new sun every day, as Heraclitus says, but a new sun every moment.[41]

Aristotle rejects the idea that the sun changes moment to moment. He rejects Heraclitus' thesis, finding it too incomprehensible to even bother refuting. He sees no similarity between what we now know to be the chemical process of a burning flame and the thermo-nuclear process of the burning of the sun.

The philosopher Karl Popper, a leading advocate of the philosophical school of fallibilism, whose epistemological outlook is nearly the same as that of Pyrrhonism, assembled several of the fragments of Heraclitus into the following coherent whole to help explain Heraclitus's view:

> Life and death, being awake and being asleep, youth and old age, all these are the same ... for the one turned

---

41 *Meteorology*, 355a.

around is the other and the other turned around is the
first. The path that leads up and the path that leads down
are the same path. Good and bad are identical. For God
all things are beautiful and good and just, but men assume some things to be unjust, and others to be just. It
is not in the nature or character of man to possess true
knowledge, though it is in the divine nature.[42]

Xenophanes concurs with Heraclitus about the nature of truth.

The gods did not reveal, from the beginning, all things
to us, but in the course of time through seeking we may
learn and know things better. But as for certain truth,
no man has known it, nor shall he know it, neither of
the gods nor yet of all the things of which I speak. For
even if by chance he were to utter the final truth, he
would himself not know it: For all is but a woven web
of guesses.

Popper concurs with Xenophanes on this. "The realization that Xenophanes had anticipated by 2,500 years my theory of knowledge taught me
to be modest."[43]

Parmenides counters Heraclitus with an argument that change is an
illusion. He does this in a poem, of which only fragments remain. The
poem had two parts and an introduction. In the poem Parmenides is addressed by a goddess who reveals to him in part one the secret truth about
reality and in part two the mistaken opinions of men.

Part one of the poem is known as the "Way of Truth." Its contents are
surprising. The goddess gives a radically rationalist view of knowledge that
is completely contrary to the information from the senses. Popper clarifies
this hard-to-follow argument as follows:

Premise: Only what is truly the case (such as what is
known) can be the case, and can truly be [exist]
First conclusion: The non-existing cannot be [exist]
Second conclusion: Nothingness, or the void, cannot be
[exist]
Third conclusion: The world is full: It is a continuous
block without any division.

42   Karl Popper, *The World of Parmenides, Essays on the Presocratic Enlightenment*, 1998, p 16.

43   Karl Popper, *The World of Parmenides, Essays on the Presocratic Enlightenment*, 1998, p 50.

Fourth conclusion: Since the world is full, motion is
impossible.[44]

Part two is known as the "Way of Opinion." It is the world of appearances, as experienced by mere mortals. It is a world of illusion. Against
this, Democritus provides a counter-argument, which Popper outlines as
follows:

• It is false that motion is impossible, for motion exists.
• Thus it is false that the world is full, and that it is one large indivisible
  block. Thus there are many full or corporeal things, or small blocks
  which are indivisible, that is, many atoms.
• Since it is false that only the full exists, the empty, or the void, also
  exists.
• Thus the allegedly non-existing void does exist.[45]

As Democritus put it, "By convention sweet is sweet, bitter is bitter, hot
is hot, cold is cold, color is color; but in truth there are only atoms and
the void." While this highlights the difference between Parmenides and
Democritus, they both agree that people live in the world of opinions,
which is what Heraclitus and Xenophanes said, too. What Democritus
has done here is to provide a theory for why Heraclitus was correct.

Heraclitus' constant change, Parmenides' being and non-being,
Democritus' by convention, all revolve around the central idea of the difficulty of knowing anything. Aristotle's thinking about knowledge differs considerably from theirs. Here's what he says about knowledge in the
Nichomachean Ethics.

> Now what knowledge is, if we are to speak exactly and
> not follow mere similarities, is plain from what follows.
> We all suppose that what we know is not even capable
> of being otherwise; of things capable of being otherwise
> we do not know, when they have passed outside our ob-
> servation, whether they exist or not. Therefore the object
> of knowledge is of necessity. Therefore it is eternal; for
> things that are of necessity in the unqualified sense are all
> eternal; and things that are eternal are ungenerated and
> imperishable. ... Now induction is the starting-point
> which knowledge even of the universal presupposes,

---

44   Karl Popper, *The World of Parmenides, Essays on the Presocratic Enlightenment*, 1998, p 118.

45   Karl Popper, *The World of Parmenides, Essays on the Presocratic Enlightenment*, 1998, p
     119-120.

while syllogism proceeds from universals. There are therefore starting-points from which syllogism proceeds, which are not reached by syllogism; it is therefore by induction that they are acquired. ...Let this, then, be taken as our account of knowledge.[46]

Here, laid bare, are the rotten foundations of all of Aristotelian knowledge. The objects of knowledge are not eternal; they are undergoing continuous change. Furthermore, induction is not reliable.

Aristotle was not invested in controlling the narrative as Plato was. He considers Democritus to be a worthy rival; albeit one that Aristotle can decisively demonstrate is wrong. Aristotle addressed Democritus' ideas about how the material world was comprised of atoms and empty space. Aristotle argued that this was ridiculous and insisted that matter was made of the four elements: earth, air, water, and fire.

In his *Metaphysics* Aristotle refutes the Heraclitean-Democritean view of that everything is always changing. If it were, as Aristotle puts it

> ...to seek the truth would be to follow flying game. ... while there is some justification for their thinking that the changing, when it is changing, does not exist, yet it is after all disputable; for that which is losing a quality has something of that which is being lost, and of that which is coming to be, something must already be. And in general if a thing is perishing, will be present something that exists; and if a thing is coming to be, there must be something from which it comes to be and something by which it is generated, and this process cannot go on ad infinitum. ... we shall make to them also the same reply that we made long ago; we must show them and persuade them that there is something whose nature is changeless. Indeed, those who say that things at the same time are and are not, should in consequence say that all things are at rest rather than that they are in movement; for there is nothing into which they can change, since all attributes belong already to all subjects.

In other words:
1. Things that are changing retain the quality being changed.
2. The process of change cannot go on forever.

---

46   Book 4, Section 3.

3. There is something whose nature is changeless.
4. Arguing that things change is saying that the same thing is simultaneously in and not in a particular state. That's a contradiction; therefore it must be wrong.

Aristotle believed that in every change there is something which persists through the change, and something else which did not exist before, but comes into existence as a result of the change. Therefore everything around us is a composite of two things: matter and form. Matter changes; form is eternal. Matter is in itself undifferentiated. Particular things arise from matter through being differentiated, which is the process of acquiring particular forms. The classic example of this is the relationship between the soul and the body. It is the soul that is the form, that which is differentiated to make the person. The soul is eternal. The body is just changeable matter.

What underlies the differentiation of forms Aristotle calls "substance," which is the essence of each thing that allows it to be differentiated from other things. It is the differentiation of the substances that allows us to judge one thing from another so that we can have knowledge – knowledge of that which is eternally true, knowledge of reality. This is Aristotle's reworking of Plato's theory of forms – those supposedly "true" things that one can see if one leaves Plato's cave.

Pyrrho picked up where his predecessor, Democritus, left off and defended his philosophical lineage's line of thought against this new attack from Aristotle. Pyrrho repurposed the Buddha's Three Marks of Existence to argue that Aristotle's conception of logical differentiation based on the substances was unsound because things had no such way of being logically differentiated, that they had no permanent form, and that they were inherently unjudgeable. Therefore, the knowledge Aristotle claimed was neither truth nor falsehood.

In antiquity there was a well-known illustration of this problem known as the Ship of Theseus paradox. It was about an actual ship that had been preserved in Athens for hundreds of years, exactly the way the United States Navy preserves in Boston Harbor the USS Constitution, which served in the War of 1812. Plutarch recorded it as the standing example among philosophers on the logical question of identity.

If the ship on which Theseus sailed has been so heavily repaired over the centuries that every part has been replaced, is it still the same ship? If not, at what point did it stop being the same ship?

Aristotle would say it is the same ship, that there's some "substance" behind the ship that gives it an identity and allows it to be differentiated.

In logic this is called *differentia*, from Latin. Aristotle's Greek word for this was *diaphora*. According to Aristotle, the diaphora exist out of necessity; they are essential to every subject.

The paradox can be extended to be even trickier. Suppose all of the replaced parts are later assembled into a second ship. Which ship is the ship of Theseus?

Aristotle has no answer for this one.

Pyrrho points out that Aristotle's differentia and "substances" don't actually exist. Identity is a matter of convention; it is not a feature of reality. The notion that there is a ship of Theseus exists in our minds, not in the things. The foundations of Aristotelian knowledge are plainly false. We are deluding ourselves if we believe that we know things in the way Aristotle says we do. Identity isn't real in the sense that Aristotle has provided as a rationalization for what most people naively believe. It is this false belief in identity that underpins myriad other false beliefs.

To be fair to Aristotle, these two fundamental errors – induction and definitional substance – did not originate with him. Aristotle credits Socrates with them in the *Metaphysics*:

> Now, regarding the Ideas, we must first examine the ideal theory itself, not connecting it in any way with the nature of numbers, but treating it in the form in which it was originally understood by those who first maintained the existence of the Ideas. The supporters of the ideal theory were led to it because on the question about the truth of things they accepted the Heraclitean sayings which describe all sensible things as ever passing away, so that if knowledge or thought is to have an object, there must be some other and permanent entities, apart from those which are sensible; for there could be no knowledge of things which were in a state of flux. But when Socrates was occupying himself with the excellences of character, and in connexion with them became the first to raise the problem of universal definition (for of the physicists Democritus only touched on the subject to a small extent, and defined, after a fashion, the hot and the cold; while the Pythagoreans had before this treated of a few things, whose definitions – e.g. those of opportunity, justice, or marriage – they connected with numbers; but it was natural that Socrates should be seeking the essence, for he was seeking to syllogize, and 'what a thing

is' is the starting-point of syllogisms; for there was as yet none of the dialectical power which enables people even without knowledge of the essence to speculate about contraries and inquire whether the same science deals with contraries; for two things may be fairly ascribed to Socrates – inductive arguments and universal definition, both of which are concerned with the starting-point of science)....[47]

The problems with Aristotle's thinking will be explored in more detail later in this book. For now this seems sufficient for contrasting Pyrrhonism with Aristotle's thinking and dispelling the idea that Heraclitus, Democritus, and the others should be considered intellectually vanquished "pre-Socratics."

Now what would be most useful for clarifying Pyrrhonism is to compare it with similar philosophies, highlighting the differences and similarities. Some of these philosophies are likely obscure to modern readers. These will be explained in enough detail for those unfamiliar with them to understand the comparisons. Many of these philosophies have direct connections to Pyrrhonism. Some are antecedents to Pyrrhonism and influenced Pyrrho's thinking, such as those of Heraclitus, Democritus, and Protagoras. Some were in turn influenced by Pyrrhonism.

---

47   Aristotle, *Metaphysics*, Book 13, Part 4.

23
Pyrrhonism and Buddhism

Although a Greek, [Pyrrho] was a Buddhist, even a
Buddha.   *Nietzsche*[48]

The world in general, Kaccaayana, grasps after systems
and is imprisoned by dogmas. But [one with the highest
wisdom] does not go along with that system-grasping,
that mental obstinacy and dogmatic bias, does not grasp
at it, does not affirm.... He knows without doubt or
hesitation that whatever arises is merely dukkha, and
such knowledge is his own, not depending on anyone
else. This, Kaccaayana, is what constitutes right view. ...
Avoiding both extremes the Tathagata teaches a doctrine
of the middle.   *Shakyamuni Buddha,*
Kaccaayanagotto Sutta

I got a surprise as I delved into researching Pyrrhonism after reading *Outlines of Pyrrhonism* and starting to practice Pyrrhonism. I encountered
the works of a scholar who argued that there were connections between
Pyrrhonism and Nagarjuna's Madhyamaka Buddhism. That was Adrian
Kuzminski, who gives full articulation to his argument in his 2008 book
Pyrrhonism: How the Ancient Greeks Reinvented Buddhism. In 2015 Christopher Beckwith's book, *Greek Buddha: Pyrrho's Encounter with Early Buddhism in Central Asia* was published, containing a remarkable philological
analysis connecting Pyrrhonism to Buddhism.[49]

As you may recall, the biography of Pyrrho preserved by Diogenes
Laertius said that Pyrrho developed his philosophy in India. Pyrrho appears to have encountered early Buddhist teachings and reinterpreted
them from a Greek philosophical viewpoint, most particularly the viewpoint of the Democritean tradition. Perhaps here it is no coincidence that
Democritus also is said to have traveled to India about 100 years before

---

48 Nietzsche, *The Will to Power*, p. 437.

49 Some scholars maintain that Pyrrho either did not, or could not have met with
Buddhists or people knowledgeable about Buddhism, or if he did, the language barriers were too great for philosophical understanding, or the date was before the creation of the Buddhist doctrines that appear similar to Pyrrho's philosophy. None of
these things matter with regard to the central thesis of this chapter which is about the
evident similarities between Pyrrhonism and Buddhism.

Pyrrho did. None of Democritus' books have survived, but we know about many of his ideas that were quoted by later writers. These give insight into what Pyrrho may have been thinking when he encountered Buddhist philosophy. Some of the most relevant ideas include:

- Man should know from this rule that he is cut off from truth.
- This argument too shows that in truth we know nothing about anything, but every man shares the generally prevailing opinion.
- Now, that we do not really know of what sort each thing is, or is not, has often been shown.
- Verily we know nothing. Truth is buried deep.
- In fact we do not know anything infallibly, but only that which changes according to the condition of our body and of the [influences] that reach and impinge upon it.
- By convention sweet is sweet, by convention bitter is bitter, by convention hot is hot, by convention cold is cold, by convention color is color. But in reality, there are atoms and the void. That is, the objects of sense are supposed to be real and it is customary to regard them as such, but in truth they are not. Only the atoms and the void are real. We know nothing accurately in reality, but [only] as it changes according to the bodily condition, and the constitution of those things that flow upon [the body] and impinge upon it.
- Medicine heals diseases of the body; wisdom frees the soul from passions.
- Men achieve tranquility through moderation in pleasure and through the symmetry of life. Want and superfluity are apt to upset them and to cause great perturbations in the soul. The souls that are rent by violent conflicts are neither stable nor tranquil. One should therefore set his mind upon the things that are within his power, and be content with his opportunities, nor let his memory dwell very long on the envied and admired of men, nor idly sit and dream of them. Rather, he should contemplate the lives of those who suffer hardship, and vividly bring to mind their sufferings, so that his own present situation may appear to him important and to be envied, and so that it may no longer be his portion to suffer torture in his soul by your longing for more. For he who admires those who have, and whom other men deem blest of fortune, and who spends all his time idly dreaming of them, will be forced to be always contriving some new device because of his [insatiable] desire, until he ends by doing some desperate deed forbidden by the laws. And therefore one ought not to desire other men's blessings, and one ought not to envy those who have more, but rather, comparing his life with that of those who fare worse, and

laying to heart their sufferings, deem himself blest of fortune in that he lives and fares so much better than they. Holding fast to this saying you will pass your life in greater tranquility and will avert not a few of the plagues of life—envy and jealousy and bitterness of mind.
- One no more exists than the other.

Although Sextus Empiricus' style of writing was cautious and legalistic, the first Pyrrhonist author, Timon, had a style that was direct, enthusiastic, and sometimes satirical. Timon laid out a summary of Pyrrhonism in a now-lost book titled *Python*. The book described a series of discussions he had with Pyrrho during a journey to Delphi to watch the Pythian Games. These were one of the four Panhellenic Games of Ancient Greece, a forerunner of the modern Olympic Games, held every four years at the sanctuary of Apollo at Delphi, on a cycle that was two years off of that of the Olympic Games. A key section of *Python* was quoted by Aristocles of Messene, a Peripatetic philosopher from around 50 CE who wrote a now-lost history of philosophy. Eusebius, an early historian of Christianity, had access to a copy of that book, and quoted it often and at length in his book *Praeparatio Evangelica*. Consequently, the quote Eusebius preserved from the *Python* is now known as the "Aristocles Passage." It is Pyrrho's direct assault on Aristotle's fallacious justifications for knowledge. It is a tightly packed piece of philosophy, the understanding of which depends heavily on the understanding of the key terms. Another factor to consider in understanding the passages is that not only is it a quote of a quote, but both Eusebius and Aristocles were writing against Pyrrhonism. Aristocles was arguing against philosophies that contradicted Aristotle and Eusebius was arguing for the superiority of Christianity over pagan philosophy. These authors could have misunderstood what Timon said or twisted it to suit their purposes.

The passage is preceded with a description of Pyrrho's philosophical predecessors, starting with Xenophanes going through Anaxarchus, the same lineage as described by Diogenes Laertius. Then comes the following commentary identifying that the refutation about to be presented is in defense of Aristotle

> … we may learn how they were refuted by those who held an opposite opinion, from the book before mentioned, speaking word for word as follows:
> Before all things it is necessary to make a thorough examination of our own knowledge; for if it is our nature to know nothing there is no further need to inquire about

other things. Some then there were even of the ancients who spoke this language, and who have been opposed by Aristotle. Pyrrho indeed, of Elis, spoke strongly in this sense, but has not himself left anything in writing.

After this introduction comes the Aristocles passage. It should be noted that the passage cannot be given a neutral translation into English. It is open to wide variation of interpretation. To mitigate this to some degree, I leave key terms in Greek, with definitions of those terms in parentheses.

> Whoever wants to achieve eudaimonia must consider three [questions]:
> First, how are pragmata (issues, matters, things, disputed issues concerning what is true/false, or ethically good/bad or just/unjust) by nature?
> Secondly, what attitude should we adopt towards them?
> Thirdly, what will be the outcome for those who have this attitude?
> As for pragmata, Pyrrho apophainein (professes to show, declares, declares to show):
> - Adiaphora (not differentiable by logical differentia, i.e. Aristotle's "diaphora." In other words, the logical categories for classifying the pragmata, to divide the pragmata do not have any real existence. There are no clear ways of consistently classifying the elements of pragmata. Hence, undefinable, unclassifiable, uncategorizable, without distinguishing characteristics, and non-dualistic.)[50]
> - Astathmeta (unstable, unbalanced, unmeasurable)
> - Anepikrita (undecidable, unfixed, unjudged)

---

50 "Adiaphora" is a term used heavily in Stoicism, and that usage came after its usage by Pyrrho. The term is usually translated as "indifferent." This is a seriously misleading translation, both for understanding Stoicism and even more so for understanding Pyrrhonism. In English "indifferent" is normally about a person's feeling state about a matter. In Greek "adiaphora" describes a property of an object, not the attitude of a person towards the object. "Adiaphora" means that the object itself lacks the characteristics that would allow it to be classified, not that the person doing the classifying doesn't care how they classify the object. Thus in Stoicism the concept of preferred and dispreferred adiaphora sounds nonsensical when rendered into English as "indifferents." These "indifferents" are things that cannot be classified with respect to virtue, but can be classified on a metric unrelated to virtue. Hence, one is not indifferent to them.

Therefore, neither our sense-perceptions nor our doxai (views, opinions, theories, beliefs) tell us what is true or false about pragmata; so, we certainly should not rely on them to do so.

Rather, we should be:

- Adoxastous (without opinions, beliefs, views)
- Aklineis (uninclined towards one side or another)
- Akradantous (unwavering)

Saying about every single one that it no more is than it is not,[51] or it both is and is not, or it neither is nor is not.

The outcome for those who have this attitude will first be aphasia (non-assertion, unspeakingness) and then ataraxia (a mental state of being unperturbed, untroubled).

To paraphrase this into something more easily understood in English:

If you want to have a good life, you need to consider what is the nature of all those matters people dispute about. Next, you need to figure out what is the best attitude to have towards those matters. Finally, you should understand what the outcome of that attitude will be.

As for the nature of those disputed matters, they're all based on issues that cannot be clearly defined, they are about things that are unstable, impermanent, and unmeasurable, and they ultimately cannot be judged.

Therefore, neither our senses nor our ideas tell us what is true or false about these matters, and consequently we should be without beliefs or even leanings about them. We should be unwavering in our refusal to have beliefs or leanings, saying about every single issue, that it is not more this than that.

The outcome for those who adopt this attitude will first be aphasia (speechlessness, a state of not making assertions), and then ataraxia (inner peace, a state of not being perturbed).

This summary of Pyrrho's teaching appears to be a metaphysical or epistemological statement of the kind that later Pyrrhonists would avoid

---

51   Or more literally translated, "it no more is or it is not."

making, as the statement can be interpreted to be an expression of belief, albeit a belief that there is no basis for having beliefs. It also should be considered that the passage is Aristocles' summation of Timon's chief points, and Aristocles may have worded things differently from how Timon actually did.

Pyrrho's argument here against Aristotle is grounded upon not only existing thinking from Heraclitus and Democritus, who are mentioned by Aristocles just prior to this passage, but from another source – a surprising source: Buddhism. The first hint about the Buddhist influence on Pyrrho is to compare the style of presentation between the Aristocles Passage with the style used for Buddhist teachings, such as the Four Noble Truths, the Three Marks of Existence, the Three Poisons, and the Eightfold Path. Buddhist teachings are often rendered as pithy numbered lists, which facilitates oral transmission.[52]

According to Buddhist tradition, the Buddha taught the Four Noble Truths in the very first teaching he gave after attaining enlightenment, as recorded in the *Dhammacakkappavattana Sutta* ("The Setting in Motion of the Wheel of the Dharma Sutta" or "Promulgation of the Law Sutta"). Four verses in this discourse present the four noble truths:

> ... the noble truth of dukkha: birth is dukkha, aging is dukkha, illness is dukkha, death is dukkha; union with what is displeasing is dukkha; separation from what is pleasing is dukkha; not to get what one wants is dukkha;
> ....

> ... the noble truth of the origin of dukkha: it is this craving which leads to re-becoming, accompanied by delight and lust, seeking delight here and there; that is, craving for sensual pleasures, craving for becoming, craving for disbecoming.

> ... the noble truth of the cessation of dukkha: it is the remainderless fading away and cessation of that same craving, the giving up and relinquishing of it, freedom from it, non-reliance on it.

> ... the noble truth of the way leading to the cessation of dukkha: it is this noble eightfold path; that is, right view, right intention, right speech, right action, right livelihood,

52   Christopher I. Beckwith, *Warriors of the Cloisters*, pp 52-53.

right effort, right mindfulness, right concentration.

How might the Four Noble Truths be rephrased as questions?
1. What is the nature of the problem of human existence?
2. What is the origin of this problem?
3. What is the outcome of dealing with this problem?
4. How should we deal with this problem?

This structure is similar to the three questions that the Aristocles Passage begins with:
1. How are pragmata by nature?
2. What attitude should we adopt towards them?
3. What will be the outcome for those who have this attitude?

Following this in the Aristocles Passage are two more lists. In these lists more than just a stylistic similarity to Buddhism is visible.
   Consider the three qualities of pragmata:
1. Adiaphora (not differentiable)
2. Astathmeta (unstable)
3. Anepikrita (undecidable)

These three qualities align closely with the Buddhist Three Marks of Existence,[53] which the Buddha says are characteristics of all dharmas. The meaning of "dharmas" includes ethical distinctions, factors, and characteristics, similar to the meaning of "pragmata." The Three Marks of Existence are:
1. All conditioned things are impermanent (anicca)
2. All conditioned things are unstable and unsatisfactory (dukkha)
3. All things lack self-essence (anatta)[54]

---

53 See Christopher Beckwith, *Greek Buddha: Pyrrho's Encounter with Early Buddhism in Central Asia*, chapter 1 for his insightful analysis.

54 Exactly what "anatta" means is the subject of considerable debate. It is typically translated as "not self," or "no self" but other translations are possible, including "no essence", and these translation differences reflect differences in interpretation. Pyrrho plausibly encountered any of these interpretations. Despite the current popularity of the "no-self" .interpretation, it is important to understand that one of the largest Buddhist sects in the time of Pyrrho was the Pudgalavada sect, which explicitly accepted that there was a self, and so did not subscribe to the "no self" interpretation. The important thing for this discussion is that Pyrrho took what he understood of the Three Marks of Existence, based on explanations of the Three Marks that likely could have been provided to him. As there is no consensus on exactly what the Three Marks of Existence means, there should be no expectation that Pyrrho's understanding should exactly match other understandings.

Consider how Pyrrho might have looked at and understood these three propositions given his existing understanding of the teachings in the Heraclitean-Democritean philosophical lineage, and the arguments against that lineage that had just a few years earlier been made by Aristotle.

Proposition #1 – *anicca* (impermanence) – is well-attested to in Greek philosophy, starting with Heraclitus, who is still well known for saying, "you cannot step into the same river twice." The word for impermanence in Sanskrit includes the meaning "unfixed," which is also one of the meanings of the Greek term Pyrrho chose. Pyrrho appears to have just translated this proposition into Greek choosing the term *anepikrita* (unfixed, undecidable, unjudged) to emphasize that things in the process of changing cannot be properly judged.

Proposition #2 is about dukkha. To this day Buddhist teachers will refer to the etymology of dukkha from wheelwrighting, where it refers to an axle or a wheel that isn't true,[55] such that it is unstable and it wobbles. Pyrrho gives a close translation here using *astathmeta* (unstable, unbalanced, unmeasurable). The word he chose picks up the additional sense that things are unmeasurable, as the etymology of the word comes from balance scales used for weighing. An unstable scale cannot measure things. That *pragmata* are unstable and unmeasurable is an extension of their being impermanent. It's easy to imagine Heraclitus or Democritus concurring with this.

Astathmeta is not the only term Pyrrho used that related to balance. Another term he used was *equipollence*. While this term isn't part of the Aristocles Passage, it is part of an extended metaphor in Pyrrho's teaching in which ideas are expressed in terms related to balance and leaning. Pyrrho's choice of this metaphor may have some basis in one of the two Pali terms used for equanimity: *tatramajjhattata*. This word is a compound made of simple Pali words. *Tatra* means "there," and it sometimes refers to "all these things." *Majjha* means "middle." *Tata* means "to stand or to pose." Putting these words into a compound word produces the meaning "to stand in the middle of all this." The Buddhist Pali scholar Gil Fronsdal explains this term as referring "to balance, to remaining centered in the middle of whatever is happening."[56] That's what equipollence is. It is taking a stand in the middle of two arguments, accepting neither. This idea is also reflected in the traditional image associated with Pyrrhonism, of a balance scale that stands in the middle between two equally weighted arguments.

55 It's interesting that this concept in wheelwrighting is rendered in English as "true," giving "dukkha" here the sense that the experience of life is that it is not true, which is indeed what Pyrrho concludes. Our thoughts and our sensations neither tell the truth nor do they lie.

56 http://www.insightmeditationcenter.org/books-articles/articles/equanimity/

Incidentally, the other Pali word translated as "equanimity" is *upekkha*, which means "to look over." Gil Fronsdal says that it also can "refer to the ease that comes from seeing a bigger picture." Colloquially, the word was sometimes used to mean "to see with patience."[57] These ideas appear in the Pyrrhonist practice of inquiry, which involves looking over the arguments, looking for an ever-greater picture about the arguments, and doing so patiently. Indeed, being so patient about the arguments to point out that there may be a good argument that won't be thought of until some future date.

While *Astathmeta* fits well with the metaphor Pyrrho uses elsewhere in his teachings, it appears to miss something about the concept of dukkha. While "dukkha" has a range of meanings, it is commonly translated into English as "suffering." Other meanings of "dukkha" include "craving," "clinging," and "grasping." While these senses of "dukkha" don't appear in the term *astathmeta*, these other senses show up elsewhere in the Aristocles Passage. Eudaimonia and ataraxia are opposites of dukkha. Pyrrho conveys "grasping" in the sense of grasping onto beliefs. "Clinging" is similar to "inclining" as both describe actively connecting oneself to something. "Inclining" fits better with Pyrrho's prescription of equipollence and *astathmeta*, which are both about balance; whereas "clinging" fits better with the Buddha's prescription of meditation and letting go, but the two terms are essentially about the same action. "Craving" is related to believing that something is good by nature. Without such a belief, desire is diminished. So, Pyrrho captured the various senses of "dukkha" in the Aristocles Passage, but not all packed into one word, as no one Greek word conveyed the entire concept.

Not only is it disputed whether the English term "suffering" is a good translation of how the term "dukkha" is presently understood, it is also disputed whether "dukkha" meant "suffering" back in Pyrrho's era. Given the overall content of the Aristocles Passage, Pyrrho's choice to use as a translation a word that conveyed one of the meanings of dukkha other than "suffering" is not a reason to conclude that Pyrrho was not conveying the meaning of "dukkha" in the Aristocles Passage.[58]

Proposition #3, *anatta*, non-self, or that things lack self-essence, was likely to have been particularly interesting and novel to Pyrrho. Greek philosophy and religion, unlike that of India, had little concern about the nature of the self, beyond concerns about the immortality of the soul. What the Greek philosophy of Pyrrho's era had a great concern about was

57   http://www.insightmeditationcenter.org/books-articles/articles/equanimity/

58   See Christopher Beckwith, *Greek Buddha: Pyrrho's Encounter with Early Buddhism in Central Asia*, starting on page 29 for an elaboration of this issue.

the nature of knowledge. It appears that Pyrrho interpreted the Buddhist arguments about *anatta* to be exactly what he needed to counter Aristotle, as the self-essence of the self is just a case of the self-essence of any defined thing. Further encouraging the choice of *adiaphora* as the most useful translation for *anatta* Pyrrho also likely encountered the Buddhist doctrine of dependent origination: that everything is connected to everything, and everything affects everything. No beings or phenomena exist independently of other beings and phenomena.

Given that Aristotle was in Pyrrho's day the primary adversary to those in the Heraclitean/Democritean tradition, it made sense for Pyrrho to reorder his version of the Three Marks of Existence by starting it with a provocative claim against Aristotle's doctrine of diaphora. Without diaphora, all definitions are in some sense delusionary because nothing is ever truly separate from other things. Pyrrho's negation of the existence of diaphora points out that Aristotle and his predecessors, Plato and Socrates, were fundamentally mistaken.

While Sextus Empiricus avoids declaring things are *adiaphora*, whenever he talks about the Pyrrhonist usage of definitions, he is careful to say that Pyrrhonists use words "loosely." The Greek term he uses to describe this loose approach to the definition of words is *adiaphoros, a cognate of adiaphora, indicating a lack of clear differentiation.*

Given how dissimilar Greek is from the Indian languages, and the possibility that communications between Pyrrho and the Indian gymnosophists may have involved going through a third language, these propositions given by Pyrrho are close enough to those of the Three Marks of Existence that they can be considered translations. Further, what Pyrrho said was recorded in his lifetime in a written language that we have good understanding of. What Buddha said was kept alive as an oral tradition. It wasn't written down until another three hundred years after what Pyrrho said in the Aristocles Passage was put into writing. Over that time the meanings may have shifted. Without a written record, we cannot know whether that happened. We do know that in Greek the meanings of some terms changed over similar time frames. Hence, it is possible that what Pyrrho understood was closer to what the Buddha meant than what is now received as Buddhist teaching. But that's for other people to argue about, which indeed they do.

Sometimes things like this can be clearer when they're turned into a joke. There's a Buddhist joke that goes:

> Dukkha, Anicca, and Anatta walk into a bar. Dukkha (suffering) says, "life sucks." Anicca (impermanence)

replies, "this will pass!" Anatta (no-self) turns around and says, "you talking to me?"

The Pyrrhonist version of the same joke is:

> Adiaphora, Astathmeta, and Anepikrita walk into a bar. Anepikrita (unjudgable) says, "I can't figure this out!" Astathmēta (unstable) replies: "it's unstable and unmeasurable!" Adiaphora (undefinable) turns around and says, "what are you talking about?"

These two versions of the same joke point to how the same fundamental ideas end up being applied differently between the two philosophies. The Buddhist is concerned about the nature of suffering; the Pyrrhonist is concerned about the nature of truth, but the issues are nearly the same.

The next section of the Aristocles Passage also appears to be based on Buddhist ideas. That section is:

Rather, we should be:
- Adoxastous (without opinions, beliefs, views)
- Aklineis (uninclined towards one side or another)
- Akradantous (unwavering)

This list seems related to the Buddhist concept of the Three Poisons and their antidotes, which are:[59]
- delusion/non-delusion
- desire/non-attachment
- hatred/non-aversion

These antidotes are similar to what Pyrrho prescribes:
- don't have beliefs, because they are delusions (*adoxstous*)
- don't have inclinations towards things (*aklineis*)
- remain unwavering (*akradantous*)

Pyrrho would likely have understood the Pali word for delusion, *moha*, as the Greek term *amathia*. *Amathia* is the opposite of wisdom. It is usually translated into English as "ignorance", but it is sometimes translated as "stupidity." *Amathia* can mean an inability or unwillingness to learn, and it can mean faulty learning, as in believing in false things.[60] Pyrrho

---

59   I am indebted to John G. Douglas for pointing this out.

60   Massimo Pigliucci provides an excellent analysis of how to understand the term *amathia* in *How to Be a Stoic*, 2017, Chapter 8, pp 109-122.

points out that the cause of our *amathia* is our *doxai* (views, opinions, and judgments). The term in Buddhism that corresponds to *doxai* is *ditthi*, which is translated into English as "view" or "position," but that does not give a clear sense of the term. In Buddhism *ditthi* is not a simple, abstract collection of propositions, but a charged interpretation of experience which intensely shapes and affects thought, sensation, and action. In the *Atthakavagga Sutta* the Buddha clearly instructs that one should have no views. He rejects the teaching of "right" views and "the highest knowledge" as "the false science of those who are still attached to views.[61] Having the proper mental attitude toward views is therefore considered an integral part of the Buddhist path. Pyrrhonism is similar, except that it defines dogma not on the basis of it being a charged interpretation of experience, but as assent to non-evident propositions. These are about the same thing, except that the Buddhist view is based on internal feeling states and the Pyrrhonist view is defined more dispassionately.

For the poison of desire, Pyrrho appears to have seen it as an inclination to prefer one thing over another. Timon remarked that "desire is the first of all bad things."[62] Unfortunately we don't have the rest of Timon's statement. It may have named the other two poisons, too.

In Hellenistic philosophy, *pathé* was considered to be cause of suffering. The *pathé* are the passions and the disturbing emotions, such as anger. It would make sense for Pyrrho to equate the poisonous emotion of anger with *pathé*, in the face of which one should be unwavering, a stance which precludes aversion.

The last recommendation Pyrrho gives is "Saying about every single one that it no more is than it is not, or it both is and is not, or it neither is nor is not." That's a formula known as the "tetralemma." It is used in Buddhist and other Indian philosophies. It also echoes a maxim "no more" from Democritus about things being no more X than not X. Democritus, of course, may have brought that back from his trip to India.

Finally, we come to what Timon gives as Pyrrho's conclusion: "The outcome for those who adopt this attitude will first be *aphasia* and then *ataraxia*." No other Hellenistic philosophy claimed to offer a transformative experience that left one speechless then unperturbed. This is a description of an enlightenment experience. To convey the idea of nirvana, Pyrrho had to use a term that was previously not associated with philosophy. Before Pyrrho used the term, "ataraxia" was associated with the ideal mental state for troops entering battle.

---

61   Christopher I. Beckwith, *Greek Buddha: Pyrrho's Encounter with Early Buddhism in Central Asia*, p. 37.

62   Athenaeus 337A

We have some other clues that Pyrrho was influenced by Buddhism. Diogenes Laertius' biography of Pyrrho tells us some things about how Pyrrho lived. We can compare that with two Buddhist sutras which have been identified as being among the oldest Buddhist prescriptions on how to live. They are our best glimpse of Buddhist teachings at the type of Pyrrho. These are:

- *Khaggavisana Sutta – Rhinoceros Sutra*
- *Atthakavagga Sutta – Chapter of the Eights* (because of the poetic structure of the verses)

The *Rhinoceros Sutra* encourages seekers of wisdom to wander alone, like a rhinoceros. The *Chapter of the Eights* is about truth and finding truth. It advises seekers of wisdom to:

- Give up having opinions and beliefs (this is by far the major topic of the sutra)
- Avoid arguments
- Detach from sensual pleasures (this is also a common theme in Greek philosophy)
- Abstain from sex
- Avoid violence

Compare these teachings with some of the things Diogenes Laertius tells us about how Pyrrho lived:

- …he would go away for a time, without telling anyone beforehand….
- …he used to walk out into the fields and seek solitary places, very rarely appearing to his family at home; and that he did this in consequence of having heard some Indian reproaching Anaxarchus [Pyrrho's teacher who also went to India] for never teaching anyone else any good, but for devoting all his time to paying court to princes in palaces.
- He also lived in a most blameless manner with his sister, who was a midwife….
- …he always maintained the same demeanor, so that if anyone left him in the middle of his delivery of a discourse, he remained and continued what he was saying; although, when a young man, he was of a very excitable temperament.
- In his investigations he was never despised by anyone, because he always spoke explicitly and straight to the question that had been put to him. On which account Nausiphanes was charmed by him even when he was quite young. And he used to say that he should like to be endowed with the disposition of Pyrrho, without losing his own

power of eloquence. And he said too, that Epicurus, who admired the conversation and manners of Pyrrho, was frequently asking him about him.

It would appear that Pyrrho, upon returning from India, lived a life much in accordance with the Buddhist teachings of his day.

Hence, at its core, Pyrrhonism is a philosophical offspring, cousin, or interpretation of Buddhism, viewed from the perspective of Greek philosophy, most particularly that of Democritus and Heraclitus. It seems to me that Pyrrho took Buddhist metaphysical ideas developed via analyses of introverted feeling states and transformed them into ideas about extraverted thinking states. Extraverted thinking states can be logically described, and are closer to objectivity. Pyrrhonism is, in a sense, the original Western Buddhism.

Thomas McEvilley, the great scholar of how ancient Eastern and Western philosophies influenced each other in antiquity, suspects that there was another, later point of contact between Pyrrhonism and Buddhism in which Pyrrhonism influenced Buddhism, with the point of influence going through Nagarjuna, who is considered one of the greatest Mahayana Buddhist philosophers. His impact on Mahayana Buddhism was so great that some consider him second only to the Buddha in terms of influence. McEvilley argues that Nagarjuna's philosophy is not only discontinuous with previous Buddhist thought, but it also has substantial overlap with that of Sextus Empiricus. The two men were roughly contemporaries. While the writing styles of Nagarjuna and Sextus are dissimilar – Sextus is verbose, precise, legalist, and technical, whereas Nagarjuna is poetic, elliptical, and religious – their subject matter, arguments, examples, and conclusions, have a tremendous amount in common – too much to be a coincidence. What McEvilley says is most striking about Nagarjuna's work is that it contains formal dialectic, a staple of Greek philosophy that prior to Nagarjuna did not exist in Indian philosophy. Further, McEvilley points out that the list of subjects covered in Aenesidemus' *Pyrrhonian Discourses*, a now-lost book of which we have a thorough summary written by Photius, matches well with the list of subjects covered by Nagarjuna in his book, *Verses of the Middle Way*. Sextus' writing project was to update Aenesidemus' work and to incorporate ideas developed by later Pyrrhonists, most notably Agrippa.

McEvilley suspects that *Pyrrhonian Discourses* or some similar book was imported into India and that Nagarjuna used it as an inspiration for his work. McEvilly points out that during this era trade flourished between the Roman Empire and India. Chinese silk was popular among the

Roman elite, and much of it passed through India on its way to Rome. Other books have been identified that appear to have been passed between the two regions.[63] A small ivory Indian statue of the goddess Lakshmi was found in a middle-class home in the excavations at Pompeii.[64]

Nagarjuna even admitted that his work was inspired by texts he received from a divine source. While he was seated by a lake one day, a *naga* (a legendary great snake) came from the depths and invited him to Potala to teach the serpentine water spirits. As a parting gift, they presented him with the 12 volumes known as the *Prajnaparamita Sutta*, saying that this teaching had been hidden and entrusted to them by Ananda, the Buddha's assistant who memorized the Buddha's discourses.

Timon's now-lost book describing Pyrrho's philosophy was titled "*Python.*" In Greek mythology the Python is a great snake, living at the center of the world, which for the Greeks was Delphi, where the Pythian priestess prophesied in the Temple of Apollo. The *Python* takes place on a trip to Delphi. Timon meets Pyrrho outside a temple of Amphiaraus, one of the Greek prophetic deities.[65] Pyrrho is also going to Delphi. During their trip Pyrrho tells Timon of his philosophy. Perhaps Nagarjuna could not say he cribbed his ideas from the Pyrrhonists, but in the legend he gave, perhaps he left us a clue about where he got his books from.[66]

An exploration of the historical influence of Pyrrhonism on Buddhism is beyond the scope of this book, but the aim of this book is to resume that influence. Some later chapters in this book will compare Pyrrhonist and Buddhist practices.

---

63 Thomas McEvilley, *The Shape of Ancient Thought*, 2002, pp 499-505.

64 http://www.sanskritimagazine.com/history/ancient-pompeiis-lakshmi-statuette/

65 Amphiaraus was favored by both Zeus and Apollo. Zeus gave him oracular powers. He was compelled to join a military expedition he knew would fail. In the battle, Amphiaraus sought to flee from Periclymenus, the son of Poseidon, who wanted to kill him, but Zeus threw his thunderbolt, and the earth opened to swallow Amphiaraus together with his chariot. Thus chthonic hero Amphiaraus came to be propitiated and consulted at his sanctuary.

66 Matthew Neale provides an illuminating discussion of how Nagarjuna explained how he obtained Pyrrhonist texts from Greek sources in his unpublished 2014 doctoral dissertation, "Madhyamaka and Pyrrhonism." While Neale's lengthy analysis and explanation has some similarities to the one given here, it is more fully thought out and seems to me to be more plausible. In outline, Neale proposes a plausible argument that "naga" was originally a term applied to the Bactrian Greeks (i.e., the Greeks who lived in northwestern India). After the extermination of the Bactrian Greeks, the meaning of the term evolved. As a scholar, Nagarjuna was aware of the history of the term and used it to hint about where he got his ideas from.

24

Pyrrhonism and Democritean Philosophy

If in some cataclysm, all of scientific knowledge were to be destroyed, and only one sentence passed on to the next generation of creatures, what statement would contain the most information in the fewest words? All things are made of atoms.   *Richard Feynman*[67]

Such is the wise Democritus, the guardian of discourse, keen-witted disputant, among the best I ever read.

Timon

Democritus gets called a "Pre-Socratic" philosopher although he was actually slightly younger than Socrates. Democritus visited Athens once, but did not bother to seek out Socrates. During Socrates' life, the common opinion of him was so poor he was the butt of jokes in popular plays.

Plato despised Democritus and argued that all of his books should be burned. Plato eventually got his wish. All we have of Democritus are quotes and comments from later writers.

Democritus was the philosopher Pyrrho admired most. In antiquity, some people did not consider Pyrrho to be the first to practice what we now call Pyrrhonism. Some claimed that Xenophanes, Zeno the Eleatic, or Democritus should be considered the originators of the philosophy. While it is true that their philosophies had major similarities with Pyrrhonism, and it seems that Pyrrho was highly influenced by these philosophers in developing his philosophy, there are differences.

Democritus is well-known for having proclaimed "By convention sweet is sweet, bitter is bitter, hot is hot, cold is cold, color is color; but in truth there are only atoms and the void." It also appears to Pyrrhonists that much is by convention. We share with Democritus these observations about the appearances.

Democriteans share with Pyrrhonists the use of the maxim "not more," and the longer version of the maxim, "not more this than that." The Democriteans and the Pyrrhonists, however, do not mean quite the

---

67   Richard Feynman, *The Feynman Lectures on Physics*, Vol. 1.

same thing with these maxims. The difference is that the Democriteans use it to mean that neither alternative is, in truth, the case. This is a dogmatic view of a non-evident matter. In contrast the Pyrrhonists use it to refer to our experience of not knowing whether either one is the case, both are the case, or neither is the case.

The difference between the Democriteans and the Pyrrhonists becomes clearer when Democritus' statement about atoms and void are considered. When he made it, it was a dogmatic truth claim about a matter that was non-evident. It should be noted, however, that modern Pyrrhonists take into account the increase in our ability to perceive the appearances provided to us by technology. Some things that were non-evident for Democritus are now, with modern technology, in the realm of the evident. As pointed out earlier, Pyrrhonists do not deny the experience of our senses. What we are concerned about is rash judgment about the non-evident. Democritus' idea of atoms and void was just one of many conflicting ideas at his time. That his idea should match (and in only broad outlines) appearances that were later revealed is not something that could have been demonstrated at the time.

Perhaps, though, because on so many other things Democritus was able to avoid rash dogmatism it improved his chances of being right when he did succumb to it, and he succumbed on a matter that had the potential to be later revealed. But that's only a speculation. While perhaps the practice of Pyrrhonism may allow one to make decisions about actions that are closer in accordance with reality than those decisions made by those who practice dogmatism, this is not the purpose of Pyrrhonism. The purpose of our practice is eudaimonia.

25
Pyrrhonism and Cyrenaicism

Those who eat most, and who take the most exercise, are
not in better health than they who eat just as much as is
good for them; and in the same way it is not those who
know a great many things, but they who know what is
useful who are valuable men.   *Aristippus*

Consider what effects, that might conceivably have practical bearings, we conceive of our conception to have.
Then our conception of these effects is the whole of our
conception of the object.   *Charles Sanders Peirce*

Like the philosophies of Heraclitus and Democritus, we know little about
the Cyrenaics because none of their books have survived.[68] Worse, what
we know of Cyrenaic philosophy is all through surviving comments about
them mostly by hostile writers, whereas the writers who quoted and commented on Heraclitus and Democritus usually respected them.

The Cyrenaic School was founded by Aristippus, one of Socrates' students. Aristippus was from Cyrene, the oldest and largest of the Greek
colonies in what is now Libya. He returned there after the execution of
Socrates. Plato unflatteringly includes Aristippus as a minor character in
the Socratic dialogs. Cyrenaicism had few followers outside of Cyrene,
and interest in the philosophy collapsed sometime before 200 BCE.

In antiquity some people argued that Cyrenaicism and Pyrrhonism
were the same, because both express similar views on our ability to perceive the world. Both philosophies point out that the only thing we directly grasp is our own experience of sensations, thoughts, and feelings.
This is a major point of agreement, and one not shared with many other
schools of philosophy. However, the Cyrenaics dogmatically claimed that
reality could not be grasped whereas the Pyrrhonists suspend judgment
on this question.

An even greater point of difference arises about the goal of pursuing
philosophy. The Cyrenaics say the goal is pleasure and, for the body,

---

68   Kurt Lampe achieves a particularly insightful reconstruction of Cyrenaicism in his
book, *The Birth of Hedonism: The Cyrenaic Philosophers and Pleasure as a Way of Life.*
While this chapter relies on the testimony of Sextus Empiricus, my own understanding of Cyrenaicism relies heavily on Kurt Lampe's incomparable book.

smooth transitions from state to state; whereas the Pyrrhonist goal is ataraxia. These goals are incompatible. The Cyrenaic, in firmly maintaining that pleasure is the goal undergoes mental torments about pleasure, whether or not pleasure is present. The Pyrrhonist, in lacking this belief about pleasure, seems to be able to escape these torments.

26

Pyrrhonism and Protagorean Philosophy

The result of our discussion appears to me to be singular. For if the argument had a human voice, that voice would be heard laughing at us and saying: "Protagoras and Socrates, you are strange beings; there are you, Socrates, who were saying that virtue cannot be taught, contradicting yourself now by your attempt to prove that all things are knowledge, including justice, and temperance, and courage,—which tends to show that virtue can certainly be taught; for if virtue were other than knowledge, as Protagoras attempted to prove, then clearly virtue cannot be taught; but if virtue is entirely knowledge, as you are seeking to show, then I cannot but suppose that virtue is capable of being taught. Protagoras, on the other hand, who started by saying that it might be taught, is now eager to prove it to be anything rather than knowledge; and if this is true, it must be quite incapable of being taught."

Socrates,
Protagoras

"Truth" itself is a rhetorical term. *Paul Karl Feyerabend*[69]

Protagoras lived in Abdera, where he became a student of Democritus. Like Democritus, Protagoras was a contemporary of Socrates who gets called a "pre-Socratic." Protagoras's books have been lost; however, Plato wrote a dialog between Protagoras and Socrates, *Protagoras,* which is a major source for what we now know of Protagrorean philosophy.

Protagoras famously argued that "man is the measure of all things; of things that are, that they are; and of things that are not, that they are not." By "measure" Protagoras means what he thinks is the criterion of truth. By "things" he means objects or facts. In effect he is saying that each person's judgment is the criterion of truth about everything, and thus all truth is relative. You have your truth, I have my truth, and those truths don't need

---

69 https://blogs.scientificamerican.com/cross-check/
    was-philosopher-paul-feyerabend-really-science-s-worst-enemy/

to be the same thing.

Protagoras' idea in this regard remain popular in the modern era in the guises of moral relativism, which argues that moral judgments are not absolute, but relative to the moral standards of some person or group of persons; and of postmodernism, which argues that empirical reality cannot be separated from the experiences and biases of the observer. It's also popular with a variety of modern Buddhists and other spiritual teachers. For example, Timber Hawkeye, author of the best-selling book, *Buddhist Boot Camp*, says

> It is important to remember that other people's perspective on reality is just as valid as your own. This is why the first principle of Buddhist Boot Camp is that the opposite of what you know is also true.[70]

Superficially this aspect of Protagorean philosophy appears similar to Pyrrhonism. However, while both accept that one must rely on the appearances, Protagoras dogmatically declares that each individual has a criterion of truth for themselves, whereas we Pyrrhonists say that no criterion of truth has yet been shown to have been found. Hence, the Protagorean dogmatically considers his decisions to be justified whereas the Pyrrhonist holds no such belief.

Protagoras made other dogmatic claims as well, which mark dissimilarities between his philosophy and ours. These dogmatic claims include the following:

- Matter is in flux, and as it flows additions are continuously made, replacing the effluvia.
- The senses are restructured and altered depending on the age and other structural features of our bodies.
- The explanations of all appearances are founded on matter, as matter in itself is capable of being in all respects such as it appears to anyone.
- People apprehend different things at different times depending on the different conditions they are in. People who are in a natural condition apprehend those features of matter that can appear to people who are in a natural condition, while those who are in an unnatural condition apprehend what can appear to people in an unnatural condition. The same applies in relation to age and with regards being asleep or awake, and for each other type of condition. Thus, man is the criterion of existence, since whatever appears to somebody exists, and what does not appear to anybody does not exist.

---

70 Timber Hawkeye, *Buddhist Boot Camp*, p 65

In contrast, for Pyrrhonists these are all non-evident matters about which we suspend judgment.

27
Pyrrhonism and Academic Skepticism

The stone-cutter[71] turned away from the evident to
become a babbler on justice, an inventor of subtle arguments, the enchanter of Greece, a snotty-nosed sneerer
whose mock humility lessened him as a citizen of Attica.
Timon

...Plato's hatred of the rhetoricians was part of a much
larger struggle in which the reality of the Good, represented by the Sophists, and the reality of the True, represented by the dialecticians, were engaged in a huge struggle for the future mind of man. Truth won, the Good
lost, and that is why today we have so little difficulty
accepting the reality of truth and so much difficulty accepting the reality of Quality, even though there is no
more agreement in one area than in the other.
Robert M. Pirsig,
Zen and the Art of
Motorcycle Maintenance

The teachings of Plato's Academy changed over time, with certain points
marking abrupt, major changes in position. Even though there was
continuity with regard to the institution, up to the end of the New Academy, there was not continuity with regard to philosophical position. Hence
it is useful to consider each phase as representing a different philosophy.

The first phase was the Old Academy, created by Plato and his followers. The second was the Middle Academy, which began when Arcesilaus took charge. The third was the New Academy, led by Carneades
and Cleitomachus. The fourth was during Philo's tenure, which was a
transition period marking the end of undisputed leadership of the Academy. Following that was a fifth Academy, initially lead by Antiochus. Later
came the Neoplatonists, who held forth yet another type of philosophy.

Old Academy
From the beginning, people had differing interpretations of Plato's discourses and the overall meaning of Plato's philosophy. Some people claim

---

71   Socrates.

that Plato was dogmatic, others say he was aporetic, and still others that he was aporetic in some respects and dogmatic in others. To be "aporetic" means to be uncertain, to not to come to conclusions, to be at a logical impasse. It is a quality associated with Pyrrhonism.

Some of Plato's works have been described as "training" discourses, like exercises one would do in a gym. These discourses have aporetic attributes in situations where Plato uses the character of Socrates either as making sport of someone or as contending with sophists. They also have dogmatic attributes where Plato speaks seriously through Socrates or Timaeus or some other character. (To be clear, while Plato did base his characters on real people and some things that actually happened, to a large degree Plato wrote fiction. During Plato's lifetime it was widely commented by people who had known Socrates that Plato was putting words in Socrates's mouth.)

Those who interpret Plato to be dogmatic, or that he was dogmatic in some respects and aporetic in others, concede that Plato's philosophy is different from Pyrrhonism. The question then is whether Plato's philosophy is non-dogmatic. Just because his discourses include characters who make dogmatic statements doesn't necessarily entail that Plato's philosophy is itself dogmatic.

Historically, some Pyrrhonists, such as Menodotus and Aenesidemus, argued that it seemed to be the case that Plato's philosophy was non-dogmatic, but Sextus Empiricus disagreed with them. The argument that Plato was non-dogmatic is based on the idea that whenever Plato makes statements about the Platonic Forms or about the existence of providence or about the virtuous life being more choiceworthy than the wicked, he assents to these as being more plausible[72] than not. Some argue that this kind of assent, based on plausibility or provisionality, is non-dogmatic. Sextus argued that because it abandons the central feature of Pyrrhonism – epoché – this type of non-dogmatism is incompatible with Pyrrhonism because it gives preference to one thing over another with regards to credibility and incredibility.

Sextus Empiricus argued that just because Plato put forward some points in his "training" discourses just as a Pyrrhonist would do, that did not make him a Pyrrhonist. Anyone who dogmatizes about any single thing,

---

72   The concept I render here as "plausible" is commonly translated as "probable." The interpretation of this term is crucial to understanding the nuances between the Pyrrhonists and the Academic Skeptics. The ancient Greeks did not have the developed conception of statistical probability that we do today, which makes "probable" confusing with regard to what they actually meant. The term they used for this concept could be more closely rendered as "verisimilitude," or "truth-likeness." Using "probable" later in the discussion would be particularly confusing. See the next footnote.

or who judges one view of things superior to all the others with regard to credibility, or who makes a firm assertion about something non-evident, is not practicing Pyrrhonism and is consequently not a Pyrrhonist. Sextus demonstrated that his position on this matter was not a new observation within the Pyrrhonist school by citing what Timon, Pyrrho's student, said about Xenophanes. After Timon praised Xenophanes in many respects, even dedicating his book *Satires* to him, he portrays Xenophanes as making this lamentation:

> I, too, should have had wisdom of mind when I was vacillating. But, being old and not completely versed in epoché, I was deceived by the treacherous pathway. For in whichever direction I turned my mind, everything was resolved into one and the same; and everything, continually drawn in all directions, wound up in a single common nature.

Timon also said:

> Xenophanes, fairly free from delusion, mocker of Homer's fiction, invented a god far removed from human kind, spherical in shape, unshakeable, unblemished, and surpassing thought in his thinking.

By calling Xenophanes "fairly free from delusion" Timon is saying that there are some points on which he is deluded. That while he mocked Homer's fiction by ridiculing Homer's stories about the gods and their tricks, he fell into delusion by asserting dogmatically that everything is one, that god coalesces with everything, that god is unchangeable, reasonable, spherical, and devoid of unpleasant emotions. These are all assertions of belief about the non-evident.

So, Sextus concluded that even though Plato, like Xenophanes, acted like a Pyrrhonist under many circumstances, because he appears to have expressed beliefs about the existence of non-evident things, and that he appeared to have preferred one non-evident thing over another with regard to credibility, Plato, like Xenophanes, cannot be considered a Pyrrhonist, regardless of how otherwise similar or admirable he may have been.

Middle Academy

Arcesilaus, the head and founder of the Middle Academy seems to share the Pyrrhonian outlook, so his version of Platonism appears to be almost the same as Pyrrhonism. One does not find him making any assertion about the existence or nonexistence of anything, nor does he prefer one thing to another with regards credibility. Rather, he suspends judgment about everything. He asserts that the goal of his philosophy is epoché, which, we say, is accompanied by ataraxia, and which is what we say the goal is. So, these are effectively equivalent. He further says that individual cases of suspension are good and that individual cases of assent are bad. One small difference is that while we make these points in accord with what is apparent to us, and we do not firmly maintain them, he says them as holding in nature, so as to mean that the suspension itself is good and the assent is bad.

It is reported, however, that Arcesilaus merely appeared to be a Pyrrhonist, but in truth he was a dogmatist because he tested his associates using the aporetic method to see whether they were naturally fitted to receive the Platonic dogmas. This made him seem to be a Pyrrhonist, but in fact he passed on the Platonic dogmas to those he thought were naturally fitted.

Ariston said of him: "He is Plato in front, Pyrrho in back, and Diodorus in the middle." Diodorus was philosopher and dialectician connected with the Megarian school (a school that Pyrrho also studied in). He was most notable for logic innovations and his work with the theory of proof and of hypothetical propositions. So Aristo is saying that Arcesilaus gave the outward appearance of being a Platonist while actually being a Pyrrhonist, but on a day-to-day basis most of what Arcesilaus taught had to do with logic and dialectics and not Platonism or Pyrrhonism.

New Academy

The members of the New Academy say that all things are acataleptic (non-apprehensible). This would at first glance make them appear to be like the Pyrrhonists, but upon closer inspection of this, they differ, for they firmly maintain this position as a belief whereas the Pyrrhonists do not do so. It occurs to us that some things may turn out to be apprehensible.

Regarding the issue of good and evil, it is even clearer that the New Academy differs from Pyrrhonism. The New Academy makes claims about good and evil on the basis of plausibility, whereas Pyrrhonists do not do this. Pyrrhonists say things about good and evil not based on judgments about plausibility, but without any belief, following ordinary life, in order to make decisions that are necessary for the actions entailed in the common course of life.[73]

---

73   In other words, not based on any distinction between whether one thing looks more like it could be true than another in order to support assenting to a provisional belief about what is true. A Pyrrhonist does not assent to a provisional belief. For purposes of decision-making about actions, however, Pyrrhonists do take into account what

About the impressions[74] (the effect the appearances have on the mind), the New Academy says some are plausible and others are implausible. In contrast, Pyrrhonists find them to be equal with regard to credibility. Among the plausible impressions, the New Academy further distinguishes among the merely plausible, the plausible and tested, and the plausible, tested, and stable. For example, when a rope is lying coiled up in a dark room, a person who enters the room suddenly gets a merely plausible impression that it is a snake. A person who looks around carefully and considers the circumstances – for example, that the object does not move, that it is colored like a rope – gets a plausible and tested impression that what appeared is a rope.

Impressions that are also stable are like this story about Heracles: After Alcestis had died, Heracles is said to have brought her up again from Hades and to have shown her to Admetus, who got a plausible and tested impression of Alcestis; but since he knew that she had died, his intellect withdrew the assent and leaned toward disbelief.

The New Academics prefer plausible, tested and stable impressions to those only plausible and tested, and they prefer those to impressions that are simply plausible. Although the New Academics and the Pyrrhonists say that certain things persuade them, there is a distinction between them based on the different senses of "to be persuaded." On one hand it means to follow without resistance or much proclivity or strong feelings, as children said to be persuaded by or be obedient to their parents. On another hand it means to assent to something by choice, and with strong desire, as a profligate person is persuaded by someone who approves of extravagant living. The followers of Carneades and Cleitomachus (influential teachers in the New Academy) say that they are strongly persuaded and that things are strongly persuasive, whereas the Pyrrhonists say we just make a concession to the necessities of making decisions in life, without any feeling of favoring one over the other. The New Academics say they conduct themselves in accordance with what is plausible and use that in everyday life. Pyrrhonists, in contrast, live without belief about what is plausible. We follow the local laws and customs and our own naturally arising feelings.

Philo's Academy
Philo's Academy had little similarity with Pyrrhonism. Under Philo the

---

appears to them to be probabilities regarding the likely outcomes of those actions. Hence, the usual translation of "probable" for the term I render here as "plausible" can be exceptionally confusing for understanding the differences between the Academic Skeptics and the Pyrrhonists.

74   The technical Greek philosophical term is *phantasiai*.

Academy transitioned towards views that were essentially Stoic. Under Antiochus the Academy had for all purposes become Stoic except in its preference for showing that the Stoic dogmas came from Plato rather than from the Stoics. However, during this period a number of Platonists, to a greater or lesser degree, retained positions that were closer to Academic Skepticism, most notably Plutarch and most particularly Plutarch's student Favorinus.

28
Pyrrhonism and Taoism

Then, on impulse, Phædrus went over to his bookshelf and picked out a small, blue, cardboard-bound book. He'd hand-copied this book and bound it himself years before, when he couldn't find a copy for sale anywhere. It was the 2,400-year-old *Tao Te Ching* of Lao Tzu. He began to read through the lines he had read many times before, but this time he studied it to see if a certain substitution would work. He began to read and interpret it at the same time.

He read:

The quality that can be defined is not the Absolute Quality.

That was what he had said.

The names that can be given it are not Absolute names.

It is the origin of heaven and earth.

When named it is the mother of all things –

Exactly.

Robert M. Pirsig,
Zen and the Art of
Motorcycle Maintenance

But spontaneity is not by any means a blind, disorderly urge, a mere power of caprice. A philosophy restricted to the alternatives of conventional language has no way of conceiving an intelligence which does not work according to plan, according to a one-at-a-time order of thought. Yet the concrete evidence of such an intelligence is right to hand in our own thoughtlessly ordered bodies. For the Tao does not 'know' how it produces the universe just as we do not 'know' how we construct our brains.

Alan W. Watts,
The Way of Zen

In the *Tao Te Ching*, Lao Tzu explains that people who are wholly in harmony with the Tao behave in a completely natural, uncontrived way. The Pyrrhonist view is that the contrivances Lao Tzu says one has gotten rid of are dogmas, as it is dogmas that are contrived and unnatural. When speaking of actions, dogmas are firm convictions that there is a particular right way, and a particular right outcome that must be imposed on nature. Thus dogmatic action is contrived and unnatural.

The Taoist concept of "wu wei" has similarities with the Pyrrhonist concept of epoché. "Wu wei" has a variety of interpretations. "Wu" is a negation, meaning "does not exist" or "does not have," or "nothing." That part of the term is clear. Understanding "wei" is more difficult because of all the things that "wei" can mean. It usually means "intending to do," but in some usages it may be interpreted to mean: "do," "act," "serve as," "govern," "effort," "purpose," "for the sake of," "regard," "interpret," "deem," "artificial," "false," or – most interestingly with respect to Pyrrhonism – "beliefs."

While "wu wei" is commonly understood as being about non-doing, or doing without intention, it is also interpretable as action taken without beliefs. The concept of intention is related to belief. The definitions for the noun "intention" include "concept" and "a concept considered as the product of attention directed to an object of knowledge." The verb "intend" means "to direct the mind to" or to "mean" or "to have in mind a purpose or goal." Concepts are often dogmas. What is often considered to be knowledge is actually dogma. What is understood as meaning is often dogma. Our ideas of purposes and goals are often based on dogma. Thus intention can be understood as action based on dogma.

Another way to look at it is that "wu wei" is about doing things in accordance with nothing – that "nothing" being the absence of intellectual contrivances, i.e., beliefs. Consider that Lao Tzu also said, "those who know do not speak and those who speak do not know." This may be interpreted as meaning that no one knows; hence they say nothing. Everything that is said comes from people who do not know, as reality is acataleptic.

To clarify the relationship between intention and belief, note that one of the dogmatists' arguments against Pyrrhonism is the claim that epoché precludes action. This is the famous "apraxia" argument against Pyrrhonism – that Pyrrhonism is impossible in practice. The dogmatists base this claim on the premise that motivation involves beliefs; therefore, for there to be action a person must believe that they should perform some action, or believe that some outcome is good. In other words, action requires dogmatic intention.

Pyrrhonists argue that actions do not require beliefs. Thus the actions of the Pyrrhonist, actions without dogmatic intention, are the same as the wu wei actions of the Taoist. While the ways the Taoists and the Pyrrhonists talk about this concept differ, it seems we're talking about the same thing. Understanding wu wei to mean "doing without doing" is paradoxical and, perhaps, nonsensical. Understanding it to mean "doing without believing" is neither paradoxical nor nonsensical: it's Pyrrhonist.

The *Zhuangzi* (an ancient Chinese compilation of stories exemplifying the nature of the Taoist sage) portrays Lao Tzu as opposing knowledge. Given the ambiguities of Classical Chinese, what is being translated as "knowledge" may well have meant "dogma." Lao Tzu's reason for abandoning knowledge is based on his concern about names, which he expresses in the opening verses of the *Tao Te Ching*:

> The Tao that can be told
> is not the eternal Tao.
> The name that can be named
> is not the eternal Name.
>
> The unnamable is the eternally real.
> Naming is the origin
> of all particular things.

The core idea is that knowledge is based on names and thus relies on social conventions. Taoism is suspicious of social conventions, which in contrast are favored by Confucianism. Allowing conventions to control us amounts to losing our natural spontaneity.

The Pyrrhonist view is that names are signs. We have one kind of sign that's just fine: the mnemonic sign. It is the other kind of sign that is the source of our troubles: the indicative sign. In this respect, Pyrrhonism and Taoism say much the same thing. Pyrrhonism, however, accepts social conventions, although just in general, and undogmatically.

People get committed to an outcome in their actions if they believe that certain outcomes are by nature good or bad. A Pyrrhonist, however, would shake off any such thought. In a situation where action is called for, while A may seem better than B, and hence a Pyrrhonist would pursue A and avoid B, the Pyrrhonist would have no belief that A is in reality better than B. B may turn out to be better than A. With this in mind, the Pyrrhonist is not psychologically invested in the outcome of the action like the dogmatist is. Whether it is A or B, it is okay. Consequently, what drives action for a Pyrrhonist has a different character from what drives action for a dogmatist. It's so different that the dogmatists can't seem to understand it, causing them to protest that Pyrrhonism entails inaction. According to the dogmatists, Pyrrhonists cannot act because they don't have beliefs to act on. Therefore, from the dogmatist's perspective, the explanation of the actions of Pyrrhonists is seen as a paradox, as a kind of acting without acting.

The *Tao Te Ching* talks about this similarly:

> The Master leads
> by emptying people's minds
> and filling their cores,
> by weakening their ambition
> and toughening their resolve.
> He helps people lose everything
> they know, everything they desire,
> and creates confusion
> in those who think that they know.
>
> Practice wu wei,
> and everything will fall into place.
> The Tao is like a well:
> used but never used up.
> It is like the eternal void:
> filled with infinite possibilities.

Pyrrhonist masters lead by emptying people's minds of beliefs. They weaken commitments to dogmatic goals while simultaneously improving the ability to tolerate adversity. They help people lose everything they believe and the idea that things are good or bad by nature. They create confusion among the dogmatists through applying the Pyrrhonist modes. Practice not believing and everything will fall into place. The Pyrrhonist way is filled with infinite possibilities.

> The Tao doesn't take sides;
> it gives birth to both good and evil.
> The Master doesn't take sides;
> he welcomes both saints and sinners.
>
> The Tao is like a bellows:
> it is empty yet infinitely capable.
> The more you use it, the more it produces;
> the more you talk of it, the less you understand.

The Pyrrhonist way is undogmatic. It is before dogmatic conceptions of good and evil. The Pyrrhonist doesn't accept dogmas, and so has no reason to reject anyone. The cure by argument is like a bellows. It contains no content, yet it is infinitely capable. The more you use it, the more it produces, and the less convinced you are that you understand.

According to Lao Tzu, the goal of spiritual practice for the human being is the attainment of a purely natural way of behaving, like how the planets revolve around the sun. The planets effortlessly do this revolving without any sort of control, intention, or attempt to revolve themselves, instead engaging in effortless and spontaneous movement.

The first of the four Pyrrhonist criteria of action is to follow the guidance of nature for making decisions about actions. The second criterion is to use the feelings that naturally arise in us in making decisions. So, nature is twice a criterion, first as outer nature, second as inner nature. Only after that comes general conformity with customs, laws, and institutions, and last about developing know-how to do useful things.

While how the Taoists describe acting naturally is different from how we Pyrrhonists describe it, what we are describing appears to be much the same thing.

29

Pyrrhonism and Heraclitean Philosophy

We know nothing accurately in reality, but [only] as it changes according to the bodily condition, and the constitution of those things that flow upon [the body] and impinge upon it.

Democritus

Experience in its immediacy seems perfectly fluent. The active sense of living which we all enjoy, before reflection shatters our instinctive world for us, is self-luminous and suggests no paradoxes. Its difficulties are disappointments and uncertainties. They are not intellectual contradictions. When the reflective intellect gets at work, however, it discovers incomprehensibilities in the flowing process. Distinguishing its elements and parts, it gives them separate names, and what it thus disjoins it cannot easily put together. Pyrrhonism accepts the irrationality and revels in its dialectic elaboration.

William James,
Essays in Radical Empiricism

In the middle of the sixth century BCE one of the world's greatest sages was born. He was born into wealth and power, which he abandoned to pursue wisdom. Little is known about his early life and education, but he was a pioneer of wisdom, which he achieved by inquiring within, spending much time in solitude. He is most famous for his teachings on impermanence and non-duality. Upon achieving wisdom, he despaired of ever being able to teach it to others, yet he tried.

Some will recognize this as the story of the Buddha, but it also happens to be the story of the Greek philosopher Heraclitus, whose teachings were a major influence on nearly all of the Hellenistic philosophies. His influence would have likely been greater had he shared the Buddha's compassion and love of people, and spent his life teaching. Instead, Heraclitus was a misanthrope who preferred to live in solitude. His teachings were confined to a book he wrote, entitled *On Nature* which he deposited in the temple of Artemis, in his hometown of Ephesus. This now-lost book contained three discourses, one on the universe, one on politics, and a third on theology. Because Heraclitus was so influential, we have a good idea of what his philosophy was about via the citations and comments of other writers.

Heraclitus' book was considered enigmatic, full of riddles and paradoxes. What was clear was that he insisted that ever-present change was the fundamental essence of the universe, as conveyed in his famous saying, "No one ever steps in the same river twice." This position was complemented by his commitment to the unity of opposites in the world, as conveyed in his saying "the path up and down are one and the same." Heraclitus characterized all existing entities by pairs of contrary properties, whereby no entity may ever occupy a single state at a single time. His cryptic utterance that "all entities come to be in accordance with this logos" (logos means "word," "reason," or "account") has acquired numerous interpretations throughout history.

We don't have any citations from Heraclitus about knowledge and beliefs, but Heraclitus' teaching can be inferred from discussions about them in the Platonic dialogs.

In *Cratylus,* Plato's character Socrates says this to Cratylus, who was a follower of Heraclitus:

> Nor can we reasonably say, Cratylus, that there is knowledge at all, if everything is in a state of transition and there is nothing abiding; for knowledge too cannot continue to be knowledge unless continuing always to abide and exist. But if the very nature of knowledge changes, at the time when the change occurs there will be no knowledge; and if the transition is always going on, there will always be no knowledge, and, according to this view, there will be no one to know and nothing to be known: but if that which knows and that which is known exists ever, and the beautiful and the good and every other thing also exist, then I do not think that they can resemble a process or flux, as we were just now supposing. Whether there is this eternal nature in things, or whether the truth is what Heraclitus and his followers and many others say, is a question hard to determine....

Plato's character, Theodorus, says this about Heraclitus in the *Theaetetus*:

> About these speculations of Heraclitus, which, as you (Socrates) say, are as old as Homer, or even older still, the Ephesians themselves, who profess to know them, … [do not] allow of any settled principle either in their arguments or in their minds, conceiving, as I imagine, that any such principle would be stationary; for they are at war with the stationary, and do what they can to drive it out everywhere.[75]

Consider now what the early Pyrrhonists said about pragmata being adiaphora, astathmeta, and aneprikita. If everything is in a state of transition, that's much the same as saying it is unstable (astathmeta), not firmly definable (adiaphora), and unjudgable (aneprikita). The Heracliteans (the Ephesians mentioned by Theodorus above) know what Heraclitus said. They do not allow any settled principle (i.e., dogma), and they do everything they can to drive out dogmas. These Heracliteans seem much like Pyrrhonists.

Diogenes Laertius, who was quite likely a Pyrrhonist, organized his book, *The Lives of the Eminent Philosophers,* according to what he saw as lineages of philosophical thought. The lineage that ends with Sextus' successor begins with Heraclitus, and includes three of the five philosophers whose philosophies Sextus considers to be similar to Pyrrhonism: Heraclitus, Democritus, and Protagoras. The two others that Sextus considered to be similar are Arcesilaus, who was a closet Pyrrhonist who by happenstance became head of Plato's Academy, and Aristippus, one of Socrates' students, who was in little agreement with Socrates' other famous students.

How Pyrrhonists should understand Heraclitus turns out to be one of the great controversies about ancient Pyrrhonism. In *Outlines of Pyrrhonism* Sextus reproaches his predecessor, Aenesidemus, for saying that Pyrrhonism was a way to understand Heraclitean philosophy, possibly also meaning that Pyrrhonism was a path for becoming a Heraclitean. What Aenesidemus said on this matter has been lost. We only have Sextus' criticism of it.

It seems plausible that Aenesidemus saw in Heraclitus a philosophy similar to Pyrrhonism, and he saw that Heraclitus' enigmatic statements started to make sense once one started practicing Pyrrhonism. My inference is that Aenesidemus is likely to have claimed that epoché makes it easier to see how pairs of opposites fuse together to be one thing. The mind in the state of epoché has nothing to push one to believe that only one out of any pair contradictory propositions is true. Instead, the opposites are

---

75 Section 179e.

held together at the same time. This state of mind allows one to become receptive to the view expressed by Heraclitus.

Sextus, who was vigilant against exposing any element of Pyrrhonism to attack from the dogmatists, argued that opposites' appearing to be the case about the same thing is not a dogma of the Pyrrhonists. It is just something that appears to us. It doesn't just appear to Heraclitieans and Pyrrhonists, it appears to other philosophers, and indeed, to all of mankind. For example, you may have had the experience of a food tasting good at one point in time and bad at another point in time. So, on this matter the Heracliteans are commenting on an experience that is common to everyone. It's interesting to note in his arguments that Sextus doesn't actually refute Aenesidemus or Heraclitus. He just distinguishes between dogmatic and non-dogmatic expressions of the same idea. He faults Heraclitus for believing in the idea and he faults Aenesidemus for how he talks about the idea.

In the intervening nearly two centuries between Aenesidemus and Sextus, the Pyrrhonists came under increasing attack from the other schools of philosophy, accusing Pyrrhonism as being dogmatic, and therefore self-refuting. Hence we see the transition from Timon's enthusiastic poetic and pithy phrasings to cautious and legalistic style used by Sextus, who puts far more effort into separating Pyrrhonism from dogmatism than he does in making Pyrrhonism understandable for beginners. Perhaps he thought that Timon and Aenesidemus had already done this and that the most important thing was to defend Pyrrhonism from attack. Consequently, Sextus sees Heraclitus as a dogmatist, and his teachings on impermanence and the unity of opposites to be dogmatic positions about non-evident matters.

However, because of Heraclitus' paradoxical phrasings, that his clear statements have to do with ever-present change and instability in nature, and the implications of such change on the idea of having secure knowledge about the nature of reality, the early Pyrrhonists likely saw great similarity between the two philosophies. And because they were not under as much attack from the dogmatists, they were not as bothered by Heraclitus's dogmatic phrasings, if not his actual dogmatism. Perhaps this was because the ways the earliest Pyrrhonists expressed their philosophy were not as cautiously worded as those of the later Pyrrhonists. Good ways of wording non-dogmatic statements about indeterminacy had not yet been developed. Hence, some of the early Pyrrhonists' statements were made in ways that could be interpreted to be firm claims about non-evident matters. Examples of this can be seen in the Pyrrhonist maxims, most of which are from the earliest period of Pyrrhonism.

Over time these wording problems became an increasing point of criticism of Pyrrhonism. The dogmatists pointed them out and claimed that we were self-contradictory. By the time Sextus was writing, about 500 years after the start of Pyrrhonism, more careful wording had been developed to allow Pyrrhonist ideas to be expressed in clearly non-dogmatic terms. (Albeit perhaps less clearly). Hence it was likely that Heraclitus appeared more dogmatic to Sextus than he did to the early Pyrrhonists, and that the early Pyrrhonists saw Heraclitus trying to say something very similar to what they were saying.

Taoism shares the Heraclitean view that opposites are one, most famously expressed in the yin-yang symbol, representing that not only does one opposite yield to the other, but at the core each opposite is created by the other.

Hence, there's no good without bad. The good is good only because of the bad. The bad is bad only because of the good. This is not the same as the Pyrrhonist view, but it seems to result in a similar sort of epoché.

30
Pyrrhonism and Science

... [The empiricist] will stay away from all other arguments which deal with matters which are not evident, keeping in mind that each of these sophisms has a persuasive power which is so difficult to resist that even the dialecticians do not readily solve them. The empiricist will not be a man of many words or of long speeches but will talk little and rarely, just like Pyrrho. Pyrrho had looked for the truth, and, not finding it, was in doubt about all things non-evident, but in his daily activities he followed what is evident, whereas concerning everything else he remained in doubt. The empiricist's attitude towards medical matters is like the Pyrrhonist's attitude towards the whole of life. He does not lack in reputation, but he also is not arrogant; he is unassuming and not boastful, just as Timon claims Pyrrho to have been. People will be full of admiration for his techne, just as Hippocrates' contemporaries were for his.... *Galen,*
An Outline of Empiricism

Bad religion is arrogant, self-righteous, dogmatic and intolerant. And so is bad science. But unlike religious fundamentalists, scientific fundamentalists do not realize that their opinions are based on faith. They think they know the truth. *Rupert Sheldrake*

Many views exist about how the ideas of modern science came about, all of which involve an interplay of causes and events taking place over centuries. Two of the most important influences that culminated in the fundamental ideas of modern science that emerged during the Enlightenment are associated with Pyrrhonism. One of these was the recovery and transmission of the works of Sextus Empiricus, most particularly the Ten Modes of Aenesidemus and the Five Modes of Agrippa as tests of truth.

The other was the thinking of the ancient Empiric school of medicine, which was closely affiliated with Pyrrhonism. The physician and philosopher Galen, whose writings are our greatest source on ancient medicine, said the Empirics were just like the Pyrrhonists, and so closely connected to Pyrrhonism that they could have named their school of medicine after Timon[76] – and Timon wasn't even a physician. Many of the well-known Pyrrhonist and Empiric teachers were teachers of both, including Sextus Empiricus, Herodotus of Tarsus, Heraclides, Theodas, and Menodotus. The school of medicine which competed with the Empirics was known as the "Dogmatic" or "Rationalist" school of medicine. Thus Pyrrhonism and early Empiricism are so deeply intertwined that they represent two aspects of the same line of thinking, with early Empiricism representing how Pyrrhonists approach practical matters, such as medicine, and Pyrrhonist philosophy representing their approach to wisdom.

The view of the Empiric school of medicine was that it was necessary to understand the evident causes of disease, but they considered inquiry into non-evident causes to be useless. They considered this inquiry useless as there was no clear understanding of non-evident causes, as demonstrated by the manifold controversies among philosophers and physicians, and by large variation in methods of practice from place to place, one method being used in Rome, another in Egypt, and another in Gaul. Even in cases where causes are evident, such as wounds, the Empirics observed that if the evident cause does not suggest a method of curing, then much less so do non-evident methods. Their conclusion was that it is much better to rely on remedies that had been tested through experience, as since the beginning of medicine all treatments had been deduced from experience, starting with simple observations of differing behaviors among the sick in the era prior to physicians. For example, some of the sick either ate or fasted in the first days of their illness. Observers noticed that the illness was more quickly alleviated in one group than the other. This and other instances occurring regularly were observed by people diligent enough to realize which method was best to cure particular conditions. Hence the art of medicine arose. Medicine was not invented through reasoning about the non-evident, but it was theories about the non-evident that arose after the discovery of medicine. What matters is not what causes, but what cures illness. It does not matter why a treatment works, only that it works. They named their approach to medicine the "Tripod of Medicine" –

Observation: The observations which the patient had made in the course of the illness concerning the course of the disease and results of any treatments.

History: A written collection of observations made by others.

Analogy: When treating a new illness, selecting a plan of treatment by comparing it with a known disease which most resembled it.

---

76 Galen, *An Outline of Empiricism*, section 43

Galen was heavily influenced by the Empirics. His attempt to synthe-
size the Empiric and Dogmatic approaches was an important forerunner
of modern science. Galen is credited with being the first person ever recorded to have settled a philosophical argument through empirical means,
by severing nerves to demonstrate how the nervous system works. The
Emperor and Stoic philosopher Marcus Aurelius held Galen in such high
esteem that he appointed Galen to be his personal physician – despite
Galen's vocal opposition to Stoicism. Galen continued to serve as the
personal physician for the next two emperors.

Pyrrhonism and science are philosophically fundamentally related. As
Arne Næss put it, "the close connection between twentieth-century empiricism and Sextus's Pyrrhonism is obvious."[77] However, Pyrrhonism and
science do not have the same goals. The goal of Pyrrhonism is psychological. It is eudaimonia and ataraxia – a happy, fulfilled life without mental
perturbance. The goal of science is to obtain better observations of the
appearances and to make better predictions (i.e., to identify what works)
via hypothesis formation and experimentation.

Pyrrhonism argues that no criterion of truth has been found. Science
accepts this, but points out that we are able to identify things that are
false. Through a process of elimination we can asymptotically approach
the truth.[78] Science makes no absolute declaration that any particular
theory is definitively true, but it does, like Academic Skepticism, accept
arguments for plausibility and holds well-tested theories supported large
amounts of data to be provisionally true. Still, such theories occasionally
get overturned by new theories that fit the appearances better, as Thomas
Kuhn engagingly detailed in *The Structure of Scientific Revolutions*.

Some of the things said by the ancient Pyrrhonists suggest that, with
regard to suspension of belief about non-evident matters, they implicitly
meant *possible* non-evident matters. What was impossible could be rejected outright. This appears to be a primitive form of scientific fallibilism
promoted by philosophers such as Karl Popper. The best examples of this
kind of Pyrrhonist thinking can be seen in a work by Sextus Empiricus
entitled *Against the Astrologers*. Sextus' choice of words shows that he's
not suspending judgment about the astrologers' claims. He thinks those
claims are impossible and he rejects them outright.

- "superstition" (section 2)
- "…it is not possible to perceive the time of birth…" "The doctrine is
  without substance… (section 55)
- "…it is quite plain that it is not possible for a horoscope to be set up

---

77 Arne Næss, *Selected Works of Arne Næss*, Volume 2, p 19.

78 The belief that science yields truth is a dogma called "scientism."

from the time of conception." (section 64)
- "…the clearest disproof of astrology…" (section 82)
- "…the most conclusive argument of all…" (section 83)
- "…we have established by proofs sufficient in themselves that it is not possible…" (section 85)
- "…the results themselves will be enough to refute them…" (section 88)
- "…appears to confute the Chaldeans very completely." (section 90)
- "But this is false…" (section 91)
- "Nor yet is it possible to say…" (section 92)
- …it is nonsense…" (section 97)
- "But this again is impossible…" (section 99)
- "…we have proved that accuracy…is not to be had." (section 99)
- "… is of all things the most absurd." (section 102)

Well-tested, no-longer-disputed scientific theories can also be seen as just more complex examples of things the ancient Pyrrhonists explicitly accepted, for example, the relationship between smoke and fire, and scars and wounds.

In the ancient world, issues that we now consider to be in the domain of science were considered to be closely related to ethics in ways that are now not immediately obvious. For example, Epicurean ethics required a universe where the gods did not intervene in human affairs whereas Stoic ethics required a universe consistent with divine providence. Hence, they had different dogmas about the state of nature. The modern equivalent of these ancient debates can be seen in issues where science gets politicized – for example, on matters such as global warming, gender, race, and abortion – where people take views on science that conform with their views on ethics. This is really the point about the Pyrrhonist attitude towards science. People fall into dogmatic positions for either ethical or egotistical reasons. Without one of those motivations, no one gets perturbed by science. It is this perturbance that Pyrrhonism is the remedy for.

31
Pyrrhonism and Postmodernism

Postmodern irony and cynicism's become an end in itself,
a measure of hip sophistication and literary savvy. Few
artists dare to try to talk about ways of working toward
redeeming what's wrong, because they'll look sentimen-
tal and naive to all the weary ironists. Irony's gone from
liberating to enslaving. The postmodern founders' pat-
ricidal work was great, but patricide produces orphans,
and no amount of revelry can make up for the fact that
writers my age have been literary orphans throughout
our formative years.   *David Foster Wallace*

Obscurity is of two kinds: intentional and unintention-
al. It is intentional when one has nothing to say and conceals the poverty of his thought by obscure language that
he may seem to say something useful. Connected with
this is the use of many digressions, poetic images, recon-
dite allusions and archaic language. Solecisms prevent
the hearer from understanding many things. Only the
true philosopher is free from these faults....

                                        Philodemus,[79]
                                        Rhetorica

Some people on encountering Pyrrhonism see it as similar to Postmodernism. While some areas of similarity exist, overall the two are
dissimilar.

Postmodernism is difficult and contentious to summarize as it represents a basket of related ideas propounded by various thinkers who were
not all in agreement with each other. Hence, definitions and descriptions of Postmodernism are disputed. As the purpose of this chapter is to
demonstrate that Pyrrhonism differs from Postmodernism, and not to establish exactly what Postmodernism is, the description of Postmodernism
used in this chapter is the one provided by the *Encyclopedia Britannica.*
Readers who do not think that the *Encyclopedia Britannica's* description is
correct are encouraged to work out their own analyses of the differences

---

79   An Epicurean philosopher who lived circa 110 – 35 BCE, and whose works were
      discovered in charred scrolls in the Villa of the Papyri in Pompeii.

between Pyrrhonism and what they think Postmodernism is.

The *Encyclopedia Britannica* outlines eight philosophical positions taken by Postmodernism.[80] These are as follows, each contrasted with Pyrrhonism.

Reality

Postmodern: The idea of there being an objective natural reality – a reality whose existence and properties are logically independent of human beings – is a kind of naive realism that should be dismissed.

Pyrrhonist: None of the Hellenistic philosophies, Pyrrhonism included, dismiss that there is an objective natural reality. All of them seek to gain knowledge and understanding of that reality. Pyrrhonism differs from the other Hellenistic philosophies in that it criticizes the dogmatic philosophies for jumping to rash conclusions about reality. Similarly, the conclusion that there is no objective reality would also be considered a dogmatic rash conclusion about reality which should not be accepted.

Statements about Reality

Postmodern: Since there is no objective natural reality, the descriptive and explanatory statements of scientists and historians cannot be objectively true or false. Therefore there is no such thing as truth.

Pyrrhonist: Pyrrhonism does not at all reject the concept of truth. In limited ways, it accepts that we have truths. Pyrrhonism simply proposes a high degree of intellectual humility about descriptive and explanatory statements about non-evident matters associated with objective natural reality, pointing out the tremendous degree of uncertainty associated with such statements. The Pyrrhonist attitude towards such statements is that while they may be used as needed for decision making, they should not be firmly assented to, i.e., they should not be believed. Pyrrhonism holds that some statements about non-evident matters can be objectively determined to be false, for example, by breaking rules of reason. This is different from Postmodernism's dogmatic claim that such statements cannot be true or false.

Faith in Progress

Postmodern: The Enlightenment faith in science and technology as instruments of human progress is misguided.

Pyrrhonist: While faith in anything non-evident is unwarranted, science

---

80   https://www.britannica.com/topic/postmodernism-philosophy, update of 14 July 2017.

and technology produce things that are evident. While good and bad do not exist by nature, they do exist by convention and as matters of individual preferences. While many of the things produced by science and technology are seen as good, such as the fact that machines inexpensively and accurately create copies of books rather than books having to be manually transcribed, the outcome of it all is ultimately uncertain. However, many of the Postmodernists go beyond doubting to taking up the dogmatic position that science and technology are by nature evil. Pyrrhonism rejects such dogmatic conclusions. For practical matters, which is what science and technology are about, Pyrrhonism recommends following the natural order of things and conventional thinking. In the example of how books are manufactured, that would be to prefer inexpensive and accurately mass-produced books over hand-copied manuscripts.

Reason and Logic

Postmodern: Reason and logic are merely conceptual constructs and are therefore valid only within the established intellectual traditions in which they are used.

Pyrrhonist: The Postmodern position is dogmatic.

Human Nature

Postmodern: There is no such thing as human nature. Everything is socially determined.

Pyrrhonist: The Postmodern position is dogmatic.

Language

Postmodern: Language is incapable of referring to and representing things outside itself.

Pyrrhonist: The belief that language cannot mirror nature is not only dogmatic, it is contrary to Pyrrhonism. Pyrrhonism explicitly accepts the usage of mnemonic signs, which are based on language referring to and representing things outside itself.

Knowledge

Postmodern: Human beings cannot acquire knowledge about natural reality, and such knowledge cannot be justified on the basis of evidence or principles that are, or can be, known immediately, intuitively, or otherwise with certainty.

Pyrrhonism: The Postmodernist position regarding knowledge is the same as that of the Academic Skeptics. It is negative dogmatism. Pyrrhonism rejects negative dogmatism in the same way it rejects the more common positive dogmatism. Things may be acataleptic to one now, but that does not mean those things are inherently acataleptic.

Theories

Postmodern: It is impossible, even in principle, to construct general theories that explain aspects of the natural or social world within a given domain of knowledge. Furthermore, even proposing such theories is not worthwhile. Such theories are pernicious not only because they must be inherently false but also because they oppress, marginalize, and silence other perspectives.

Pyrrhonism: Declaring that it is impossible even in principle for general theories to be true is dogmatic. Believing that such theories are pernicious is also dogmatic.

....

Book IV
Practicing Pyrrhonism

32
The Cure by Argument

Likewise it would seem that the equality of opposite rea-
sonings is the cause of aporia (being at a loss, perplexity);
for it is when we reason on both [sides of a question] and
it appears to us that everything can come about either
way, that we are in a state of aporia about which of the
two ways to take up.   *Aristotle*[81]

The shuttling to and fro of arguments and affects represents the transcendent function of the opposites. The
confrontation of the two positions generates a tension
charged with energy and creates a living third thing –
not a logical stillbirth in accordance with the principle of
tertium non datur [the law of the excluded middle] but a
movement out of the suspension between the opposites,
a living birth that leads to a new level of being, a new
situation.   *Carl Jung,*
                          The Transcendent Function[82]

The most remarkable thing about Pyrrhonism is the central use of
argument in its practice. I refer to this practice as the "cure by argument" based on a passing use of that phrase by Sextus. While other
wisdom traditions, particularly the other Hellenistic philosophies, use arguments to induce states of mind, only Pyrrhonism makes argument its
central practice. It is without parallel in other wisdom traditions, and it is
commonly overlooked or misunderstood. Some people look at Pyrrhonism and seem overcome with an inability to understand its fundamental ideas. For example, Linda Johnsen, writing about Pyrrhonism in *Lost
Masters: Rediscovering the Mysticism of the Ancient Greek Philosophers* said
that Pyrrho:

> ...taught his students to be skeptical of – that is, not to
> accept at face value – knowledge provided by the mind]
> or senses. One point of view explains the world one way,
> another explains it a different way. Who can tell which is

---

81   *Topics* 6.145b 12-20.

82   Carl Jung, *The Transcendent Function*, p. 90.

correct? The real truth, he explained, is beyond the reach of rational inquiry. Therefore it is best not to lose oneself in logical analysis but rather to cultivate a state of inner peace, free from craving and attachment.[83]

That's nearly the opposite of Pyrrhonism. The technique of Pyrrhonism is to lose oneself in logical analysis – the cure by argument – as this is what cultivates a state of inner peace, and indeed, a kind of losing of one's self. By engaging in the cure by argument we see that for any one point of view about non-evident matters there's a contrary view. Instead of not accepting at face value the knowledge provided by the mind or the senses, Pyrrhonism accepts the appearances at face value – but nothing more. More than that would be to say they represented truth. Instead the Pyrrhonist view is that the appearances are simply what we have available to us to guide us in our day-to-day actions.

The cure by argument appears to have been part of Pyrrhonism from the start. Diogenes Laertius' biography of Pyrrho said of him, "In debate he was looked down upon by no one, for he could both discourse at length and also sustain a cross-examination." In the same context, the biography says, "On being discovered once talking to himself, he answered, when asked the reason, that he was training to be useful." It would appear then that Pyrrho may have debated out loud with himself. Excellence at argument was characteristic of Pyrrho's students.

Timon produced ridicules and satires of his philosophical opponents as a way of demonstrating the unsoundness of their arguments. One effect of epoché is that one often not only finds the beliefs of the dogmatists funny, but their emotional commitment to those beliefs as hilarious. Socrates loved playing mind games with such people, showing them to be rather ridiculous. It's always useful to remember that Socrates ended up getting himself executed.

Nausiphanes was said to be a master of rhetoric.[84] Philo was said to be fond of arguing.[85] Arcesilaus was famous for his argumentation skills, and his arguments were said to have been delivered with kindliness.[86] Cicero tells us that Arcesilaus would invite members of his audience to state their opinions, and that he would then argue against them.[87] This approach for

83   Linda Johnsen, *Lost Masters: Rediscovering the Mysticism of the Ancient Greek Philosophers*, p 95.

84   Sextus Empiricus, *Against the Professors*, Book 1, Section 2.

85   Diogenes Laertius, *Life of Pyrrho*.

86   Eusebius, *Praeparatio Evangelica*, Book 14, Chapter 6.

87   *De Finibus*, Book 2, Section 1.

helping rid people of their beliefs appears to have been unique to Arcesilaus.

It would seem that proper training for a Pyrrhonist would be in logic, rhetoric, and debate. These were critical components of *paideia* (pronounced PAY-dee-uh) – the ancient Greek method of education. Sextus notes that some of Plato's Socratic discourses can be instructive to Pyrrhonists, specifically the aporetic discourses such as *Laches, Euthyphro, Meno, Charmides,* and *Protagoras.* These are all discourses about divesting the pretense of knowledge, doing so via logic and rhetoric.

While Pyrrhonists must readily engage in debate with themselves, they should be cautious about engaging in debate with others. This is not only because it can be disturbing, but there's a tendency to end up taking a position regarding the non-evident. Besides, beliefs have a way of acting like jealous lovers, driving people to act out dangerously. However, Pyrrhonists need to be prepared to debate should someone try to convince them of a non-evident proposition.

Possibly an essential element of the cure by argument is time alone so that one can argue with oneself. There may be times when the input of someone else is helpful, acting in a Socratic role, but ultimately epoché is something one has to achieve for oneself. It doesn't happen if one is not actively engaged in it, and it's not a task one can delegate to someone else.

An interesting side effect of the cure by argument is that it places Pyrrhonism within the rational tradition. While Pyrrhonists occasionally use weak arguments, a fact that Sextus admits to, the objective is to come up with whatever arguments are readily at hand for producing equipollence. There's always at least a *prima facie* effort to make a good argument, and there's always the understanding that better arguments may be required. While a Pyrrhonist would accept an argument that something appears to have contradictory attributes, they would not accept a logical contradiction. Pyrrhonism works within the ancient Greek philosophical constraint of requiring that all arguments at least try to make rational sense. Buddhism, however, does not work within this constraint. Consider this text from the *Maha Prajnaparamita (Heart Sutra),* which is generally considered the central text of the Zen tradition. Because of its failure to hold to this constraint, it is described as being opaque to the mind but radiant to the heart.

> Avalokiteshvara Bodhisattva, practicing deep prajna paramita clearly saw that all five skandhas are empty, transforming all suffering and distress.
> "Shariputra, form is no other than emptiness, emptiness no other than form; form is exactly emptiness,

emptiness exactly form; sensation, perception, mental reaction, consciousness are also like this.

"Shariputra, all things are essentially empty – not born, not destroyed; not stained, not pure; without loss, without gain.

"Therefore in emptiness there is no form; no sensation, perception, mental reaction, consciousness; no eye, ear, nose, tongue, body, mind; no color, sound, smell, taste, touch, object of thought; no seeing and so on to no thinking; no ignorance and also no ending of ignorance; and so on to no old age and death, and also no ending of old age and death; no suffering, cause of suffering, cessation, path; no wisdom and no attainment.

"Since there is nothing to attain, the bodhisattva lives by prajna paramita, with no hindrance in the mind; no hindrance, and therefore no fear; far beyond delusive thinking, right here is nirvana.

"All Buddhas of past, present and future live by prajna paramita, attaining anuttara-samyak-sambodhi.

"Therefore know that prajna paramita is the great sacred mantra, the great vivid mantra, the unsurpassed mantra, the supreme mantra, which completely removes all suffering.

"This is truth, not mere formality."[88]

This sutra invokes what is essentially a deity, Avalokiteshvara, who represents compassion, who is practicing perfect wisdom (prajna paramita) who sees the nature of reality. The skandhas are the body, sensations, perceptions, mental activities, and consciousness. These things are "empty," and this emptiness is the same as form. Since all things are empty, there's a huge list of apparent things that are declared to be non-existent, among these are body parts, experience, wisdom, and attainment. Wisdom, however, is what we are told Avalokiteshvara is practicing, and all Buddhas, we are told, achieve attainment. This gets wrapped up by saying that this is a "mantra," which is basically a magic invocation that is being declared to be the "truth."

Looking at this sutra, it's hard to imagine it being accepted within Greek philosophy. While Greek philosophers occasionally invoked deities, it's almost unimaginable for them to declare a philosophical statement to be a magic spell. While Heraclitus argued that the opposites are one, and

---

88   Translation by Robert Aitkin Roshi.

the Eleatics and Pyrrhonists offered arguments against the existence of a variety of non-evident concepts whose existence was widely considered to be obvious, it's hard to imagine a Greek philosophical text denying obvious physical things, such as the existence of eyes, or to be so obviously self-contradictory. Either there is wisdom or there isn't. Either people attain things or they don't. You are not allowed to violate the law of non-contradiction.

To be fair to Buddhism, it too has the cure by argument, but in how Buddhism is commonly taught in the West, little attention is given towards it. To find it one has to look for it in the ancient texts. It's in the *Upadana Sutta*, for example.

> Just as if a great mass of fire were burning, and into it a man would time and again throw dried grass, dried cow dung, and dried timber, so that the great mass of fire — thus nourished, thus sustained — would burn for a long, long time. In the same way, in one who keeps focusing on the allure of clingable phenomena, craving develops.... Such is the origin of this entire mass of suffering and stress.
>
> Now, in one who keeps focusing on the drawbacks of clingable phenomena, craving ceases.... Such is the cessation of this entire mass of suffering and stress.

A later example can be found in the *Platform Sutra of the Sixth Patriarch*:

> If someone asks you about the Dharma, answer in dichotomous fashion making constant use of opposition pairs to demonstrate their mutual dependency. Do this, and eliminate dualistic dharmas once and for all, leaving them with no place at all to go.[89]

Perhaps the cure by argument was more prominent in the Buddhism that Pyrrho saw and he just copied it. Whatever the case, we have ancient Buddhist texts attesting to its use. There doesn't seem to be any reason for modern Buddhists not to avail themselves of this technique.

Not only should Buddhists and Pyrrhonists avail themselves of the cure by argument, everyone should, because the utility of the cure by argument extends beyond individuals to entire societies. Michael Schmidt-Salomon, a philosopher and commentator on the philosophy of Karl Popper, describes the societal situation well:

---

89 *Platform Sutra*, Chapter 45.

Historical experience shows that societies which penalize any deviation from the norm are doomed to cultural standstill. At least a part of mankind has learned a lesson from this.

Thus, modern societies don't consider the conflict of opinions primarily as an undesirable disruptive factor, but as fertile soil for civilizational progress. This is expressed in the beautiful term, "culture of dispute", indicating what the modern era is essentially about, namely a culture of having disputes. Indeed modern societies are characterized by not only allowing, but actively supporting, the debate about "the true, beautiful and good."

However, they should not do this in an unregulated way, but according to clearly defined cultural guidelines, which could be called the game rules of civilized conflict.[90]

Practiced collectively, the cure by argument heals societies of their dogmas.

---

90 *Die Grenzen der Toleranz – Warum wir die offene Gesellschaft verteidigen müssen.* (translation by Janosch Rydzy) http://grenzen-der-toleranz.de/the-limits-of-tolerance

33
Styles of Pyrrhonist Practice

Socrates told us, "the unexamined life is not worth living." I think he's calling for curiosity, more than knowledge. In every human society at all times and at all levels, the curious are at the leading edge.   *Roger Ebert*

It is evident that skepticism, while it makes no actual change in man, always makes him feel better.

Ambrose Bierce

Pyrrhonism can be practiced in three different approaches or styles. They are:
- Refutation style (traditional term *aporetic*)
- Suspension style (traditional term *ephectic*)
- Seeking style (traditional term *zetetic*)

These style differences likely have to do with differences in the practitioner's experience with Pyrrhonist practice, their personality and temperament, and differences in situations. Due to the nature of their philosophical objectives, the books Sextus Empiricus and Aenesidemus wrote were mostly in the refutation style. Sextus Empiricus mentions the three styles but does not elaborate on them. Recognition of the three styles may go as far back as Timon, who created three neologisms to describe Pyrrhonist practice. These translate to "speaking about things from both sides," "thinking about things from both sides," and "looking at things from both sides." These neatly match refutation, suspension, and seeking.[91]

In the Refutation style, focus is placed on developing arguments against non-evident propositions as the means for inducing epoché. It seems to me that this style is attractive to people who are particularly prone to developing beliefs, and who enjoy rhetoric and logic.[92] The situations that this style is most suited for are those where the practitioner feels a strong urge to accept a dogma.

---

91   Dee L. Clayman, *Timon of Philus*, p 86.

92   In the Five Factor model of personality, I suspect these practitioners might be high on conscientiousness and low on agreeableness. In the Enneagram system, I suspect these would likely be Type 1s (Reformers), 4s (Individualists) and 8s (Challengers). In the Myers Briggs system these might be thinking and judging types.

In the Suspension style, focus is placed on going directly to epoché via the use of the Pyrrhonist maxims. I suspect that this style is attractive to people who don't feel the need to argumentatively oppose the intruding belief. They just need to remind themselves of the desirability of suspending judgment. These individuals likely have a weaker attraction to developing beliefs and a strong attraction to ataraxia.[93] The situations that this style is most suited for are those where the practitioner feels a slight urge to accept a dogma.

In the Seeking style, focus is placed on inquiry and investigation. This technique involves ongoing questioning and perspective shifting as a method of avoiding coming to conclusions. Another way of thinking about it is as an injunction to just investigate pragmata (issues about non-evident matters) without coming to conclusions about whether they are true, or whether they are good or bad. Just investigate. That is the essence of the zetetic (seeking) process. It seems that individuals who are most attracted to the seeking style have a high level of curiosity, which is a natural impediment to coming to a judgment.[94] The situations that this style is most suited for are those where the practitioner feels little urge to accept a dogma because there are so many competing dogmas readily available to explore and because the exploration itself is satisfying.

The Seeking style gets little direct discussion in the surviving Pyrrhonist texts. I suspect that this is because it seemed to need no explanation. However, if one is aware of its existence, references to it abound, some of which are prominent. Sextus begins *Outlines of Pyrrhonism* by saying that seeking is the defining characteristic that sets Pyrrhonists apart from the dogmatists. It's also central to the term the ancient Pyrrhonists used to refer to themselves: *skeptikoi*, which translates to "inquirers" or "investigators."

Underlying the cure by argument is seeking. The process of coming up with arguments requires one to seek out and research opposing views so that one may set them against the non-evident proposition one is tempted to believe.

---

93   In the Five Factor model of personality, I suspect these practitioners would be high on agreeableness. In the Myers Briggs system these might be feeling and perceiving types. In the Enneagram system, these would likely be Type 9s (Peacemakers), 2s (Helpers), and 6s (Loyalists). In the Enneagram system the Type 6 is also known as the "Doubter" or "Skeptic." The Type 6 combines loyalty to what has been demonstrated over time and doubt towards new ideas and change. This matches the Pyrrhonist approach to ethics and decision making with regard to following experience and a default preference for convention.

94   In the Five Factor model of personality, I suspect these practitioners would be high on openness. In the Enneagram system, these would likely be Type 5s, (Investigators), 3s (Achievers), and 7s (Enthusiasts). In the Myers Briggs system these might be intuitives and perceivers.

The Pyrrhonist emphasis on seeking is an interesting point of comparison with Buddhism. Some Buddhists hold that "right view is no view," a paradoxical statement open to multiple interpretations. The corresponding Pyrrhonist prescription is that the "right" view of non-evident matters is to have multiple plausible views and that one should suspend judgment among them.

To achieve the multiple views, one must have curiosity, one must inquire. Aristotle famously said, "it is the mark of an educated mind to be able to entertain a thought without accepting it." Pyrrhonism is like that, but it goes further. In Pyrrhonism it is the mark of a eudaimonic mind to seek out and entertain multiple thoughts without accepting any of them. In contrast with Buddhism's inward focus on the nature of the self, Pyrrhonism is an outwardly oriented practice. Ataraxia is achieved through curiosity about the world.

The Zen Master Shunryu Suzuki famously expressed something similar to the Pyrrhonist concept of seeking: "In the beginner's mind there are many possibilities, but in the expert's there are few." But Pyrrhonism doesn't see the expert's mind as constrained like this. It is the dogmatist's mind that is constrained like this. One can be an expert without being a dogmatist. Similarly one can be a beginner and a dogmatist due to preconceived notions. Indeed, it is though developing expertise that beginners learn that things that they did not think were possible can in fact be done. Sextus was an expert about the matters he wrote about. He didn't fall into believing them. Think about the great minds of history. These people were all experts, not beginners. Why do we consider them to be such great minds? It is often because they rejected one or more commonly accepted beliefs and explored other possibilities.

Peter Thiel, the co-founder of PayPal who has gone on to become a highly successful investor, innovator, and thought leader, credits part of his success to a technique he calls – quite surprisingly – "Pyrrhonian skepticism." [95] In this technique Thiel seeks out non-evident propositions that are commonly assumed to be true. Thiel then proposes: what if they're not true? What if the opposite or something else contrary to the proposition is true? Theil reports that this process is a key secret to his success. Thiel is an expert investor, but in this expert's mind the possibilities are obviously not few.

Think about how you feel when you develop curiosity about something. How does this make you feel? The curiosity is a feeling that is opposite being anxious or perturbed. It is an enjoyable feeling. When one

---

95   https://www.electronicsweekly.com/blogs/mannerisms/genius/
pyrrhonian-scepticism-2017-01/

is freed from beliefs – dogmas that must be defended – the mind is free to inquire about all sorts of things. Children are naturally curious, but curiosity is lost as their minds are filled with dogmas. Emptying the mind of dogmas returns the mind to its natural and happier state of curiosity. As Plutarch put it, "the mind is not a vessel to be filled, but a fire to be kindled."

34
Beliefs and Appearances

The foolish reject what they see and not what they think;
the wise reject what they think and not what they see.
Huang Po

All philosophies are mental fabrications. There has never
been a single doctrine by which one could enter the true
essence of things. *Nagarjuna*

As discussed previously, some people insist that a life without beliefs is not only impossible, it is inconceivable. To a large degree, this is either a word game – meaning that one party defines a word one way and the other party defines it another way and the two parties are just arguing about words – or a failure or a refusal to see the Pyrrhonist point of view. Here are some examples of the types of beliefs some people have claimed Pyrrhonists must have, contrasted with the Pyrrhonist view of why those things do not constitute "beliefs" as we define the term.

• The "belief" that it is day outside, where this "belief" is formed immediately from the perceptual appearance to you that it is day outside.

Pyrrhonist view: That's not a belief. The experience of daytime is an appearance that is forced upon one. Things that are forced upon us are not choices. One chooses to believe non-evident things. If one cannot choose it, it cannot be a belief.

• The "belief" that 1+1=2.

Pyrrhonist view: That's not a belief. The experience of taking one thing and adding another to it is an appearance that is forced upon one. Alternatively, it can be viewed as an ability. It's an ability that is not uniquely human. For example, dogs can do this kind of math with small numbers, as for that matter, so can a pocket calculator.

• The "belief" that you should eat something right now, where this "belief" is formed immediately from the feeling you have of being hungry.

Pyrrhonist view: That's not a belief. The experience of one's body signaling hunger is forced upon us. Besides, if hunger is a belief, then creatures with the most minimal nervous systems would therefore have beliefs. Even mechanical devices that have been programmed to refuel or recharge as needed would qualify as having beliefs.

- The "belief" that you, as a carpenter, should construct a table in a particular way, where this "belief" is formed from your craft-experience.

Pyrrhonist view: That's not a belief; that's either a convention about how tables are made, or an appearance about what tables people buy. If buyers of tables expect or want tables to be a particular way, a Pyrrhonist carpenter would observe this and see that's the kind of table people want.

Some people who seem to be simultaneously too clever and too dense for their own good argue that the description of Pyrrhonism in this book represents a belief about Pyrrhonism, and based on that insist that a dilemma exists: I either cannot be a Pyrrhonist, or I don't believe what I'm saying. Therefore why should you believe any of this? This is just a word game, but there's a good reason the dogmatists would insist on this word game. The dogmatists want to make "belief" so fundamental to cognition as to make cognition impossible without "beliefs." This masterfully hides what they're doing. By making people think that evident experiences are "beliefs" in the same category as "beliefs" about non-evident matters, it allows the dogmatists to more easily justify their dogmas.

As this is a book about Pyrrhonism, we get to use the Pyrrhonist definition of "belief," not that of the dogmatists. For a Pyrrhonist a "belief" is assent to a non-evident proposition about reality. Appearances are not only evident; they are in a tautological sense true for the person experiencing them. In the various debates on this subject among scholars, it amazes me that they missed Sextus' clear statement on this matter. Perhaps it was because that statement is in a place where they did not think to look for it, because it is in a section of text contrasting Pyrrhonism with Cyrenaicism:

> Some people say that Cyrenaicism is the same as Pyrrhonism, since it too says that only pathé are apprehensible.[96]

In other words, one is capable of knowing the truth about how one feels. People can make true statements about their own experiences. This is

---

96 *Outlines of Pyrrhonism*, Book I, Section 32.

knowledge, not belief. It would become a belief if one were to extrapolate from one's experience to asserting that it was a true statement about reality. This book is about what is evident to me. I do not firmly maintain it is a description about reality.

Correspondingly, some people interpret the Pyrrhonist rejection of belief to mean that Pyrrhonists accept only "facts." This is also a misunderstanding. While it is true that Pyrrhonists focus on the evident, what is evident to one person may well not be evident to another person. The ways that perception of the evident could be distorted was covered in detail in the chapter on the Ten Modes of Aenesidemus. To call something a "fact" is just a matter of convention. It is an agreement that the parties to a conversation agree on something evident. Just because the parties agree doesn't mean that the "fact" is true with regard to reality.

Some people say that one has to believe in ataraxia in order to become a Pyrrhonist. This too is a misunderstanding of "belief." Ataraxia is simply a psychological state of being unperturbed. Anyone old enough to read this book will have experienced periods in their life where they were perturbed and periods when they were not perturbed. Ataraxia is a state everyone is familiar with, if only temporarily. It's like how Buddhists say that samsara (the world of suffering) is nirvana (the world of bliss). The difference is in how you look at it, with deluded mind or with enlightened mind. Pyrrhonism is a system for changing how one looks at things so that one experiences them as less troubling.

How do you know when you have a belief? The most effective thing you can do is to be attuned to detecting your own feelings of perturbance or being troubled. Anytime you are suffering from something that's not physical, that suffering can be traced to a belief. Here's recent example from my life.

Another aspiring writer on Hellenistic philosophy I know engaged a professional editor with a personal interest in philosophy to do developmental editing on their manuscript. Developmental editing deals with matters such as whether the thesis and concepts are clear and are optimally organized. It is not about copyediting. The editor's advice was excellent. I decided to hire this editor to review my own manuscript. The result was upsetting.

What I found was troubling me was that I believed that it was my responsibility as an author to make my points clear, and that I should expect myself of being capable of delivering my message to any motivated reader – most certainly one who was a professional and being paid to do so. What I got back from this editor barely discussed anything in the manuscript that they found confusing or unclear. Instead, their comments indicated that they misunderstood the book. I'd seen nothing like this among the many other people who had previously reviewed my manuscript. I was perturbed. What had I done wrong?

It took some time for me to realize it, but what I had done wrong was to believe that I was responsible. Whether a book is understood is just as much a function of the reader as it is the author. The editor's interest in philosophy was an impediment. The editor was a practicing Stoic. Their psychological investment in Stoic dogma appears to have produced a mental block so great that it distorted not only their comprehension, but also their awareness of whether they were comprehending. Those are well-known symptoms of the disease of dogmatism. Not only in antiquity did dogmatic philosophers misunderstand Pyrrhonism, the writings of many modern scholars on ancient Pyrrhonism demonstrate that they do not understand the material about which they claim to be experts. How could they understand it? They don't practice Pyrrhonism. It's like trying to understand water without ever taking a drink.

I'm suspect that some people in the midst of reading this book will hurl it against the wall in rage as they come to realize what a threat Pyrrhonism is to their cherished dogmas by which they define themselves. This sort of reaction has been happening since antiquity. Epictetus, the ancient Stoic philosopher, is the author of the famous slogan, "bear and forbear." In *The Enchiridion* he says: "Remember that it is not he who gives abuse or blows who affronts, but the view we take of these things as insulting. When, therefore, anyone provokes you, be assured that it is your own opinion which provokes you."[97] His writings are full of advice on how to avoid any upsetting emotion, most particularly anger. But, what is his reaction to Pyrrhonism? Here it is, overflowing with anger:

> If I were slave to one of these men, even if I had to be soundly flogged by him every day, I would torment him. "Boy, throw a little oil into the bath." I would have thrown a little fish sauce in, and as I left would pour it down on his head. "What does this mean?" "I had an external impression that could not be distinguished from olive oil; indeed, it was altogether like it. I swear by your fortune." "Here, give me the gruel." I would have filled a side dish with vinegar and fish sauce and brought it to him. "Did I not ask for the gruel?" "Yes, master; this is gruel." "Is not this vinegar and fish sauce?" "How so, any more than gruel." "Take and smell it, take and taste it."

---

97 Epictetus, *Enchiridion*, Section 20.

"Well, how do you know, if the senses deceive us?" If I had three or four fellow-slaves who felt as I did, I would have made him burst with rage and hang himself, or else change his opinion. But as it is, such men are toying with us; they use all the gifts of nature, while in theory doing away with them.[98]

Epictetus has convinced himself that he knows the truth about reality. The idea that he might not is such an affront to him that he totally loses his highly proclaimed self-control to go out of his way to torment someone merely because that person holds an opinion different from his own. As Nietzsche said, "Oh, you noble Stoics, what fraud of words!"

The most glaring example I've encountered of a modern scholar failing to understand Pyrrhonism comes from Jonathan Barnes, professor of ancient philosophy at Oxford, then later University of Geneva. He's the author of many books on ancient philosophy, several of which are on Pyrrhonism. Below are some examples of his fundamental misunderstanding of Pyrrhonism. If a scholar of Pyrrhonism can have such misunderstandings of Pyrrhonism, it's reasonable to expect readers of this book to have similar misunderstandings.

Sextus makes no attempt to find the best, or the clearest, or the most plausible interpretation of a Dogmatic position. It is for the Dogmatists to state their opinions as best they can: Sextus will destroy them. Why should a skeptic hold out a hand to his enemies? Well, he should do so in the interest of truth. But – this is my chief criticism of him as a philosopher – it is difficult to believe that Sextus ever seriously searched for truth.[99]

The problem here is that Barnes believes that coming up with opinions on the non-evident is what the search for truth is about. The type of search for truth that Sextus is engaged in is a removal of that which is believed but which is not true. If you want to find the truth, you have to get rid of everything that isn't truth. Barnes is blind to this way of searching for truth, even when it's described and demonstrated to him, as Sextus repeatedly does.

From our distant perspective, one can easily see the value of what Sextus did. On the subjects of natural philosophy, almost every dogmatic

---

98 Epictetus, *Discourses*, Book 2, Section 20.

99 From Barnes' introduction to *Outlines of Scepticism*, by Sextus Empiricus, edited by Julia Annas and Jonathan Barnes, 2000, pp xxx.

belief that Sextus calls into question has been demonstrated by later scientific inquiry to have been partially or totally false. In many cases the criticisms described by Sextus were instrumental in correcting these errors. Sextus seriously searched for the truth.

Barnes doesn't even comprehend the point of Pyrrhonism. He says:

> Skepticism is offered as a recipe for happiness. After all, skepticism is an ancient philosophy, and ancient philosophies were, in general, offered as recipes for happiness. What is the point of studying logic, say, or of investigating the nature of numbers if not to become happy?
>
> I find it difficult to take this sort of thing seriously; and doubly difficult in the case of skepticism.
>
> ... do not read philosophy if you want to be happy. There are many things in life more interesting and more desirable than happiness. Knowledge, for example, and understanding.[100]

Barnes should of course be aware that the concept he is presenting here as "happiness" is actually eudaimonia. Eudaimonia is about living a fulfilling life. It's not merely about happiness. One must wonder what kind of defect of the soul Barnes suffers from that he would advise people to eschew having a fulfilling life, to disregard happiness, and to provide as a substitute the accumulation of "knowledge" – "knowledge" of the kind for which it is plain see has great propensity to be false. Do you want to live a good life, or do you want to live a lie? Barnes recommends the lie. Barnes misunderstands the cure by argument as follows:

> Suppose that I suspect that I have a fatal disease: unsure, I worry, I become depressed; and in order to restore my peace of mind I decide to investigate – and I visit my doctor. What does Dr. Sextus say? "My dear chap," he says, "on the one hand there are several clear signs that you are not ill at all; on the other hand, I can produce compelling argument to show that you will die within a month." – "What am I to do?" – "Plainly, you will and must suspend your judgment on the matter. You must neither morbidly suppose that you are fatally infected nor cheerfully imagine that you are in perfect health.

---

100 From Barnes' introduction to *Outlines of Scepticism*, by Sextus Empiricus, edited by Julia Annas and Jonathan Barnes, 2000, pp xxx-xxxi.

And then, mark my words, you will find that you have nothing to worry about." Thus Dr. Sextus lets me leave the surgery in the very state of uncertainty which induced me to enter it. He is a quack.... Sextus' advertisement for skepticism is false: do not read him if you want to be happy.[101]

It appears that Barnes prefers false certainty over the truth. Suppose you do have a fatal disease that cannot be diagnosed. You knew before you saw the doctor that you were eventually going to die. Nothing has changed. The ancient philosophers, at least since Socrates, viewed the study of philosophy as preparation for death. Barnes somehow missed that. He wants certainty, but that is not how life works.

What is it about death that worries Barnes? He doesn't tell us. Perhaps he is worried that he has wasted his life. Perhaps he is worried that all of that "knowledge" he has spent his life accumulating will disappear with his death, and that it was all in vain. About these matters we can speculate, but we must suspend judgment. It is Barnes here who needs to search for the truth, to inquire, to have curiosity about the matter. Why is he worried about that which is certain? It is for this that Dr. Sextus' prescription applies.

It's an interesting coincidence that Barnes has a brother who is a famous novelist, Julian Barnes. About her two sons, their mother once remarked, "one writes books I can read, but cannot understand. The other writes books I can understand, but cannot read." Jonathan Barnes' books can be read, but not understood because he doesn't understand what he's writing about. Julian Barnes' books can be understood, but some people would not want to read them because they are disturbing. One of them, *A Sense of an Ending*, deals with troubling matters concerning what the protagonist knows, doesn't know, what he doesn't know about what he doesn't know, and how he fills those gaps in with beliefs. It's a novel dealing with Pyrrhonist issues. Another of them is a memoir, *Nothing to be Frightened of*. It is a meditation on death.

Nassim Nicholas Taleb coined a term for people like Professor Barnes. He calls them "intellectual-yet-idiots." Barnes presents himself as an expert on Pyrrhonism when in fact he doesn't understand the fundamentals of his subject. To turn the tables on what Barnes concludes in his remarks about Sextus being a "quack:" Professor Barnes' advertisement for knowledge is false. Do not read him if you want to understand reality. There are

---

101 From Barnes' introduction to *Outlines of Scepticism*, by Sextus Empiricus, edited by Julia Annas and Jonathan Barnes, 2000, pp xxxi.

many things in life more interesting and more desirable than acquiring beliefs regarding non-evident matters, for example, the taste of an apple, how to ride a bicycle, the eyes of your lover.

In many of the Zen lineages it is customary to have the chant leader mark the end of each day of a retreat by chanting, solo, the following:

> Let me respectfully remind you,
> Life and death are of supreme importance.
> Time swiftly passes by and opportunity is lost.
> Each of us should strive to awaken. . .
> . . . awaken,
> Take heed. Do not squander your life.

35

Against Aristocles of Messene

But if someone else were to produce a thesis which purported to be a major breakthrough between Eastern and Western philosophy, between religious mysticism and scientific positivism, he would think it of major historic importance, a thesis which would place the University miles ahead. In any event, he said, no one was really accepted in Chicago until he'd rubbed someone out. It was time Aristotle got his.   *Robert M. Pirsig,*
                Zen and the Art of Motorcycle Maintenance

Indeed neither life nor science bothers about "essences" – they leave "essences" to metaphysics, which is neither life nor science.   *Alfred Korzybski,*
                Manhood of Humanity

Aristocles of Messene was the Peripatetic philosopher who was quoted by Eusebius, who preserved the Aristocles Passage as part of Aristocles' arguments against Pyrrhonism. To understand both the Aristocles Passage and the arguments against Pyrrhonism better, it seems useful to consider those arguments.

We have no surviving records from antiquity of a Pyrrhonist defending Pyrrho's statement against Aristocles' arguments. Sextus Empiricus does not appear to have taken up the matter. His approach in describing Pyrrhonism is to make it as hard to attack as possible. He streamlines out of it things such as what Pyrrho said in the Aristocles Passage in favor of cautious and legalistic wordings.

Aristocles makes clear that he is arguing on behalf of Aristotle, and that the target of his argument is not only Pyrrho, but Pyrrho's whole philosophical lineage:

> Such then were the followers of Xenophanes.... Now a hearer of Xenophanes was Parmenides, and of Parmenides Melissus, of him Zeno, of him Leucippus, of him Democritus, of him Protagoras and Nessas, and of Nessas Metrodorus, of him Diogenes, of him Anaxarchus, and a disciple of Anaxarchus was Pyrrho....

…who have been opposed by Aristotle.

Here again is my paraphrase of Pyrrho's argument – the Aristocles Passage – the argument that is opposed by Aristocles and the other followers of Aristotle:

> If you want to have a good life, you need to consider what is the nature of all those matters people dispute about. Next, you need to figure out what is the best attitude to have towards those matters. Finally, you should understand what the outcome of that attitude will be.
>
> As for the nature of those disputed matters, they're all based on issues that cannot be clearly defined, they are about things that are unstable, impermanent, and unmeasurable, and they ultimately cannot be judged.
>
> Therefore, neither our senses nor our ideas tell us what is true or false about them, and consequently we should be without beliefs or even leanings about these matters. We should be unwavering in our refusal to have beliefs or leanings, saying about every single issue, that it is not more this than that.
>
> The outcome for those who adopt this attitude will first be a state of not making assertions, and then inner peace.

Aristocles begins his argument as follows:

> These then are the chief points of their arguments: and now let us consider whether they are right in what they say. Since therefore they say that all things are equally adiaphora, and bid us for this reason attach ourselves to none, nor hold any opinion, I think one may reasonably ask them, whether those who think things differ are in error or not. For if they are in error, surely they cannot be right in their supposition. So they will be compelled to say that there are some who have false opinions about things, and they themselves therefore must be those who speak the truth: and so there must be truth and falsehood. But if we the many are not in error in thinking that things differ, what do they mean by rebuking us? For they must be in error themselves in maintaining that they do not differ.

By saying that these are the "chief points" of the Pyrrhonist arguments, Aristocles implies that he has left out other points that he doesn't consider important. Let's first consider what those may have been.

I suspect one thing he has left out is the characteristic way Pyrrhonists say things. Pyrrhonists say things "appear" to be such, or they "seem" to be such, or they are "perhaps" such. They do not say that things "are" such when all they have to go on is an appearance. So, it's probable that in this respect Aristocles has distorted Pyrrho's argument. Pyrrho's argument was likely worded as a description of the appearances, whereas Aristocles assumes that this distinction is irrelevant: the appearances and the nature of reality are essentially the same. For Pyrrhonists, this is a critical distinction; for Aristotelians, it all but doesn't exist. Aristocles likely edited these qualifiers out.

Another thing Aristocles likely edited out was the Pyrrhonist distinction between evident and non-evident. By *pragmata*, it is likely that Pyrrho was referring specifically to non-evident things. Understanding this distinction is essential for understanding Pyrrhonism. Aristocles' arguments show no indication of taking this distinction into account. Hence, Aristocles may have distorted or misunderstood what Pyrrho meant by *pragmata*. Pyrrho uses the term to refer to the things people dispute over, i.e., non-evident matters. Aristocles seems to understand it to mean absolutely everything. This seems unlikely to be what Pyrrho meant. Contrary to the modern stereotype of a skeptic being someone who wants to refute everything, this is not true about Pyrrhonists, and it was not a stereotype of Pyrrhonists in antiquity. Pyrrhonists were not concerned with refuting what everyone agreed upon. It was the Cynic philosophers who were known for doing that. In contrast with the Cynics, the Pyrrhonists recommend following custom and convention. Aristocles certainly should have been aware of how the Cynics and Pyrrhonists differed on this issue. On the things everyone agreed upon, the Pyrrhonists were only concerned that agreement on the appearances should not be extrapolated to being considered to be construed to be a true statement about the nature of reality. Pyrrho was likely remarking on the issues about non-evident matters people disagreed about, not necessarily taking a position on the fundamental nature of reality.

One way that Aristocles distorts Pyrrho's argument is that he insists on taking it as a metaphysical argument. Pyrrho's aims are, however explicitly psychotherapeutic. He tells people what attitudes to have and how to see things to achieve eudaimonia. For Pyrrho, it doesn't matter what is true about the ultimate nature of reality. He explicitly says one should not have an opinion about that kind of thing. What matters for Pyrrho is what allows people to have happy, fulfilling lives.

Aristocles, however, shows no concern about eudaimonia. He is only concerned about the ultimate nature of reality – i.e., non-evident matters. So, Aristocles is arguing against a position Pyrrho did not take and insists on taking Pyrrho's statement in a way that Pyrrho did not mean.

To look at the matter another way, imagine the advice a person who found their job was maddening might receive from a counselor. The counselor might tell them it would appear that getting unclear, contradictory, and ever-changing instructions from management was the norm, and that the attitude they should take is to not get psychologically wrapped up in the apparent insanity of the workplace. The situation itself is not fixable. What can be done is to change one's attitude towards the job. Just show up, do whatever it is you're told, and don't worry that it contradicts the prior thing you were told. At the end of the day, go home and forget about it. Focus on enjoying your life and be thankful that you have an income to do so. Pyrrho's intent appears to be closer to the intent of the counselor in this example – a psychological intent – rather than an intent regarding diagnosing the organization's ills – a metaphysical intent.

In taking Pyrrho's claim as metaphysical, Aristocles assumes that the differences people perceive in things are in the things themselves. He leaves out the possibility that differences may be generated by the perceiver, despite the fact that he references not only Timon's work, but also that of Aenesidemus, specifically mentioning the Ten Modes, which are about differences among perceivers accounting for differences in the appearances. Presumably Aristocles was also aware of the rest of Aenesidemus' book, *Pyrrhonian Discourses*. While that book did not survive, a summary of it does, which says:

> The overall aim of the book is to establish that there is no
> firm basis for cognition, either through sense-perception,
> or indeed through thought.[102]

Aenesidemus' main point was that aspects of the perceiver are a critical source of what it is that the perceiver perceives. This point is of long standing in Pyrrho's lineage, going back as far as Xenophanes, who noted that people projected attributes of themselves onto the gods:

> Ethiopians say that their gods are flat-nosed and dark,
> Thracians that theirs are blue-eyed and red-haired.

---

102 Photius, *Myriobiblion.*

Aristocles should have been aware that the issue at stake here is not about the nature of reality – the metaphysics – but the nature of cognition – the human mind. Consequently, it appears that the best interpretation of what Pyrrho's intent was that it was about providing practical psychological advice, not metaphysical dogma. But since Aristocles insists on taking it as metaphysical dogma, I'll propose an answer about the non-evident matters he raises.

The answer I would give to Aristocles' question, whether those who think things differ are in error or not, is that Pyrrhonists don't dispute that things appear different. We dispute whether there's some substance inherent in each thing that produces the apparent differences. Some people say a thing is one way. Other people say the same thing is another way. If what differentiated a thing was inherent in the thing, then everyone inspecting the thing should be able to agree. However, they don't agree. Consequently, there's a problem. In diagnosing that problem we find ample evidence that perceivers differ. So, these permanent essential substances Aristotle says are there that allow things to be differentiated no more seem to be attributes of the things themselves as they are attributes of those perceiving the things and the conditions under which those perceptions are made; otherwise there would not be these disputes. Therefore, the attitude one should take about *pragmata* is that they have no inherent essential differentiators, that they are unstable, and they are unjudgeable. In this way we say that those who, like Aristotle, claim that the *diaphora* inherently differentiate the *pragmata* are in error. Aristotle's *diaphora* seem to be mental creations that allow our minds to freeze ever-changing reality and see in it differences that are useful for practical purposes.

Aristocles implies that Pyrrhonists don't accept the idea of truth and falsehood. That's an error. We say that our senses and opinions are not powerful enough for giving us assured knowledge about things non-evident. We have knowledge of the appearances, and we can make truth claims about them, so long as those claims are limited to being about what we experience.

Aristocles' next argument is:

> ...those who assert that all things are uncertain must do one of two things, either be silent, or speak and state something. If then they should hold their peace, it is evident that against such there would be no argument. But if they should make a statement, anyhow and by all means they must say that something either is or is not, just as they certainly now say that all things are to all men

matters not of knowledge but of customary opinion, and that nothing can be known.

Aristocles here simply refuses to acknowledge the answer he knows full well was given. The answer was that things are uncertain, yet he insists that the only answers possible are that something is or is not. In other words, the answerer must be certain. He refuses to accept uncertain.

From there Aristocles plunges into sophistry:

> The man therefore who maintains this either makes the matter clear, and it is possible to understand it as spoken, or it is impossible. But if he does not make it clear, there can be absolutely no arguing in this case either with such a man. But if he should make his meaning clear, he must certainly either state what is indefinite or what is definite: and if indefinite, neither in this case would there be any arguing with him, for of the indefinite there can be no knowledge. But if the statements, or any one of them whatever, be definite, the man who states this defines something and decides. How then can all things be unknowable and indeterminate? But should he say that the same thing both is and is not, in the first place the same thing will be both true and false, and next he will both say a thing and not say it, and by use of speech will destroy speech, and moreover, while acknowledging that he speaks falsely, says that we ought to believe him.

Pyrrho said pragmata should be viewed as indefinite. Aristocles claims that Pyrrho's statement is definite; therefore, something is definite. And if something is definite, then things aren't indefinite, because that's a logical contradiction. Aristocles follows that argument with one that is structurally identical to the one above: that Pyrrho cannot be certain about his uncertainty. Such arguments are just refusals to understand Pyrrho's position.

Aristocles' next argument says that Aenesidemus, in describing the modes, must either speak with knowledge about the modes or without knowledge.

> But when he was making these and other such fine speeches, one would have liked, I say, to ask him whether he was stating with full knowledge that this is the

condition of things, or without knowledge. For if he did not know, how could we believe him? But if he knew, he was vastly silly for declaring at the same time that all things are uncertain, and yet saying that he knew so much.

Aristocles simply cannot fathom that knowledge of the appearances is not tantamount to knowledge of reality, and that Pyrrhonists make a distinction here that he insists on remaining oblivious to. Aenesidemus is saying that since people cannot even agree on the appearances, it is inappropriate to assume that knowledge of the various perceptions of the appearances are tantamount to knowledge of reality.

As for the next part of Aristocles' argument:

> For if they [we Aristotelians] are in error, surely they [the Pyrrhonists] cannot be right in their supposition. So they will be compelled to say that there are some who have false opinions about things, and they themselves therefore must be those who speak the truth: and so there must be truth and falsehood.
>
> Why trouble yourself, poor fellow, in writing this, and relating what you do not know?

This is a standard misinterpretation of Pyrrhonism. It intentionally mixes up the Pyrrhonists' assertion that they do not know reality to be an assertion that they don't know anything at all. Either Aristocles doesn't understand what he is arguing against, or he does understand it and is intentionally distorting it for rhetorical effect.

While the metaphysics of whatever reality might be are likely complicated – complicated to the point of being unfathomable – whatever useful guidance there can be for helping people live their lives in the most fulfilling way must be pretty simple. At its core it must be a few ideas people can memorize. Pyrrhonism invites you to set aside silly fixations such as those Aristocles gets caught up in and to focus on what's really important: eudaimonia.

In Buddhism there's a parable about a poisoned arrow. The parable starts with a monk being troubled by the Buddha's silence on what are known as the fourteen unanswerable questions, which include issues about the nature of the cosmos and life after the death of a Buddha. The monk then meets with the Buddha and asks him for the answers to these questions. He tells the Buddha that if the Buddha fails to answer these questions, he will renounce the Buddha's teachings. The Buddha replies that he never promised he would reveal such metaphysical truths, and then he tells a story of a man who has been shot with a poisoned arrow to illustrate the irrelevance of those questions.

> It's just as if a man were wounded with an arrow thickly smeared with poison. His friends and companions, kinsmen and relatives would provide him with a surgeon, and the man would say, "I won't have this arrow removed until I know whether the man who wounded me was a noble warrior, a priest, a merchant, or a worker." He would say, "I won't have this arrow removed until I know the given name and clan name of the man who wounded me...until I know whether he was tall, medium, or short...until I know whether he was dark, ruddy-brown, or golden-colored.. until I know his home village, town, or city...until I know whether the bow with which I was wounded was a long bow or a crossbow...until I know whether the bowstring with which I was wounded was fiber, bamboo threads, sinew, hemp, or bark...until I know whether the shaft with which I was wounded was wild or cultivated...until I know whether the feathers of the shaft with which I was wounded were those of a vulture, a stork, a hawk, a peacock, or another bird...until I know whether the shaft with which I was wounded was bound with the sinew of an ox, a water buffalo, a langur, or a monkey." He would say, "I won't have this arrow removed until I know whether the shaft with which I was wounded was that of a common arrow, a curved arrow, a barbed, a calf-toothed, or an oleander arrow." The man would die and those things would still remain unknown to him.[103]

Like the Buddha, Pyrrho is offering to remove that arrow and provide an antidote to the poison. They're talking about the same arrow, and the same poison. The Buddha's prescription is meditation. Pyrrho's prescription is the cure by argument.

---

103 *Cula-Malunkyovada Sutta: The Shorter Instructions to Malunkya.*

....

36
Is There a Self?

Nothing is so firmly believed as that which we least
know.   *Montaigne*

We step and do not step into the same rivers; we are and
are not.   *Heraclitus*

Plutarch gives an ancient Greek view on the self in discussing the three
maxims inscribed over the entrance to the Temple of Apollo at Delphi,
where he was a priest. The first of these is the famous "know thyself." The
second was the nearly as famous "nothing in excess." The third was the
now all-but-forgotten "make a commitment, delusion is nearby."[104] These
are the first three of the Delphic maxims – the three most important out
of the total set of 147 that were inscribed inside the temple. These maxims
were known and revered all over the Greek-speaking world. Archeologists
have found inscriptions of them as far away as Afghanistan.

Above these three maxims at the entrance to the temple was inscribed
the letter "E", which is also a word in Greek, meaning "you are." Plutarch
quotes his teacher, Ammonius, who says that this is what the worshiper is
to say upon entering the temple. This phrase renders unto the god:

> ...the designation which is true and has no lie in it, and
> alone belongs to him, and to no other, that of BEING.
> For we have, really, no part in real being; all mortal na-
> ture is in a middle state between becoming and perish-
> ing, and presents but an appearance, a faint unstable im-
> age, of itself. If you strain the intellect, and wish to grasp
> this, it is as with water; compress it too much and force
> it violently into one space as it tries to flow through, and
> you destroy the enveloping substance; even so when the
> reason tries to follow out too closely the clear truth about
> each particular thing in a world of phase and change, it

---

104 This maxim is difficult to translate. The first clause is about a legal and financial
pledge, like co-signing a loan. In ancient Greece, there was not only no such thing as
limited liability, there was also chattel slavery. That meant the counter-party for the
pledge could collect by taking everything one had – including one's freedom. The second clause is about a mistake, delusion, an evil thing. An idiomatic paraphrase of the
maxim into modern English might be "You would be crazy to be making promises."

is foiled, and rests either on the becoming of that thing or on its perishing; it cannot apprehend anything which abides or really is.

"It is impossible to go into the same river twice," said Heraclitus; no more can you grasp mortal being twice, so as to hold it. So sharp and so swift its change; it scatters and brings together again, nay not again, no nor afterwards; even while it is being formed it fails, it approaches, and it is gone. Hence becoming never ends in being, for the process never leaves off, or is stayed. From seed it produces, in its constant changes, an embryo, then an infant, then a child; in due order a boy, a young man; then a man, an elderly man, an old man; it undoes the former becomings and the age which has been, to make those which come after. yet we fear (how absurdly!) a single death, we who have died so many deaths, and yet are dying. For it is not only that, as Heraclitus would say, "death of fire is birth of air," and "death of air is birth of water;" the thing is much clearer in our own selves. The man in his strength is destroyed when the old man comes into being, the young man was destroyed for the man in his strength to be, so the boy for the young man, the babe for the boy. He of yesterday has died unto him of today; he of today is dying unto him of tomorrow. No one abides, no one is; we that come into being are many, while matter is driven around, and then glides away, about some one appearance and a common mold.

Else how is it, if we remain the same, that the things in which we find pleasure now are different from those of a former time; that we love, hate, admire, and censure different things; that our words are different and our feelings; that our look, our bodily form, our intellect are not the same now as then? If a man does not change, these various conditions are unnatural; if he does change, he is not the same man. But if he is not the same man, he is not at all; his so-called being is simply change and new birth of man out of man. In our ignorance of what being is, sense falsely tells us that what appears is.

For to say of that which has not yet come into being, or has already ceased from being, that it "is" is silly and absurd. But at the very moment when, trying to fix our perception of time, we say "it is present," "it is here," and "now," our reason slips away again from this and loses it. For it is thrust aside into the future and into the past, just as a visual ray is distorted with those who try to see what is necessarily separated by distance.

And if the nature which is measured is subject to the same conditions as the time which measures it, this nature itself has no permanence, nor "being," but is becoming and perishing according to its relation to time.

Hence nothing of this kind may be said of "being," such as "was" or "will be:" for these are a kind of inflexions, and transitions, and alternations of that which is not fitted by nature to continue in "being."[105]

Such is the nature of the self. It has no being.

It's an interesting coincidence that Eusebius quotes this long passage (and more) from Plutarch in the same book he quotes Aristocles' argument against Pyrrhonism. Eusebius praises what Plutarch says here as corroborating what the Hebrews say of God. He totally misses that Plutarch makes an argument here in support of what Pyrrho claims – that everything is unstable – and what the implications are of Plutarch's argument with respect to the immortality of the soul.

I speculate that the Temple of Apollo at Delphi was an important element in Timon's book, *Python,* which was the first book to describe Pyrrhonism. Before going into more detail on that speculation, it would be useful to review more of what Plutarch says about the temple.

That the God [Apollo] is no less philosopher than he is prophet appeared to all to come out directly from the exposition which Ammonius gives us of each of his names. He is "Pythian" (The Inquirer) to those who are beginning to learn and to inquire; "Delian" (The Clear One) and "Phanaean" (Disclosing) to those who are already getting something clear and a glimmering of the truth; "Ismenian" (The Knowing) to those who possess the knowledge; "Leschenorian" (God of Discourse) when they are in active enjoyment of dialectical and philosophic intercourse. "Now since," he continued, "Philosophy embraces inquiry, wonder, and doubt, it seems natural that most of the things relating to the God

---

105 Plutarch, *On the "E" at Delphi.*

should have been hidden away in riddles…. These problems when suggested to persons not altogether wanting in reason and soul, lure them on, and challenge them to inquire, to listen, and to discuss. Look again at those inscriptions, KNOW THYSELF and NOTHING TOO MUCH; how many philosophic inquiries have they provoked! What a multitude of arguments has sprung up out of each, as from a seed! Not one of them I think is more fruitful in this way than the subject of our present inquiry."[106]

Evidence of the philosophical inquiries these maxims have provoked appears in Plato's *Charmides*, a dialog about wisdom, knowledge, and temperance, in which Critias gives his interpretation of the maxims to support his argument that the foundation of wisdom and temperance are in self-knowledge.

The opening of *Python* has Timon encountering Pyrrho outside a temple of Amphiaraus, who was one of the heroes from the era just prior to the Trojan War. He was favored by both Zeus and Apollo. He was persuaded by his wife to join a military expedition which, due to the oracular talent given to him by Zeus, he knew would result in his death. This story has similarities with Alexander the Great's Indian expedition, which Pyrrho participated in, and which resulted in Alexander's death. Amphiaraus knew his wife was corrupt and had been bribed to persuade him to join the expedition. Following Amphiaraus death, intra-family conflict arose, a metaphor for the breakup of Alexander's empire following his death. This choice of location suggests that Timon used it as a literary device for getting Pyrrho to talk about the expedition and to position Pyrrho as an oracle.

We know from other sources that Pyrrho was a priest, most likely in a line of seer priests who interpreted the oracle at the Temple of Zeus at Olympia. Timon likely leveraged this to position Pyrrho as being like the oracle Amphiaraus. Later writers who had access to Timon's books tended to use an unusual word in reference to Timon's relationship to Pyrrho. Instead of the usual terms associated with a philosophical lineage, such as "student," "follower," or "hearer," for Timon they used "prophet," suggesting a religious aura around Pyrrho and Timon's testimony of Pyrrho.

As Timon and Pyrrho encounter each other outside the temple of Amphiaraus they learn that they are both on their way to Delphi, the location of the most important of all of the Greek temples, associated not only with prophecy but also with philosophy: the Temple of Apollo

---

106 Plutarch, *On the "E" at Delphi*.

at Delphi. The title Timon chose for his book is a reference to the vapors that arose off of the decomposition of the giant snake that was slain by Apollo. This snake was buried beneath the temple. The vapors of its decomposition were what put the Pythia – the female oracle of Apollo – into her holy trance. The choice of title alludes to the ultimate earthly source of the wisdom of Apollo, the god of truth, prophecy, and healing. The title also refers to one of the meanings of the term "pythian" as "inquirer." It is a synonym for the term the early Pyrrhonists choose for themselves: "skeptikoi" – inquirers.

Given the literary elements we know about *Python*, it would seem nearly essential that the *Python's* plotline would involve Pyrrho and Timon visiting the Temple of Apollo at Delphi. We also know from Aristocles that Timon describes what he and Pyrrho talked about at great length. Beyond this, one can only speculate about the contents of the book. I imagine the two men outside the Temple of Apollo. Pyrrho takes advantage of the setting to tell Timon about a discussion he had with one of the gymnosophists who had asked Pyrrho about what the Greeks considered to be their most important spiritual advice. Pyrrho points to the inscription on the temple and says he told the gymnosophist:

- Know yourself
- Nothing in excess
- Make a commitment, delusion is nearby

The gymnosophist says that the advice is good, and that his people have a similar bit of three-item advice:

- All conditioned things lack self
- All conditioned things are unstable and unsatisfactory
- All conditioned things are impermanent

Pyrrho goes on to explain the connection he sees between the two statements.

- To know yourself is to learn that you lack self-essence. You are a process that is interacting with everything around you. Due to this interaction, there is no clear demarcation between yourself and everything else. Who you are is a function of all sorts of things that are outside yourself, such as who your parents were or whether you were born in Greece or India. Everything is like this. Everything is a process interacting with other things. Nothing has an inherent demarcation.
- As for nothing in excess, we have a problem. To know what is in excess, one would have to be able to measure it, but we are continually foiled in our efforts to do so. Everything is unstable, and what is

unstable cannot be accurately measured. This is why life is unsatisfactory. Try as we may, we cannot even things out. Even Odysseus, using his best efforts to take the middle way between Scylla and Charybdis could only steer a course such that he lost a few men to Scylla. Life is like riding in a cart that has a bent axel. One moment the cart lifts up too high. The next moment the cart lurches down too low. Each rotation is constantly in excess.

- The reason that making a commitment means that delusion is nearby is because commitment is permanent, yet everything else is impermanent. As Heraclitus said, we cannot step into the same river twice. Commitment to anything unstable must end in calamity.

Following this, I imagine Pyrrho explaining to Timon how the appearances don't give us reality, conversationally covering most of what we now know as the Ten Modes of Aenesidemus, as some authors credit Pyrrho with those modes. It seems likely that Pyrrho expressed the basic ideas for the Ten Modes in *Python* and Aenesidemus later systematized and expounded upon them. Finally Pyrrho explains how committing to beliefs about non-evident things results in delusion. To sum up his teachings, he goes on to say what is recorded in the Aristocles Passage.

From a rhetorical standpoint, it would make sense for Pyrrho to base his arguments on the Delphic maxims. Not only were they universally accepted across the Greek-speaking world, but leveraging them would also give a religious aura to his message, just like the religious aura Pyrrho saw in India that accompanied Buddha's philosophy. Doing so would also stylistically fit in Pyrrho's philosophical lineage. Heraclitus wrote his book, *On Nature*, in the style of oracular sayings. He deposited his book as a dedication in the great temple of Artemis, the *Artemisium*, one of the largest temples of the 6th Century BCE and one of the Seven Wonders of the Ancient World. Parmenides' book, also entitled *On Nature*, takes place in an imaginary temple and involves a conversation with a goddess. Much of what Democritus taught as ethics was in the form of maxims, like the Delphic Maxims, and much of Pyrrhonist practice involves the use of maxims.

Another reason for Pyrrho and Timon to connect Pyrrho's teaching to religion could be that Pyrrho and Timon were influenced by how Buddhist philosophy is also connected to religion. We know that Pyrrho was raised to the status of high priest during the period he was active teaching Pyrrhonism. In starting Pyrrhonism, Pyrrho and Timon may have tried to connect it with religion. This would not have been unusual at the time. Plato's dialogs often have Socrates discussing the gods. Ancient Stoicism had a strong pantheistic religious orientation. A core feature of Epicure-anism was to reposition the view of the gods. Early Christians considered the Hellenistic philosophies to be competitors to Christianity; hence ref-utations of them like the one from Eusebius that preserved the Aristocles Passage. Arguably all of the Hellenistic philosophies of life functioned as kinds of covert religions structured to allow them to deny that they were religions and to avoid any overt interference with the official religions.

Regardless of this, for his book Timon would need to marshal every persuasive technique available, as Pyrrhonism is for so many people intu-itively implausible. Upon being introduced to Pyrrhonism, many people react with horror at the notion that their beliefs about what is good and bad, and about what non-evident things are true and false, could possibly be wrong. Why this should be so is a matter of speculation. Perhaps it is because, if they were to accept the Pyrrhonist view, the consequence would be that all of the beliefs they used to construct their idea of themselves would collapse. It seems to them like the prospect of death.

Some people see an extraordinary kind of passivity or psychological hollowing out implicit in following Pyrrhonism. While Pyrrhonists es-chew inclinations about belief, this cannot be done about actions, about which we must be inclined for or against in order to take them or reject them. We're aware of these actions. We watch them unfold and what hap-pens because of them. Richard Bett, a scholar on ancient Pyrrhonism, speculates that a Pyrrhonist,

> ...does not get involved with [their actions] in any way; he simply lets them do their work, watching them unfold just as if it was not him to which they were happening at all. In fact, there is a sense in which the [Pyrrhonist] is not fully an agent, or in different terminology, not fully a self. If we think of an agent or a self as having, or being, a cluster of concerns, priorities and perspectives on the world in which he, she or it is invested, and which shape one's choices and actions through that very engagement, then the [Pyrrhonist] does not qualify. True, the [Pyr-rhonist] has concerns, priorities and perspectives of a kind – these are given by the dispositions ingrained in him – but his attitude towards them is spectacularly dis-engaged. Indeed, that is the whole point. The project of suspending judgement, so that one does not come down on the side of anything's really being any particular way, in terms of its nature or its value, ensures that one will

not treat one's own concerns and priorities as tracking anything that really matters; they may push one in various directions, and hence they are not fundamental to who one is. Nor, as far as I can see, is anything else.[107]

So, in this way there is a kind of Pyrrhonist deconstruction of the self, and similarly a description of how the Pyrrhonist achieves something like the Taoist wu wei.

The description of Pyrrhonism given by Diogenes Laertius gives some other hints about the Pyrrhonist view of the self. Pyrrho would quote anything that bore on the uncertainty, emptiness, and fickleness of human affairs, particularly Homer. Pyrrho's view appears to have been to consider our own agency – our ability to create the lives we want – to be greatly limited. So much of what happens in our lives just happens to us. We did nothing to bring it about.

Why should anyone be convinced by the dogmatists who proclaim that we have robust agency, and that we are beings motivated by our beliefs? Maybe we have only the appearance of choice, the appearance of free will, but we don't actually have free will. We're just riding along in the current of life, just experiencing it. Maybe everything that happens is outside our control, including our seeming efforts at control. Or maybe we have some sliver of control, but it is far less than it seems.

Hellenistic philosophy talks about the "soul" which it differentiates from the body. It also differentiates the *nous* (intellect), which Aristotle defined as the basic understanding or awareness that allows human beings and the gods to think rationally. This was distinct from the processing of sensory perception, including the use of imagination and memory, which other animals can do. Stoicism and some other traditions add *hegemonikon*, which is the commanding faculty of the soul; the center of consciousness, the seat of all mental states, thought to be located in the heart. It manifests four mental powers: the capacity to receive impressions, to assent to them, form intentions to act in response to them, and to do these things rationally.

For this discussion we'll need to consider that the Indian concept of *atman* is the same thing as the Greek concept of the soul. Given that none of the four at-length descriptions we have of ancient Pyrrhonism – those from Sextus Empiricus, Diogenes Laertius, Eusebius, and Photios – directly address the question of whether the soul exists, we don't have a good understanding of how the ancient Pyrrhonists treated the question, but, we have some clues about it.

---

107 Richard Bett, "Living as a Skeptic", 2013, pp 17-18 http://krieger.jhu.edu/philosophy/wp-content/uploads/sites/7/2013/02/Living-as-a-Sceptic.pdf

One of the books that Sextus Empiricus wrote was titled *On the Soul*. Unfortunately it was not preserved for us, but the fact that he wrote such a book suggests the subject of the soul was important to ancient Pyrrhonists; we just don't know what they said about the matter. A hint about the contents of that book is in *Outlines of Pyrrhonism* where Sextus briefly considers arguments about the existence of the soul, not as a subject in itself, but only with regard to another subject. Surely Sextus' book *On the Soul* included arguments against the existence of the soul, and this may explain why that book was not preserved but several copies of some of his other books were preserved. While it's easy to imagine medieval Christians having interest in preserving arguments against various pagan philosophies, it's difficult to imagine them wanting to preserve arguments against the existence of the soul.

Sextus mentions that Dicaearchus the Messenian, one of Aristotle's students, said that there is no such thing as the soul. Tertullian, one of the earliest Christian writers, writing within a few decades of Sextus, provides a little more information in his book *On the Soul*,[108] showing Dicaearchus was not alone in this.

> In the first place, (we must determine) whether there be in the soul some supreme principle of vitality and intelligence which they call "the ruling power of the soul" for if this be not admitted, the whole condition of the soul

---

108 In the same work, Tertullian mentions the Pyrrhonist philosopher Aenesidemus three times about the soul, but these citations do not seem to be helpful. Aenesidemus also wrote a book about Heraclitean philosophy, and it appears to be this book Tertullian is citing because he combines the positions of Aenesidemus and Heraclitus. The citations are as follows.

> Now what color would you attribute to the soul but an ethereal transparent one? Not that its substance is actually the ether or air (although this was the opinion of Aenesidemus and Anaximenes, and I suppose of Heraclitus also, as some say of him), nor transparent light (although Heraclides of Pontus held it to be so).
>
> This example is not remote from (the illustration) of Strato, and Aenesidemus, and Heraclitus: for these philosophers maintain the unity of the soul, as diffused over the entire body, and yet in every part the same.
>
> This view is entertained by the Stoics, along with Aenesidemus, and occasionally by Plato himself, when he tells us that the soul, being quite a separate formation, originating elsewhere and externally to the womb, is inhaled when the new-born infant first draws breath, and by and by exhaled with the man's latest breath.

is put in jeopardy. Indeed, those men who say that there
is no such directing faculty, have begun by supposing that
the soul itself is simply a nonentity. One Dicaearchus, a
Messenian, and amongst the medical profession Andreas
and Asclepiades, have thus destroyed the (soul's) directing power, by actually placing in the mind the senses, for
which they claim the ruling faculty.[109]

Sextus doesn't take the position that the soul does not exist. He just presents
it as a possibility and points out that the matter is disputed. However, he
does take up the argument that we cannot apprehend the soul. He argues
that since the dogmatists say the soul is a thought object, that means the
soul cannot be apprehended via the senses and that it must be apprehended
by the intellect. But the problem is that not only is the intellect non-evident, the dogmatists disagree among themselves about the nature of the
intellect, so much so that the intellect is more questioned than the soul. In
other words, Sextus classifies the soul among the non-evident things.

Elsewhere Sextus routinely refers to the soul as if it existed. I suppose
that if Sextus were asked whether the soul existed he would probably say
that in as much as it is evident that there are individual people, it appears that souls exist; however, the non-evident properties of souls, such as
whether they are immortal, are matters about which judgment should be
suspended. If Sextus were asked whether there is any fixed essence to the
soul, I suppose he would point out that it is evident that people change
over time, that the soul of a child is different from that of an adult, and
that people who were once sane can go mad. So, if there is any fixed
essence to the soul, it is non-evident.

We have some other clues about Pyrrhonist thinking on the soul
from surviving arguments against Pyrrhonism. This argument by the Stoic
philosopher Epictetus is particularly intriguing (emphasis mine):

Let a Pyrrhonist, or an Academic, come and oppose them.
For my part, I have neither leisure nor ability to stand up
as an advocate for common-sense. Even if the business
were concerning an estate, I should call in another advocate. To what advocate, then, shall I now appeal? I will
leave it to anyone who may be upon the spot. Thus, I may
not be able to explain how sensation takes place, whether
it be diffused universally, or reside in a particular part; for

---

109 *A Treatise on the Soul*, Chapter 15 – The Soul's Vitality and Intelligence. Its Character
and Seat in Man.

I find perplexities in either case; but **that you and I are not the same person, I very exactly know.**

"How so?"

Why, I never, when I have a mind to swallow anything, carry it to your mouth, but my own. I never, when I wanted bread, seized a broom instead, but went directly to the bread as I needed it. You who deny all evidence of the senses, do you act otherwise? Which of you, when he wished to go into a bath, ever went into a mill?

"Why, then, must not we, to the utmost, defend these points; stand by common-sense; be fortified against everything that opposes it?"[110]

Lucian, a satirist whose perspective in his writings suggests he may have been a Pyrrhonist,[111] provides another clue. One of his satires was *Sale of Creeds*. In it, the gods Zeus and Hermes sell off as slaves the founders of some of the philosophies. It is likely that Lucian modeled this satire on a similar satire by Timon in the *Silloi*, about a marketplace of philosophies. That satire is now lost, but several quotes from it survive. In Lucian's satire the last slave to be sold is Pyrrho. Here is that part of the satire (emphasis mine):

> *Hermes*: There is Pyrrhonism. Come along, Pyrrho, and be put up. Quick's the word. The attendance is dwindling; there will be small competition. Well, who buys Lot Nine?
>
> *Dealer:* Tell me first, though, what do you know?
>
> *Pyrrho:* Nothing.
>
> *Dealer:* But how's that?
>
> *Pyrrho:* There does not appear to me to be anything.
>
> *Dealer:* **Are not we something?**
>
> *Pyrrho:* **How do I know that?**
>
> *Dealer:* **And you yourself?**
>
> *Pyrrho:* **Of that I am still more doubtful.**
>
> *Dealer:* Well, you are in a fix! And what have you got those scales for?
>
> *Pyrrho:* I use them to weigh arguments in, and get them

---

110 Epictetus, *Discourses*, Book 1, Chapter 27.

111 Contradicting this is one of his works praising Epicureanism. He may have been an Epicurean who switched to Pyrrhonism or vice versa, or he may have been eclectic in his philosophical attitudes. His disdain for Stoicism was common among both Epicureans and Pyrrhonists.

evenly balanced. They must be absolutely equal – not a featherweight to choose between them; then, and not till then, can I make uncertain which is right.

Dealer: What else can you turn your hand to?

Pyrrho: Anything; except catching a runaway.

Dealer: And why not that?

Pyrrho: Because, friend, everything eludes my grasp.

Dealer: I believe you. A slow, lumpish fellow you seem to be. And what is the end of your knowledge?

Pyrrho: Ignorance. Deafness. Blindness.[112]

Dealer: What, sight and hearing both gone!?

Pyrrho: And with them judgement and perception, and all, in short, that distinguishes man from a worm.

Dealer: You are worth money! What shall we say for him?

Hermes: Four pounds.

Dealer: Here it is. Well, fellow; so you are mine?

Pyrrho: I doubt it.

Dealer: Nay, doubt it not! You are bought and paid for.

Pyrrho: It is a difficult case.... I reserve my decision.

Dealer: Now, come along with me, like a good slave.

Pyrrho: But how am I to know whether what you say is true?

Dealer: Ask the auctioneer. Ask my money. Ask the spectators.

Pyrrho: **Spectators? But can we be sure there are any?**

Dealer: Oh, I'll send you to the treadmill. That will convince you with a vengeance that I am your master.

Pyrrho: Reserve your decision.

Dealer: Too late. It is given.

Although Lucian is exaggerating for comic effect, it's interesting to note that Epictetus is also exaggerating for comic effect, like he does with Pyrrhonists confusing a broom for bread. While the Pyrrhonists went into great detail to logically criticize the dogmatists – we have hundreds of pages written by Sextus doing so – the dogmatists generally just dismissed the Pyrrhonists with the type of argument you see here from Epictetus, an argument that is essentially no different from Lucian's satire. Perhaps the dogmatists had the luxury of doing so because Pyrrhonism attracted

---

112 Compare with the *Maha Prajnaparamita Heart Sutra*: "No eye, ear, nose, tongue, body, mind; No forms, sounds, smells, tastes, touchables or objects of mind; No sight-organ element, and so forth."

few adherents. Lucian placed the sale of Pyrrho at the end, noting that the attendance had dwindled. Pyrrho was sold for a mere four pounds. Chrysippus, the Stoic, sold for fifty. Aristotle sold for eighty – a price so high it required a group of buyers.

What's interesting about these passages is that they may be referencing now-lost Pyrrhonist arguments about the self. Note Epictetus' emphasis about what he very exactly knows, and Lucian's Pyrrho's comment that the thing he is most doubtful of is himself.

Epictetus makes another argument that has some implications on how the ancient Pyrrhonists might have viewed the soul.

> Are you certain that you are awake? "I am not," replies such a person, "for neither am I certain when in dreaming I appear to myself to be awake." Is there no difference, then, between these appearances? "None." Shall I argue with this man any longer? For what steel or what caustic can I apply, to make him sensible of his paralysis? If he is sensible of it, and pretends not to be so, he is even worse than dead. He sees not his inconsistency, or, seeing it, holds to the wrong. He moves not, makes no progress; he rather falls back. His sense of shame is gone; his reasoning faculty is not gone, but brutalized. Shall I call this strength of mind? By no means, – unless we allow it to be such in the vilest debauchees publicly to speak and act out their worse impulses.[113]

Epictetus was likely responding to arguments based on our inability to differentiate our experiences between being awake and dreaming. There's an interesting parallel here between Epictetus' argument and a famous story from Zhuangzi, a Taoist philosopher who espoused ideas similar to Pyrrhonism.

> Once upon a time, I, Chuang Chou (Zhuangzi referring to himself), dreamt I was a butterfly, fluttering hither and thither, a veritable butterfly, enjoying itself to the full of its bent, and not knowing it was Chuang Chou. Suddenly I awoke, and came to myself, the veritable Chuang Chou. Now I do not know whether it was then I dreamt I was a butterfly, or whether I am now a butterfly dreaming I am a man.

---

113 Epictetus, *Discourses*, Book 1, Chapter 5.

It seems likely that some Pyrrhonist made a similar, but now-lost argument to which Epictetus is responding. Perhaps the Pyrrhonist argument was that the condition of the soul when awake was not meaningfully different from dreaming. How can we be certain that what we experience is not a dream? Ultimately is there any difference between the experience of being among the appearances and the experience of being in a dream? And if this is how thin the nature of experience is, then how thin must the nature of the soul be?

Applying the Fifth Mode of Aenesidemus – all appearances involve a perception from some position and distance – to the question of the soul points out that the soul may appear to be individual, as we are close to our own souls and far from those of others. However, the soul may actually be collective, and we are all part of it. Indeed, some people claim to see it this way, but others do not see it that way because they can view only the part that is within themselves, or only the parts near them. Hence, we must suspend judgment on the nature of the soul.

Another Pyrrhonist argument might have looked like something I once heard the Zen teacher John Daido Loori Roshi say:

> You and I are the same thing, but I am not you and you are not me. Both of those facts exist simultaneously, but somehow that doesn't compute. Our brains can't deal with it. The two things seem mutually exclusive.[114]

The approach of the Buddhists and other non-dualists is that the answer to this question is through some sort of mystical experience that transcends the paradox. Pyrrhonism eschews paradox to provide a rational answer. You and I appear different – and we grant the appearances – but are we really different? That's not evident. There may be a relationship between us like that of the caterpillar and the butterfly – two manifestations of the same creature – which isn't apparent to us.

Edward O. Wilson, in his studies of social animals, argues that for highly social animals – the ones exhibiting eusociality – such as bees, ants, and humans, each colony is best understood as a kind of creature in itself, where each member of the society functions like a cell, or an organ or limb of a single animal. Aren't you and I having a social interaction right now? Therefore, doesn't that make us part of the same social colony, and therefore part of the same entity?

On the other hand, I am not you and you are not me. You are the one

114 John Daido Loori Roshi, Dharma discourse, *River Seeing River*, http://www.mountainrecord.org/dharmadiscourses/river-seeing-river/

reading this. I am the one writing it. The reverse of this is not true. Aren't we therefore different? Neither argument has any logical errors, but the arguments support opposite conclusions.

The concern about the nature of the soul seems to me to be one of the big differences between Greek and Indian philosophy. The Greeks generally assume the soul exists and have little interest in exploring the idea that it does not exist, but for the Indians, the question of the self was a major philosophical concern. It is interesting to note that René Descartes, generally considered the founder of modern Western philosophy, developed his philosophy as a reaction to the crise pyrrhonienne (Pyrrhonist crisis) in intellectual circles in France following the recovery and publication of Sextus Empiricus' works. Descartes deeply explored the problem of the lack of assurance we could know anything. He came to the conclusion that there is one thing for sure we could know: *cogito ergo sum* – "I think, therefore I am." Perhaps the inclination of the Western mind is to hit a wall on the idea of no-self. There's a joke about someone who just returned from a long, expensive meditation retreat to be greeted with the question, "so, you just spent 10 days and $5,000 to discover that you have no self. How did that work out for you?"

In reading some current Buddhist writers, one might think that the non-existence of the self was early Buddhist doctrine, but that doesn't seem to be what the Buddha's position was. The *Ananda Sutta* gives the Buddha's answer to exactly this question, which may give insight about what the Pyrrhonist perspective may have been. Here is my paraphrase of this section of the sutra.

> The wanderer Vacchagotta asked the Buddha, "is there a self?"
>
> The Buddha was silent.
>
> "Then is there no self?" Vacchagotta asked.
>
> A second time, the Buddha was silent.
>
> Then Vacchagotta the wanderer got up from his seat and left.
>
> Ananda asked the Buddha, "Why didn't you answer the question?"
>
> "Ananda, if I answered that there is a self, that would be conforming with those priests and contemplatives who dogmatize for Eternalism [the dogma that there is an eternal, unchanging soul]. And if I were to do so, might it not confuse Vacchagotta about what the self is? On the other hand, if I answered that there is no self,

> that would be conforming with those priests and con-
> templatives who dogmatize for Annihilationism [the
> dogma that death is the annihilation of consciousness].
> And if I were to do so, might it not confuse Vacchagotta
> even more? Might he not wonder, 'does the self I used to
> have now not exist?'"

These concerns seem similar to those of the ancient Greeks, about whether the soul was eternal or not. They do not seem to be about what is now commonly discussed as the idea of no-self.

Earlier in this book, the paradox of the Ship of Theseus was discussed. Another example from antiquity of this type of argument would be useful to consider here. It's from a dialog between the Greek King Milinda and the philosopher Nagasena.[115] The dialog, paraphrased here, begins with the king asking for the philosopher's name. Nagasena replies that he's known by "Nagasena." But although parents give names to their children, this word, "Nagasena," is just a denomination, a designation, a conceptual term, a mere name, because no real person can be apprehended.

King Milinda countered, "how can you tell me that you are not a real person? How can I be expected to agree with that?!" If no person can be apprehended in reality, who then, I ask you, gives you what you require by way of robes, food, lodging, and medicines? Who is it that shuns killing living beings, taking what is not given, committing sexual misconduct, telling lies, and drinking intoxicants? For, if there were no person, there could be no merit and no demerit; no doer of meritorious or unmeritorious deeds, and no agent behind them; no fruit of good and evil deeds, and no reward or punishment for them. What is this 'Nagasena'? Are perhaps the parts of your body 'Nagasena'?"

Nagasena replied "they are not."

The king asked, "is Nagasena a form, or feelings, or perceptions, or impulses, or consciousness?"

Nagasena replied "they are not."

"Then is Nagasena a combination of form, feelings, perceptions, impulses, and consciousness?"

Nagasena again says no.

"Then is Nagasena outside the combination of form, feelings, perceptions, impulses, and consciousness?"

To which Nagasena also says no.

"Then, ask as I may, I can discover no Nagasena at all. This 'Nagasena' is just a mere sound. But who is the real Nagasena? You have told a lie. You

---

115 *Milinda Panha.*

have spoken a falsehood! There is really no Nagasena!"

Nagasena said, "King Milinda, when you travel, being a king, instead of walking you normally ride in a chariot. I presume you know then what a chariot is."

The king replied that of course he knew what a chariot was.

"Then explain to me what a chariot is," said Nagasena. "Is it the pole?"

"No," said the king.

"Is then the axle the chariot?"

"No," said the king.

"Is it then the wheels, or the framework, of the flag-staff, or the yoke, or the reins, or the goad-stick?"

"No," said the king.

"Then is it the combination of pole, axle, wheels, framework, flag-staff, yoke, reins, and goad which is the chariot?"

"No," said the king.

"Then, is this 'chariot' outside the combination of pole, axle, wheels, framework, flag-staff, yoke, reins, and goad?"

"No," said the king.

"Then, ask as I may, I can discover no chariot at all. This 'chariot' seems to be just a mere sound. What is a real chariot? Your Majesty doesn't seem to know, and you are therefore mistaken in claiming to know what a chariot is. It seems there is really no chariot because you cannot establish its existence. How can one possibly approve of that? Let's see your Majesty get out of that if you can!"

The king replied, "I have not spoken a falsehood regarding my knowing what a chariot is. A chariot is in dependence on the pole, the axle, the wheels, the framework, the flag-staff, and its other parts which are assembled into the form of a chariot, which goes by the conceptual term, the designation, named 'chariot.'"

"Your Majesty has spoken well about the chariot. It is just so with me. In dependence on the parts of the body there results in this denomination 'Nagasena.' In ultimate reality, however, this person cannot be apprehended. Where all constituent parts are present, the word 'chariot' is applied. So, likewise, is it with human beings."

King Milinda was pleased with this answer. Perhaps you will be too. Incidentally, the school of philosophy Nagasena belonged to was Buddhism. This is an ancient record of how a Buddhist would explain the concept of no-self to a rationalist Greek. The explanation is still good today.

Some people have mystical experiences of there being no self. It would appear that most people don't. The matter seems to be important for people, as there is so much dogmatization about whether the self is eternal or not. It seems evident, however, that we change moment to moment, that we are born, that we die, that we are profoundly affected by things outside of ourselves, such that they change us.

I once saw a cartoon that summarized the Eastern and Western views on the self. For the Eastern view the cartoon said, "your self and this world are illusory. Do not grow attached." For the Western view it said, "You and this world are temporary, but real. You should be ashamed of yourself while you are here." The Pyrrhonist view would be: "Your self and this world are apparent, but the appearances are neither true nor false. Nothing is good or evil by nature. Don't believe in the non-evident." Pyrrhonism takes a middle way between Eastern and Western. It neither affirms nor denies the reality of the self and the world.

The Buddhist concept of sunyata, typically translated into English as "emptiness" has multiple meanings. In Theravada Buddhism, it often refers to the not-self nature of the five aggregates of experience and the six sense spheres, and it is also often used to refer to a meditative state or experience. In Mahayana Buddhism, sunyata refers to the precept that "all things are empty of intrinsic existence and nature." In Tibetan Buddhism, sunyata refers to "openness and understanding nonexistence." A Pyrrhonist way of looking at what sunyata means is that it is adiaphora plus astathmeta plus anepikrita. The English word that sums that all up is "indeterminacy"; the Greek word that does this is acatalepsia. Thus the Buddhist monk in meditating dwells in the no-self state of sunyata whereas the Pyrrhonist practitioner, in the state of epoché produced by the cure by argument, dwells in the no-belief state of acatalepsia.

Pyrrhonism's view of truth parallels the Madhyamaka Buddhist Two Truths doctrine. In Pyrrhonism the Buddhist concept of "ultimate" truth corresponds with truth as defined via the criterion of truth, which, as we covered in the chapter on the criterion of truth, does not exist. As we are without a criterion of truth, the ultimate truth of reality is non-evident; therefore nothing can with certainty be called "true" with respect to being an accurate account of reality. The Buddhist concept of "conventional" or "provisional" truth corresponds in Pyrrhonism to the appearances, which are used in Pyrrhonism for making decisions about what to do.

The striking difference between the Buddhist and Pyrrhonist interpretations is that in the Buddhist doctrine, at least with regard to how it is conventionally described in English, says that there are truths. Pyrrhonism recognizes a similar categorization but is careful and parsimonious with the term "truth." It also avoids presenting the existence of the categories as some sort of doctrine. It's just an observation available to anyone who cares to look. The Buddhist use of the word "truth" here seems to create unnecessary confusion. It also seems to be a way of perverting Buddhism, as it can be used to justify the idea that certain "enlightened" teachers know ultimate truth and that one can learn this ultimate truth from them. A good Zen teacher, however, will tell you that teaching Zen is like selling water by the river.

Just as we survive by eating food, beliefs survive by feeding off of us. We should view our minds as being infected with parasites. By ridding ourselves of beliefs we cure ourselves from our parasitical infections. When belief disappears, we are left with the appearances of the world and something some might call one's "true" self; although a Pyrrhonist would not use that word. After the self is rid of the disease of dogmatism, what's left? We have physical and emotional reactions that appear to be forced upon us by our bodies. We exist in a society where we have roles to play and decisions to make. Pyrrhonism calls for following the ordinary course of life. Ordinary mind is the way. It's practical advice for avoiding being egotistical.

....

37

Meditation

The inherent nature of mind is to process thought. To
attempt the cessation of thought goes against what is natural. The goal, therefore, is not the cessation of thought.
The goal is the cessation of identification with thought.

Wu Xin

The more I read, the more I meditate; and the more I
acquire, the more I am enabled to affirm that I know
nothing. *Voltaire*

Upon learning that Pyrrhonism is based on Buddhism, a common
question is, what are the meditation practices?

There are none, and there's no trace of there ever having been any.

While meditation-oriented forms of Buddhism such as Zen, Vipas-
sana, and Tibetan Buddhism have achieved substantial popularity in the
West, the East is full of various forms of Buddhism that do little or no
meditation, such as Pure Land and Nichiren Buddhism. In Buddhism,
meditation has traditionally been considered a practice for monks and
hermits, not for the average person.

Pyrrho spent approximately 18 months in India. One Indian gymnosophist accompanied Alexander's entourage on the long journey back
to Greece, although he became ill and committed suicide mid-journey.
Surely in all of this time Pyrrho would have had an opportunity to learn
meditation, as it was so central to the practices of Buddhism, upon which
he was basing his new philosophy. It seems we are left with a set of three
possibilities.

• Perhaps Pyrrho tried it and did not think it was worth incorporating
into his philosophy, perhaps because he did not find it suitably efficacious, or perhaps he found the cure by argument was much more
efficacious – the ancient Pyrrhonists claimed that it brought the intellect to a standstill, the same objective that meditation has – or perhaps
because the mystical element associated with meditation was contrary
to the Greek philosophical vision of progress via reason. All of these
seem plausible.

• Perhaps he tried it and it became an esoteric Pyrrhonist practice of
which there is no trace. This seems unlikely. The other schools of

philosophy openly talked about practical techniques for calming the disturbing emotions.

• Finally, there's the possibility that the early Buddhists didn't think meditation was important, and that meditation was a practice that was developed later and was projected back onto early Buddhism. Very unlikely.

The Buddhist sutras say that people became enlightened just from hearing one of the Buddha's discourses.[116] I don't hear reports of that sort of thing happening in modern times. Perhaps the sutras contain wild exaggerations, or perhaps something fundamental got changed over time. The secular Buddhist movement, with Stephen Batchelor being perhaps the most prominent advocate, suspects something indeed did happen, and that early Buddhism's practices and thinking were considerably different from what developed in later centuries.

It's also useful to consider the differences between philosophers and priests as wisdom teachers, or alternatively, to consider the difference between those who get paid directly for teaching versus those who seek contributions from others to allow them to support their work – work that generally includes little of what other people call "work." Across religions, a variety of similar practices appear to be common. Large amounts of time tend to be devoted to religious services, often including chanting or singing. Time may be devoted to religious art, studying scripture, and contemplation, in the form of prayer, if there are gods to pray to, or meditation, if there are none to pray to. So, while meditation has positive effects, and for some people it induces altered states, in a religious context one of its major functions may be simply to soak up a lot of time in a religious activity that looks like work – indeed, is work – so as to demonstrate the piety necessary for perpetuating the teachings.

Philosophers, however, are not expected to invest time in devotional activities, at least with respect to engaging in philosophy. So, even if Pyrrho had found meditation useful, and practiced it in private, his objective was to found a philosophy. Pyrrhonism not only did not need anything that looked like a devotional practice, having one might have been dangerous. Philosophers were routinely accused of impiety. It was only a few decades earlier that Socrates was convicted on charges of introducing new gods.

Although the concept of contemplation appears often in what we know of ancient Greece, there's little that could be called "meditation"

---

116 For example the "Fire Sermon" (SN 35.28 *Adittapariyaya* Sutta) concludes by saying "Now during his utterance, the hearts of those thousand bhikkhus were liberated from taints through clinging no more."

in the Eastern sense of the term. One of the closest things we have is this mention that originates with Favorinus:

> Among voluntary tasks and exercises for strengthening his body for any chance demands upon its endurance we are told that Socrates habitually practiced this one: he would stand, so the story goes, in one fixed position, all day and all night, from early dawn until the next sunrise, open-eyed, motionless, in his very tracks and with face and eyes riveted to the same spot in deep meditation, as if his mind and soul had been, as it were, withdrawn from his body. When Favorinus in his discussion of the man's fortitude and his many other virtues had reached this point, he said: "He often stood from sun to sun, more rigid than the tree trunks."[117]

Interestingly, the gymnosophists did something similar. Aristobulus of Cassandreia, who accompanied Alexander and Pyrrho to India, said he saw one gymnosophist who "stood on one leg holding aloft in both hands a log about three cubits in length, and when one leg tired he changed the support to the other and kept this up all day long...."[118]

Hundreds of years after Pyrrho, we have a comment from Cicero, who like Favorinus was an Academic Skeptic, referring to how meditation shuts down the senses and separates the soul from the body,[119] indicating that there was Western knowledge of meditative states.

Meditation appears to be something that some rare people in Pyrrho's time engaged in. We don't know anything about how it was taught, who taught it, what the motivations were, or what the techniques were.

We do know, however, that one stage in Pyrrhonist practice is *aphasia*, which means in Greek, "non-assertion," "unspeakingness," "wordlessness." This is the stage between epoché and ataraxia. This stage has similarities to meditation, as silence and motionlessness form the first step in meditation practice, with the second step being the quieting of the mind. In contrast with this, in Pyrrhonist practice, the first step is to make the mind busier, by harnessing it to generate arguments to produce equipollence. Equipollence leads to epoché, which then quiets the mind. All of those beliefs that one used to have and that one reinforced by talking about them are no longer there to inspire one to talk. Bereft of one's usual verbal content

---

117 Aulus Gellius, *Attic Nights*, Book 2, Chapter 1.
118 Strabo, Book 15, Chapter 1, Section 61.
119 Cicero, *Tusculan Disputations*, Book 1, Chapter 20.

about non-evident matters, this stage of entry into Pyrrhonist practice causes a substantial reduction in speech, and in some cases a period of actual speechlessness; although the cases I know about where that has happened have all been associated with engaging with Pyrrhonist practice during a period of emotional crisis so intense that it was also producing other physical symptoms, such as extreme sleeplessness.

Meditation practice starts with aphasia and uses this as a crucible for addressing the contents of the mind; whereas Pyrrhonist practice starts with addressing the contents of the mind so that aphasia can arise. Regardless of which practice is pursued, the ultimate fruit of the practice comes as if by chance, by accident, like a shadow.

Perhaps it is no coincidence that the Sanskrit term *dhyana*, which is the term used to describe Buddhist meditative states, derives from the same Indo-European root as the Greek term for contemplation, *theoria*, from which we get not only the English word "theory" but also "theater." This matches the notion that the Eastern object of contemplation is the self; whereas the Western object of contemplation is the world. Other related words Greek words are *theorein*, "to see," and *theoros*, "spectator." Ancient Greek theater was an act of contemplation. As Simon Critchley puts it, in his book, *Tragedy, the Greeks and Us,*

> Tragedy is, for me, the life of skepticism, where the latter
> is the index for a certain moral orientation in the world,
> an orientation that seems to emerge from the disorienta-
> tion of not knowing what to do.[120]

For the ancient Greeks, truth was external. Recall that the etymology of their word for "truth" was "not hidden." Their view was that truth is out there to be uncovered. Once it is uncovered, we are no longer ignorant. Since we start in a state of ignorance, does it make sense to go looking for truth inside ourselves? Actually, Socrates thought so. The Socratic method is built on the idea that by asking the right questions, truth can be extracted from people. While the Socratic method lives on as a teaching technique, at least starting with Aristotle the West's orientation has turned to looking outside the self for the truth. Now this view permeates Western culture. Hence, for those whose inclinations are that the truth is out there, rather than inside, Pyrrhonist techniques may work better than meditation, or, at least they may be said to be more intuitively appealing and easier to engage with.

In Buddhism, there's the concept of "thinking mind." Buddhism uses meditation to calm the thinking mind so that the practitioner fully and

---

120 Pages 3-4.

truly experiences life. The heart of meditation practice is the dethroning of the stories one compulsively tells oneself about each moment, putting in their place simply being in the moment. The stories are not eliminated, *per se*. It's the power and the compulsiveness of the stories that are eliminated. In other words, meditation erodes the attachment to dogmas, turning them into just non-evident ideas, and makes these non-evident ideas secondary to what is evident.

Pyrrhonism uses an alternative technique and alternative terminology to achieve the same ends. In Pyrrhonism dogmatic thinking (thinking mind) is directly assaulted, via the cure by argument, to disempower dogmatism and achieve epoché. Once this has been achieved, the practitioner can experience the appearances without the filtering of dogmatism.

One thing we know about Pyrrho and Democritus was that they would spend large amounts of time alone, wandering. The *Rhinoceros Sutta*, one of the earliest known Buddhist texts, encourages seekers of wisdom to wander alone, like a rhinoceros. In Zen practice the activity that is second only to seated meditation is walking meditation, at least with respect to the amount of time devoted to it. Pyrrho got to India on foot. Even the shortest route, which was not what Alexander's army took, would have required over 3,500 miles of walking just to get to India. For proof of the salutary effects of long walks, look at all of the memoirs associated with hiking the Appalachian and Pacific Crest trails.

Spending large amounts of time alone, wandering, is something I have taken up, via hiking. I highly recommend it. There may not be any wisdom on the top of mountains that you didn't bring there with you, but it seems to me that one can pick up wisdom while going up the mountains, and this is done by discarding beliefs to lighten one's load on the ascent. This kind of time alone is perfect for practicing self-argumentation. Grab onto whatever thought troubles you and develop argument after argument to disempower it. It seems that time alone is needed to get some perspective so that you can create good arguments that are efficacious against your beliefs.

Alone means just you: no companion, no music, no audio programs. You must be able to hear yourself and allow yourself to think. One exception would be you can bring your dog. You can even talk to them if you like. Just be concerned if you find them talking back to you.

The continuous need to move forward during hiking is something like paying attention to the breath in meditation. While walking alone in nature, the mind settles down. It's not a fast process, but neither is meditation for most people. The exhaustion that sets in from all of that walking helps. That's not a recommendation to push to one's limit. That's unsafe hiking, especially while hiking alone. Just get tired. Mountains are not required, but they do seem more efficient for making one tired, and the panoramic views seem to help one put things into perspective. There's also a specific structure to hiking, that's like the structure of a Zen retreat in that there's a commitment to get to the destination and back, just like there is a commitment to sit motionless on the meditation cushion until the bell rings.

Hiking isn't the only thing that works. Running, bicycling, canoeing, kayaking, cross-country skiing, or even motorcycle riding or driving a car long distances can all work. However, having to react to moving things greatly reduces effectiveness. A canoe trip on calm water works; white water rafting doesn't. A motorcycle trip in the New Hampshire White Mountains works; one on the New Jersey Turnpike doesn't. Whatever it is you're doing must leave lots of mental capacity free – the more the better.

It also seems to me that contact with nature is useful for putting the mind in the proper framework to think well. That Zen temples are famous for their spectacular gardens seems to me to be no coincidence. When I was briefly a resident at Tofuku-ji, in Kyoto, the last sit of the day was held outside on a veranda overlooking one of the beautiful gardens. The whole temple compound functioned as a spectacular park, with a tiny community of monks hidden in the middle. The daily work practice involved in maintaining the monastery was almost all outdoors work.

There's a cartoon about a person outside a Zen center, looking at a poster that says "Seeking enlightenment? Inquire within." Looking around, they see no door, but they do see a monk outside, whom they ask, "where is the door?" The monk replies, "there is no door." Hence the centrality of meditation to Buddhism: the idea that enlightenment comes from within, and there's no door to go through. Pyrrhonism is the mirror image of this. The person standing outside a Pyrrhonism center would see a poster saying "Seeking eudaimonia? Inquire!" They would look around and see there is no door. They would see a philosopher nearby, whom they would ask "where is the door?" The philosopher would reply, "what makes you believe that there should be a door?" There's no door or wall that's a barrier. The barrier is our beliefs.

There's a famous Zen story about meditation. It involves Baso, who would go on to be one of the most influential Zen teachers of all time.

> When Baso was still a monk, his teacher, Master Nangaku, one day went to visit him in his hut. Nangaku asked Baso, using an honorific that a monk would use in speaking to a master, "in practicing sitting meditation, what does your Reverence desire to attain?"

Baso responded, "to attain Buddhahood!"

Nangaku then exited the hut and picked up a roofing tile lying outside, and began to rub it against a rock. Baso, upon seeing this, asked, "what is the master doing?"

Nangaku answered, "polishing a tile."

Baso asked, "what is the use of polishing the tile?"

Nangaku replied, "I am polishing it to make it into a mirror."

Baso asked, "how can polishing a tile make it into a mirror?"

Nangaku said, "how can sitting in meditation make you into a Buddha?"

Baso inquired, "then, what must I do?"

Nangaku said, "consider the case of an ox cart. If the cart does not move, do you whip the cart or the ox?"

Baso remained silent.

Nangaku asked, "in learning sitting meditation, do you aspire to learn sitting Zen or do you aspire to imitate the sitting Buddha? If the former, Zen does not consist of sitting or lying down. If the latter, the Buddha has no fixed postures. The dharma goes on forever, and never abides in anything. You must therefore not be attached to nor reject any particular phase of it. To sit yourself into Buddha is to kill the Buddha. To be attached to the sitting posture is to fail to comprehend the essential principle."[121]

What does Nangaku mean by this? This story has many interpretations. It seems to me that he's saying that there is an essential principle to Buddhism that one has to comprehend, and that this principle is like the Pyrrhonist equipollence and epoché, that one must neither believe that meditation will make one a Buddha nor must one believe it won't. Without this epoché-like principle, meditation does not achieve its aim.

---

121 Adapted from *The Golden Age of Zen*, John C.H. Wu, World Wisdom Books, NY, 1975, p. 92.

38
Confusions About Pyrrhonist Ethics

> One almost wonders whether greater erudition and
> complexity of thought leads to more, not less, immorality.
> *Victor Davis Hanson & John Heath,*
> Who Killed Homer:
> The Demise of Classical Education
> and the Recovery of Greek Wisdom

> Do not search for the truth; only cease to cherish opin-
> ions. Do not remain in the dualistic state. Avoid such
> pursuits carefully. If there is even a trace of this and that,
> of right and wrong, the mind-essence will be lost in
> confusion. *Sengcan,*
> Xinxin Ming

The typical barrier people have in understanding Pyrrhonist ethics is
that they cannot wrap their heads around an ethics that is built on the
premise that nothing is inherently good or bad, and that there is no criterion of truth for what is good and bad. This seems impossible to them,
so they reject it out of hand, as if they were suffering from an allergic reaction. Some of the knee-jerk reactions I have seen have been remarkably
strong, with emotions blinding people to the basic ideas of Pyrrhonism.
This appears common even among academic "experts" on Pyrrhonism.

Consider this example from Allan Hazlett's *A Critical Introduction to
Skepticism:*

> Evaluative beliefs have emotional consequences – some-
> one who thinks honor is good will be frustrated when she
> fails to acquire honor – but if you remove the evaluative
> beliefs, so the argument goes, you'll remove their emo-
> tional consequences (Sextus, Outlines, I 27, III 237–8).
> But suspension of judgment is not always calming, even
> when it comes to evaluative matters: if you very much
> want to eat at the best restaurant in town, suspension of
> judgment about the question of which restaurant is the
> best will hardly bring you tranquility.[122]

---

122 Page 6.

Professor Hazlett's conclusion here is absurd. He apparently does not understand that very much wanting to eat at the best restaurant in town is an evaluative belief. The whole purpose of Pyrrhonist practice is to help the practitioner get rid of very much wanting anything and to develop detachment for judgments such as "best," particularly for such ridiculous notions such as the idea that there could be such an evaluation of something so subjective in preference as restaurants.

Consider another example, this one from Tim O'Keefe:

> If the thought that one is experiencing something bad by nature produces additional trouble, then Pyrrho and Anaxarchus can confidently assert that they are not suffering something bad by nature, whereas Sextus, it seems, would still have to worry that what he is experiencing might be bad. I myself find this whole line of thought about the psychological benefits of indifference wildly implausible – if I am drenched to the bone, it is freezing, and I am shivering violently, or if I am being pounded to death in a mortar at a tyrant's orders, I doubt that the thought "ah, yes, but at least things like cold and excruciating pain are not by nature bad" would be terribly comforting.[123]

First, Sextus repeatedly says in both *Against the Ethicists* and *Outlines of Pyrrhonism* that nothing is good or bad by nature. His position on this is no different from that of Pyrrho, who is described by Diogenes Laertius as having said this, too. There is no "might be bad" on this matter for Sextus that's different from what it is for Pyrrho and his teacher, Anaxarchus, who was pounded to death in a mortar on a tyrant's order. Nowhere do we have a report of Pyrrho saying that he confidently asserted any positive doctrine. To ascribe to Pyrrho the philosophical ability to confidently assert that he is not having an experience totally misses what Pyrrhonism is about.

Second, Sextus specifically says that Pyrrhonists are troubled by things such as being cold or beaten:

> We do not suppose, of course, that the Pyrrhonist is wholly untroubled, but we do say that he is troubled only by things unavoidable. For we agree that sometimes

---

123 Tim O'Keefe, "Anaxarchus on Indifference, Happiness, and Convention," forthcoming in *Early Greek Ethics*, ed. David Wolfsdorf, Oxford University Press. Footnote 11.

he is cold and thirsty and has various feelings like those. But even in such cases, whereas ordinary people are affected by two circumstances – namely by the pathé themselves and not less by its seeming that these conditions are by nature bad – the Pyrrhonist, by eliminating the additional belief that all these things are naturally bad, gets off more moderately here as well. Because of this we say that as regards belief the Pyrrhonist's goal is ataraxia, but in regard to things unavoidable it is having moderate pathé.[124]

So, if you feel you're having some difficulty grasping Pyrrhonist ethics, you can be comforted in the fact that Ph.Ds in specializing in Greek philosophy exhibit in their articles and books some of the same difficulties.

The psychological indifference Sextus is talking about is not an indifference to pain. Indifference to pain has never been specifically associated with the practice of Pyrrhonism. Perhaps indifference to pain is something Pyrrho and Anaxarchus learned from the gymnosophists. We have several reports from antiquity about the gymnosophists' indifference to pain, most famously the self-immolation of Kalanos, which was observed by the party of Alexander the Great on their return from India, and the self-immolation of the Indian gymnosophist Zarmanochegas, which happened in Athens around 22 BCE.

Perhaps a personal anecdote will help clarify things. The first time I went car camping with my wife, who was then my girlfriend, we went to the camp store to find something to eat. As a veteran of two entire summers spent in such campgrounds, I described what I usually bought at such camp stores when I lacked any cooking equipment or refrigeration: crackers and cheese. She pointed out that the store had prepared sandwiches. I almost always avoid such things, fearing food poisoning, but I decided not to mention this, as it seemed to me that she was saying that she wanted the sandwich rather than the crackers and cheese that I had all but declared we should buy. We bought the sandwiches.

Three hours later, I became violently sick with food poisoning. I got the usual vomiting, diarrhea, body aches, and convulsive shivering. As I had only a couple of months earlier written the first draft of this chapter, I got to meditate on the benefits of psychological indifference to pain.

I'm no gymnosophist who has been trained to be indifferent to pain. Physically the event was awful, but there was no psychological awfulness to it. I wasn't angry at the camp store for their unhygienic food preparation.

---

124 Sextus Empiricus, *Outlines of Pyrrhonism*, Book I, Chapter 12, Sections 29-30.

I wasn't angry at my girlfriend for pushing me to do something against my better judgment. I wasn't angry at myself for going against my better judgment. Outside the physical experience, I had no thought that there was anything bad about it. It's not more this than that. What do I know? No need even to construct an argument about it for creating equipollence.

In some respects the event turned out to be good. It was the first time I'd become sick around my girlfriend. I learned what a devoted caretaker she was. She and I learned something about communicating with each other. She thought she was pointing out the sandwiches because she thought I'd like them better than what I had proposed. I thought she was pointing them out because she preferred them to what I had proposed. In fact, she was also normally wary of such prepared sandwiches and would not have bought them except that she thought I would prefer them. The event made us both more aware of her approaches associated with her strong desire to please others, and my tendency to laconically say what I mean. Because I was too sick to take down the tent, I got to learn that the fussy way I normally packed the tent was unnecessary. Best of all, I got a much better way of illustrating the point about good and bad than the one I originally had in my manuscript.

I suspect that a major factor in the difficulties these Ph.D. scholars have in understanding Pyrrhonism is that it doesn't even occur to them that they should attempt to practice Pyrrhonism. For them, discussing Pyrrhonism is just an intellectual exercise. Imagine if Christianity had died out in the 3rd Century CE, never becoming more than a small movement. Then, 1,700 years later atheist scholars were writing articles about Christian practices based on just some parts of the New Testament that had survived and without themselves even considering trying to practice Christianity. Would they be credible sources of what being a Christian is like psychologically?

Some people who reject Pyrrhonist ethics mistake Pyrrhonism for moral relativism. That's a mistake that has been around since antiquity, which Sextus addresses in his comparison of Protagorean philosophy with Pyrrhonism. Moral relativism dogmatically claims that morality is relative: man is the measure of all things. If you think something is good, it is good. You have determined it to be so. You are the criterion. That's not at all the Pyrrhonist view. In the Pyrrhonist view there is no criterion of truth. Remember the Taoist story of the old farmer whose horse ran off. With each change in circumstances, the wise old farmer said, "we'll see." Think about how things that you initially thought were good turned out to be bad, and how things you initially did not like turned out to be good. Hasn't your own experience told you that you are not a good measure of all things?

One thing people are curious about is that if Pyrrhonism and Buddhism are based on essentially the same observation about the nature of knowledge, how is it that Pyrrhonism says so little about ethics and Buddhism so much? It seems to me that the answer to this is both cultural and about roles. In India, the wise people were holy men. Holiness was the supreme virtue. They eschewed wealth. They lived on donations. In Greece the wise people were philosophers. Reason was the supreme virtue. Philosophers usually made a living by either having a profession other than philosophy, charging tuition, being sponsored by someone wealthy, or inheriting wealth. For example, Sextus was a physician, Isocrates charged tuition, Plato was a wealthy aristocrat, Aristippus served a royal court, Thales got rich as a speculator, Zeno of Citium was a wealthy merchant. The exception was the Cynic philosophers, who eschewed wealth. The roles of philosopher and holy man imply a difference in attitude about ethics, with holy men being held to a much standard than philosophers.

Let's take a look at the basics of Buddhist ethics. The various schools of Buddhism espouse not only somewhat different sets of ethical precepts, but also, priests and monks are held to a more stringent set than laypeople are. As priests and monks present themselves as holy people who beg for alms, they're in a separate category that we need not consider, since Pyrrhonist philosophers do not present themselves as holy.

The oldest and simplest articulation of the Buddhist ethical precepts for everyone is found in the Pali Canon:

1. I undertake the training rule to abstain from killing.
2. I undertake the training rule to abstain from taking what is not given.
3. I undertake the training rule to avoid sexual misconduct.
4. I undertake the training rule to abstain from false speech.
5. I undertake the training rule to abstain from fermented drink that causes heedlessness.

Buddhism has another set of fundamental ethical statements, called the "Pure" or "Universal" precepts. These are given in several different wordings.

1. "Do no evil" or "to avoid all evil", or "refrain from unwholesome action" or "the precept of observing rules"
2. "Do good" or "engage in wholesome action"
3. "Save all beings" or "purify your own mind"

Is there anything in these lists that strikes you as controversial? Anything that parents worldwide would not teach their children except, perhaps, the one about alcohol? If you were told to follow your society's laws and customs, would you find yourself breaking any of them by following these precepts, except perhaps a custom about drinking alcohol? Indeed, isn't the one about doing no evil and following the rules an instruction to follow your society's laws and customs?

The third of the Pure Precepts even has a parallel in Pyrrhonist ethics. Sextus explicitly states that one of the objectives of Pyrrhonism is to cure people of the mental disease of dogmatism – an act of purifying minds – and this objective is pursued because of the Pyrrhonists' love of humanity.

Consider all of the horrible things people do to one another. Could these be possible without beliefs? Why would anyone go to much effort to hurt anyone if they were not convinced that the other person was somehow evil, or what they were doing was evil? Might not the most effective moral teaching be one that frees people of the grip of dogmatism, not only for their own sakes, but for the sake of others?

If one reads old translations of ancient Greek writers, one will encounter many words and phrases that sound rather odd. In these translations many of the philosophers talk about "incontinence," which in modern usage suggests someone peeing in their pants. The Greek word involved here is *akrasia*, which means lack of self-control. The virtue of self-control was a major theme in Hellenistic philosophy. It predates philosophy, as it is also a major theme in the Delphic maxims and the works of Homer, two of the key elements in Greek culture out of which philosophy arose. At first, I found it off-putting to see "incontinence" as the translation for *akrasia*. Now I kind of like it. It causes me to imagine watching ill-behaved people pee in their pants, for everyone to see. They cannot control themselves. They cannot follow rules of behavior. They are simultaneously ridiculous and to be pitied.

Unlike some of the other Hellenistic philosophies, Pyrrhonism makes no specific claims about helping one improve one's self-control, although Sextus does remark that the practice of Pyrrhonism allows one to live rightly with respect to virtue. As self-control is one of the virtues, it's an indirect claim. It seems to me that beliefs are a reason people lose self-control. Instead of their having ideas, ideas have them. It's harder to get angry when it only seems to you that you're right and they're wrong, rather than believing they're wrong and you're right. Since I started practicing Pyrrhonism, I have had increasingly fewer incidents where I felt that I lost self-control, as it has lowered my reactivity.

If by the end of this book you still find yourself troubled or perplexed by Pyrrhonist ethics, but you are willing to give Pyrrhonism a try, I suggest setting your concern aside, or better yet, practice equipollence against those concerns to achieve epoché. Once you start seriously engaging in

Pyrrhonist practice, the ethics will likely become clearer to you, and your concerns about them will disappear as the beliefs that underlie those concerns are gradually done away with.

39
Moral Beliefs

Peace of mind produces right values; right values produce right thoughts. Right thoughts produce right actions and right actions produce work which will be a material reflection for others to see of the serenity at the center of it all.   *Robert M. Pirsig*

[Pyrrhonism is] is a way of life that, in accordance with appearances, follows a certain rationale, where that rationale shows how it is possible to seem to live rightly ("rightly" being taken, not as referring only to virtue, but in a more ordinary sense)....   *Sextus Empiricus*

While people do get upset about theoretical matters that do not involve ethics, these seem much less frequent than matters that do involve ethics. Many of the matters that on the surface that do not seem to involve ethics, upon closer inspection do.

Moral Foundations Theory suggests that there are six dimensions on which people judge things as morally good or bad.

- Care: cherishing and protecting others; opposite of harm.
- Fairness: rendering justice according to shared rules; opposite of cheating.
- Loyalty: standing with your group, family, nation; opposite of betrayal.
- Authority or respect: submitting to tradition and legitimate authority; opposite of subversion.
- Sanctity or purity: abhorrence for disgusting things, foods, actions; opposite of degradation.
- Liberty; opposite of oppression.

This list is useful for summarizing the types of moral beliefs people hold. When one finds oneself upset about something, it's likely that it is due to a moral belief. Even to be upset that someone is wrong about a statement of fact or a theory about how things work is usually dependent on some sort of moral hazard caused by that error, typically that the error could cause harm. Explore what moral belief is bothering you, then develop arguments against it.

We have this idea that things should be fair, but isn't it evident that life isn't fair? Some people are born to good parents, some to bad parents. Some people are born into prosperity, some into poverty, some into free countries, some into tyrannies. Some are healthy, others have congenital diseases. The list goes on and on. Why should your situation be any different? Besides, the person who is treating you unfairly almost surely thinks that what they're doing is fair. Isn't that likely to be the case in this instance? How is it that your sense of fairness should supersede theirs?

On arguments like this, I find it useful to read history, memoirs, or fiction describing situations that were unfair. These people experienced unfairness. Why shouldn't I experience it, too? Isn't this just a fact of life? Pyrrho did the same thing with the literature of his day.

Buddhism has a famous parable that is similar to this technique. It is called *The Parable of the Mustard Seed*:

> A woman named Kisa Gotami had her only child die. Unwilling to accept his death, she carried him from neighbor to neighbor and begged for someone to give her medicine to bring him back to life. One of her neighbors told her to go to the Buddha, who was nearby.
>
> Kisa found the Buddha and pleaded with him to help bring her son back to life. He instructed her to go back to her village and gather mustard seeds from the households of those who have never been touched by the death. From those mustard seeds, he promised he would create a medicine to bring her son back to life. Relieved, she went back to her village and began asking her neighbors for mustard seeds.
>
> All of her neighbors were willing to give her mustard seeds, but they all told her that their households had been touched by death. They told her, "the living are few, but the dead are many."
>
> As the day became evening and then night, she was still without any of the mustard seeds that she had been instructed to collect. She realized then the universality of death. With this new understanding, her grief was calmed. She buried her son in the forest and then returned to Buddha. She confessed to Buddha that she could not obtain any of the mustard seeds he had instructed her to collect because she could not find even

one house untouched by death.[125]

Here is a passionate interpretation of what Buddha imparted upon Kisa Gotami at this point from *The Buddha: His Life Retold*, by Robert Allen Mitchell:

> Dear girl, the life of mortals in this world is troubled and brief and inseparable from suffering, for there is not any means, nor will there ever be, by which those that have been born can avoid dying. Not from weeping nor from grieving will anyone obtain peace of mind. On the contrary, his pain will be all the greater, and he will ruin his health. He will make himself sick and pale; but dead bodies cannot be restored by lamentation. And just as the fire of a burning house is quenched, so does the contemplative wise person scatter grief's power, expertly, swiftly, even as the wind scatters cottonseed.
>
> He who seeks peace should pull out the arrow of lamentations, useless longings, and the self-made pangs of grief. He who has removed this unwholesome arrow and has calmed himself will obtain peace of mind.
>
> Kisa entered the first stage of enlightenment from her experience. She decided to become a disciple of Buddha's and went on to become the first female arahant. The Buddha employs a technique here similar to the Pyrrhonist prescription. By causing Kisa to inquire with each family about death, she learns that it is an evident fact of life that everyone is touched by the death of loved ones. Harm is pervasive. Unfairness is pervasive. To think contrary to this is to have a belief in something non-evident, in this case that she and her son deserve some extraordinary intervention to "correct" the harm and injustice of his death. She comes to accept the evident fact that her son is dead and to stop judging things as good or bad by nature. This relieves her of her useless suffering.

So who hasn't experienced harm, or unfairness, betrayal, disrespect, degradation, and oppression? Perhaps some lucky few young people have been able to avoid a couple of these, but they're all as much a part of human experience as is death. No one is exempted.

---

125 Adapted from http://christicenter.org/2012/11/buddhism-parable-mustard-seed/

40

Pyrrhonist Decision-Making

It is remarkable how much long-term advantage people like us have gotten by trying to be consistently not stupid, instead of trying to be very intelligent.
        Charlie Munger, Vice-Chairman, Berkshire Hathaway

Losing an illusion makes you wiser than finding a truth.
        Ludwig Borne

The ancient Pyrrhonists do not give much advice about how to make decisions. The advice is to use the appearances, rely on customs, and to make decisions non-dogmatically. It may help to expand on that idea.

The ancient Pyrrhonists lived lives that differ greatly from those of today in some respects. Life was much simpler. The amount of information to deal with was far lower. Change happened at a much slower rate. Many tasks of daily living were far more time-consuming. Compared with modern people, they had fewer decisions to make. The matters of practical life were all much easier and straightforward then. Other than the arguments on ethics, most of what the ancient Pyrrhonist philosophers argued against had little or no practical application to daily life, except perhaps a few topics covered in some of the books Sextus Empiricus wrote, such as *Against the Grammarians*. We all still deal with grammar on a daily basis. That book contains arguments against theories of Greek grammar and word usage. Sadly, the experience of reading that book is like reading translated arguments for and against the Oxford comma, except that your own language doesn't use commas. Back then, just as now, people were judged based on grammar and pronunciation. Elite families hired grammarians to teach their sons to speak in the elite manner. The grammarians espoused dogmas on what was correct and incorrect. Some things never change. Part of the stress of my first year of college involved my efforts to lose my West Virginia accent so that I could sound like my new peers who had graduated from prep schools.

Contrary to the satirical criticisms of the Pyrrhonists about their knowing nothing, the ancient Pyrrhonists we know about were learned men. Sextus himself must have been a walking encyclopedia. He reports that Pyrrho's student, Nausiphanes, was a man of great erudition. Despite Sextus' many books of criticisms against the dogmas of the professors of arts and sciences, he said that the members of Pyrrho's school:

> … were not moved either by the view that these subjects
> are of no help to gaining wisdom (for that is a dogmatic
> assertion) or by any lack of culture attaching to them-
> selves; for in addition to their culture and their superi-
> ority to all other philosophers in breadth of experience
> they are also indifferent to the opinion of the multitude.
> Nor is the reason to be found in ill-will towards any (for
> that sort of vice is wholly alien to their gentle character),
> but in the fact that in respect of the arts and sciences they
> have met with the same experience as they did in respect
> of philosophy as a whole. For just as they approached
> philosophy with the desire of attaining truth, but, when
> faced by the equipollent conflict and discord of things,
> suspended judgment, – so also in the case of the arts
> and sciences, when they had set about mastering them
> with a view to learning here also the truth, they found
> difficulties no less serious, which they did not conceal.[126]

In many languages the concepts of ignorance and delusion overlap. They
are both about not knowing the right thing. But there's a useful distinction
between not knowing anything, knowing several options but not knowing
which is right, and believing the right thing is something other than what
it is. Pyrrhonism aims at this middle way. The life of a Pyrrhonist is a life
of inquiry. Contrary to the satirical criticisms of Pyrrhonism, Pyrrhonists
are great collectors of information. We find it useful to know about conflicting dogmas as this helps us prevent believing in any of them, and if
we ever need to make a decision under uncertainty, knowing these various
ways of looking at the situation gives some advantage in helping choose a
course that has a better chance of working out well. Yet, for people who
have spent their lives making decisions based on their dogmas, this idea of
non-dogmatic decision making seems inconceivable.

Remember the allegory of the Cave. Pyrrhonism endorses the careful
observation and recording of the appearances – what Plato calls "shadows."
Pyrrhonism endorses practical applications of that information for making predictions about past and future appearances. That's non-dogmatic
decision-making. It is pragmatic.

The first step in non-dogmatic decision-making is to collect all the
information about the appearances that you suspect is relevant to the

---

126 Sextus Empiricus, *Against the Professors*, Book 1, Section 2.

problem you face and any theories that might be relevant. Review all of this and use your judgment to attempt to predict the future. Endeavor to keep yourself honest about how good your predictions are by keeping some sort of score about how well your predictions turned out. Cultivate intellectual humility about your failed predictions. Look for patterns associated with where you have particularly good or poor predictions.

There are plenty of good books on practical problem-solving. Indeed, the books I've read that are specifically about problem-solving tend to be non-dogmatic. In contrast, books about problems and offering solutions, however, tend to be dogmatic. One book on problem solving I recommend is *How to Measure Anything: Finding the Value of Intangibles in Business* by Douglas W. Hubbard. While the examples are drawn from the business world, the book presents non-dogmatic ways of dealing with practical problems, focusing on how to convert information that is not quantified into numbers. It gives lots of rules of thumb and perspective-changing techniques to help one produce measurements of things not easy to measure. Once such information is turned into numbers, it is easier to analyze using math. Math is an alternative method to dogma. The easier something is to analyze quantitatively, the easier it is to come up with good answers based on the appearances. People sometimes resort to dogmatism because they cannot analyze the information. Another useful book is *Superforecasting: The Art and Science of Prediction* by Philip E. Tetlock and Dan Gardner. This book describes the behaviors of people who are exceptionally good at forecasting, describing in particular the ways they avoid dogmatism.

It can be instructive to consider an example of what one should not do. As an opposite example about how to deal with a problem, consider any controversial political issue and how it is addressed by partisans in the press. You'll likely get maximum clarity by picking an example on a topic you don't care much about. Read examples of pro and con. In almost every case you'll observe a writer who starts with a dogmatic view of things, does whatever is necessary to fit the appearances to the dogmatic view, leaves out anything that might plausibly contradict the writer's conclusions, and concludes that everything corroborates the view the writer started with. This is what you are to avoid in your own decision-making.

Some useful Pyrrhonist decision-making ideas can be found in Nassim Nicholas Taleb's book *Antifragile: Things That Gain from Disorder*, in particular the concept of *via negativa* (Latin for the "negative way"). The idea of via negativa is that solutions that involve avoidance or removal are unlikely to have unintended consequences. Via negativa is in many respects the opposite of dogmatism. In the dogmatic way there is belief that certain actions are right. Take this belief away, and the rationale for action goes away with it. From the Pyrrhonist perspective, inaction, or the reversal of prior dogmatic action, looks much more attractive and safer than it looks to a dogmatist.

Taleb also endorses the use of long-standing rules of thumb for decision-making rather than adopting dogmatic theories. This, too, is Pyrrhonist, reflecting the Pyrrhonist deference to customs that have been worked out over time, involving the experiences of many people from different perspectives across time, over the rash precipitancy of the dogmatists' non-evident theories.

Another suggestion Taleb has is to trust distributed systems that arise organically more than centralized systems created intentionally, as centralized systems are prone to being run dogmatically whereas distributed systems have decision-making agents who pay more attention to the appearances and who as a group do not subscribe to any particular dogma. Taleb points out that decision-makers who subscribe to dogmas tend to make bad decisions, typically with hidden or unaccounted-for risks.

41

Pyrrhonism and Religion

... always learning but never able to come to a knowledge of the truth. Just as Jannes and Jambres opposed Moses, so also these teachers oppose the truth.

Saint Paul, 2 Timothy 3, 6-8

Those who can make you believe absurdities can make you commit atrocities. *Voltaire*

One common question about Pyrrhonism is that since to be a Pyrrhonist is to be without beliefs, does that mean that Pyrrhonists have to be atheists? If one understands "atheist" to mean someone who believes gods do not exist, then a Pyrrhonist is not an atheist, as this kind of atheism is a belief: a belief about the non-existence of gods.

Then is a Pyrrhonist an agnostic? If by "agonistic" one means someone who doesn't know whether there are gods, this would be closer to the Pyrrhonist position of epoché. One might also consider Pyrrhonists to be, as many Buddhists consider themselves to be, non-theists, in which the existence or non-existence of one or more deities is not something they are concerned about. Pyrrhonists are concerned about evident matters, and the existence or non-existence of gods is a non-evident matter.

While Pyrrhonists suspend judgment about gods, we operate with general conformity to the customs and institutions of our societies. Pyrrho's own life provides an excellent example of this. The people of Pyrrho's hometown of Elis were so impressed with his wisdom that they made him a high priest. Pyrrho's Pyrrhonism did not prevent him from fulfilling this role. This is difficult for some people to wrap their heads around. They see Pyrrho as a hypocrite, serving as a priest for a god he doesn't believe in. What this conclusion misses is that Pyrrho did not believe that the god did not exist. Suspension of judgment about the existence of the god means that one has no beliefs one way or the other about the god. One cannot be hypocritical about beliefs one doesn't have.

But while the god was not evident to Pyrrho, many other things were. For example, worshipping the gods was customary in his society. Being a high priest was customary for well-respected men in his society. The temple was an important institution. These are all things that Pyrrhonists operate in general conformity to. Pyrrho also had his family to consider.

He was probably a member of the Klytidiai, a family of hereditary seers in Elis who interpreted the oracles of Zeus at Olympia.[127] Almost any reason for refusing the high priesthood would apply also to just being a priest, which he was already.

Belief is not necessary for performing the functions of a priest of a Greek pagan religion. Some religions don't require their priests to have beliefs, such as Buddhism. Some Christian ministers have reportedly done their jobs well despite secretly being atheists. Greek paganism was more concerned with orthopraxis than orthodoxy, unlike the Abrahamic religions that are better known to us today. In Greek paganism it was more important to perform the rites correctly than it was to have correct beliefs. One can perform rites correctly without having any beliefs about them.

Why should Pyrrho decide that he should not be a high priest when the people who were authorized to decide who should be a high priest had chosen him to be one? What evident reason could Pyrrho have for such a thing? It seems none. Indeed, refusing the honor of the high priesthood might be viewed negatively by those who wished to confer it upon him. This could cause needless trouble. Just a few decades earlier Socrates was killed because the citizens of Athens were concerned that he was introducing new gods. How could it in any way profit Pyrrho or Pyrrhonism or Pyrrho's community for Pyrrho to decline this honor?

So, those who accuse Pyrrho of being hypocritical because he accepted the high priesthood are expecting Pyrrho to be judged on whether he acted contrary to his beliefs. This misses the fact that Pyrrho had no beliefs, and it misunderstands how Pyrrhonists make decisions based on what is evident and in general conformity to the customs and institutions of their society. Pyrrho's acceptance of the high priesthood is an excellent example of how a Pyrrhonist can make decisions without beliefs on things that the dogmatists insist require beliefs in order to act.

The understanding of those who bestowed the honor of the high priesthood also needs to be considered. It seems implausible that they did not know what Pyrrho was teaching, yet they decided that he should be a high priest. If belief in the god was essential, might it not be said that the citizens of Elis were hypocritical in bestowing the high priesthood onto Pyrrho? Surely, they knew what they were doing and did not see their own action as inappropriate. Perhaps Pyrrho had influenced them to become Pyrrhonists, and they found that they did not have to have beliefs in order to determine that Pyrrho was suitable for the high priesthood. They, too, could use the criterion of action, just as Pyrrho did in accepting the high priesthood.

---

127 Dee L. Clayman, *Timon of Philus*, p 51.

In Montaigne's *Apology for Raymond Sebond*, Montaigne simultaneous-ly endorses Pyrrhonism and, paradoxically, the revealed truth of Christiani-ty. While Montaigne was presumably sincere, it's possible that he was not. If he was sincere, Montaigne was a man of his times, where religious belief permeated everything and divine revelation was taken as fact. If he wasn't sincere, Montaigne was still acting like a Pyrrhonist in appearing to accept the truth of the Church's teachings. Had he not done so the Church would surely have branded him a heretic and quite possibly have had him killed. Whether his position was sincere or not is a matter upon which we must suspend judgment, as we do not have access to the secrets of Montaigne's mind; although it does appear that Montaigne was a devout Catholic, who believed that while truth was inaccessible to reason and sense experience, it was revealed through the incarnation of Christ as disclosed through the Catholic Church. Pyrrhonism was, for him, entirely compatible with this belief as he interpreted Pyrrhonism as being about the truths proclaimed by man, and excluding those revealed to man by God.

42
Pyrrhonism and Politics

As a psychologist I am deeply interested in mental disturbances, particularly when they infect whole nations.... I am a neutral Swiss and even in my own country I am uninterested in politics, because I am convinced that 99 per cent of politics are mere symptoms and anything but a cure for social evils. About 50 per cent of politics is definitely obnoxious inasmuch as it poisons the utterly incompetent mind of the masses.   *Carl Jung*[128]

...every strong upsurge of power in the public sphere, be it of a political or a religious nature, infects a large part of humankind with stupidity.... The power of the one needs the stupidity of the other. The process at work here is not that particular human capacities, for instance, the intellect, suddenly atrophy or fail. Instead, it seems that under the overwhelming impact of rising power, humans are deprived of their inner independence and, more or less consciously, give up establishing an autonomous position toward the emerging circumstances. The fact that the stupid person is often stubborn must not blind us to the fact that he is not independent. In conversation with him, one virtually feels that one is dealing not at all with him as a person, but with slogans, catchwords, and the like that have taken possession of him. He is under a spell, blinded, misused, and abused in his very being. Having thus become a mindless tool, the stupid person will also be capable of any evil and at the same time incapable of seeing that it is evil. This is where the danger of diabolical misuse lurks, for it is this that can once and for all destroy human beings.   *Dietrich Bonhoeffer,*
On Stupidity[129]

---

128 *Collected Works*, Volume 18, p. 564.

129 A famous Nazi resister who was imprisoned for most of the war, and executed towards its end.

What is the proper attitude toward politics for a Pyrrhonist? The writings we have from the ancient Pyrrhonists do not directly illuminate this question because they came from an era that did not have politics like the modern world does. Our ancient Pyrrhonists whose works have survived lived in ancient empires, so they did not have the kind of political options and discourse that people who live in modern democracies have. Citizens had certain rights. Courts administered justice according to the laws. While there were political offices and councils, political power flowed from the top down. Their politics was more like what we think of as organizational politics rather than electoral politics. This kind of politics tends to be more personal and less ideological.

While the focus of all the Hellenistic philosophies was the cultivation of character, most of them addressed politics. Platonism was keenly interested in politics, as it arose in democratic Athens. Peripateticism also substantively addressed politics as it too arose in Athens. The Epicurean position on political involvement was that it should be avoided. Epicurus thought that politics was inherently psychologically disturbing, and that it led to psychologically disturbing pursuits of unnatural and unnecessary things, such as status and power. Conversely, the Stoics thought that participation in politics was about fulfilling a virtuous duty. Unfortunately we have no surviving Pyrrhonist texts about politics; however, the indirect illumination provided by the general principles of Pyrrhonism make the proper attitude toward politics for a Pyrrhonist clear enough.

Politics is largely dogma. Indeed, these days for a huge portion of mankind, politics is the most obvious form of dogma people are exposed to. Pyrrhonism is, of course, opposed to all dogmas. That various so-called experts are in contentious debate about a matter shows that the matter being disagreed about is dogma. These days some of the most contentious debates the typical person gets to observe or get caught up in are likely to be political debates. If you have political dogmas, it should be easy, upon a bit of reflection, to see how those dogmas upset you. When your candidate or political proposal wins, you are elated, most likely beyond any benefit that will actually accrue. When your candidate loses, you are upset and distraught, and prone to unwarrantedly catastrophize about the future. When you find that your friend doesn't share your viewpoint you find it threatening to the relationship. Pyrrhonist practice will help you get rid of these dogmas, and the unhelpful emotional rollercoaster associated with them.

A bit of Pyrrhonist insight about politics comes from a fragment of Timon's *Silloi*, a comedic poem that caricatured dogmatic philosophers. What Timon had to say is equally true about dogmatic politicians and political pundits.

And Strife, the plague of mortals, stalks vainly shriek-
ing, the sister of Murderous Quarrel and Discord, which
rolls blindly over all things. But then it sets its head towards men, and casts them on hope.... For who hath set
these to fight in deadly strife? A rabble keeping pace with
Echo; for, enraged at those silent, it raised an evil disease
against men, and many perished.

What Timon is saying here is that dogmatism produces strife and that this
strife has awful outcomes. People are lured to accept dogmas due to the
hopes those dogmas incite. Dogmas produce conflict among people that
is both unnecessary and tremendously damaging. Dogmatism is a disease
that kills many, a fact that should be apparent to anyone with even the
most superficial knowledge of the hundreds of millions who killed by the
dogmas of Communism and Fascism in the 20th Century.

"Echo" in the poem refers to a mythical nymph who used to engage
Hera, the wife of Zeus, in lengthy conversations to delay Hera as she
searched for Zeus among the other nymphs, with whom Zeus was being
unfaithful to Hera. These delays allowed Zeus to evade being discovered.
Eventually Hera figured out what Echo was doing and put a curse on her
that allowed her to say only the last few words of what others had just
said to her. Timon points out that the fate of Echo is like what happens
when people follow dogma. Once belief sets in, the holder of the dogma
is cursed to just mindlessly repeat fragments of what they've been told.
They also lose tolerance for those who have not taken a side. Their attitude
hardens to a stance of "you're either with us or you're against us."

What would it be like to be without political dogma?

We know from Diogenes Laertius' biography of Pyrrho that "there were
many who emulated his abstention from affairs." The Greek term translated
as "abstention from affairs," is *apragmon* – a person who refrains from taking
part in public affairs. The term can also be translated as "impassiveness."
Depending on context, the term can be either positive or negative. In a positive sense it can mean someone who has left worldly cares behind to pursue
higher pursuits, such as philosophical contemplation. In a negative sense it
can mean someone who engages in political irresponsibility.

The antonym of *apragmon* is *polupragmon*. *Polupragmon* is always pe-
jorative. It means someone who is overly involved – a busybody. Timon
uses this word in the very first verse of the *Silloi*: "Speak to me now whoever of you are busybody sophists!" Aristotle used the word also, saying
that people thought that politicians were busybodies.[130] One cannot be a

---

130 Aristotle, *Nicomachean Ethics*, Section 1142a.

Pyrrhonist and be a busybody, and while one doesn't have to be a busy-body to be a politician, busybodies sure tend to like politics.

Right after mentioning Pyrrho's abstention from affairs, his biography follows with a verse from one of Timon's poems:

> Now, you old man, you Pyrrho, how could you
> Find an escape from all the slavish doctrines
> And vain imaginations of the sophists?
> How did you free yourself from all the bonds
> Of sly chicane, and artful deep persuasion?

These days, referring to someone as a "sophist" is an accusation of intellec-tual deceit. In Pyrrho's day a sophist was a professional teacher who taught the sons of the elite how to think and speak effectively. Character, logic, and rhetoric were all equally important in this pursuit, and the ultimate use of these skills was primarily in the context of politics and the courts. And, yes, these skills included persuasive bits of trickery all designed to get someone to believe something whose truth could not be established. Such sophistry is today on exhibit daily by polemical journalists, pundits, politicians, and activists – all busybodies.

Much of what gets called "politics" is sophistic drama that is manu-factured by busybodies. These busybodies have vested interests in creating drama.[131] For journalists the drama gets attention, which sells advertising and subscriptions, and builds reputation. For politicians and activists, the drama energizes the base and keeps the donations flowing. Drama is re-warding – for them. But is it rewarding for you? Is that feeling of righteous anger that political drama stokes actually good for you? Does it make you a better person, or delude you into thinking you're better simply by creat-ing the impression that others are worse? Does it improve your relation-ships with other people, or cause people to avoid you, or at least certain topics when they are around you? Do you find that it has produced results commensurate with the time you have invested, or was it a waste of your time? Think of how much time politics can consume, and how little you can actually affect anything.

Sure, go vote, if for no other reason that it is a civic ritual that bonds the electorate with those in government. Doing so is in accordance with ex-isting customs and institutions. You can figure out who to vote for without

---

131 A fascinating and lovely analysis of how all of this drama works to make highly edu-cated people much less accurate than shear random guessing about important and fundamental facts that people are convinced that they know can be found in Hans Rosling's book *Factfulness: Ten Reasons We're Wrong About the World—and Why Things Are Better Than You Think.*

having any adherence to their dogmas.

One modern critic of the Pyrrhonist approach to politics is the theologian Angus Ritchie. He claims that "the real flaw in Pyrrhonism is that it masquerades as neutrality," based on the rationale that the Pyrrhonist attitude towards moral arguments is that they are irresoluble, and because of this, judgment is to be suspended in order to achieve ataraxia.[132] Ritchie is mistaken. First, he falls into the common error of ignoring that Pyrrhonism has a criterion of action. While we cannot know that a moral argument is true, we are still fully able to act when called upon to make a decision such as deciding which candidates to vote for, based on moral arguments.

Second, he doesn't appreciate what he calls a "masquerade." In antiquity Pyrrhonists were known to be fully capable of political decisions. For example, the thesis of Favorinus' now-lost book, *Pyrrhonean Tropes*, was to show how helpful Pyrrhonism was for those who practiced in the law courts as advocates and judges. What Ritchie calls a "masquerade of neutrality" is better understood as impartiality and dispassion, not avoidance and indecision.

With respect to decision-making, Pyrrhonism has much in common with how the law courts work. First, there's an inherent conservatism to the Pyrrhonist approach – not "conservatism" in the sense of being politically right-wing, but in the more traditional sense of conserving what has been demonstrated to work and of deferring to precedent. The burden of proof is always on the arguments for change, and proof comes from the evidence of the appearances – not theories. Existing customs, laws, and institutions receive the benefit of the doubt and are assumed to be the closest thing we have to being correct, unless it is demonstrated otherwise.

The aim of Pyrrhonism is to resist dogmatism. Extremism of any kind is characterized by a compulsion for closure and an allergy to ambiguity. Ritchie fell into the erroneous idea that Pyrrhonists suspend all aspects of moral judgment. That we do not do. Moral judgments are required for decisions we must make in day-to-day life. Pyrrhonism suspends judgment about what is by nature good or bad; it does not suspend making judgments required for actions. The Pyrrhonist Criterion of Action gives standards for these decisions:

1. Is it in accordance with appearances?
2. Is it in general conformity with local customs, laws, and institutions?
3. Is it in general conformity with the practitioner's own experience, temperament, and feelings?

---

132 Angus Ritchie, *From Morality to Metaphysics: The Theistic Implications of our Ethical Commitments*, 2013, p 38.

For example, if someone steals from you, is it not evident that something you once had has been taken away from you? Has it been your experience that being stolen from leads to outcomes that seem undesirable? Is it the local custom that theft is wrong? Are there laws against theft? Are there institutions that catch and punish thieves? Based on all of this, a Pyrrhonist would conclude that theft was wrong, and from that conclusion the Pyrrhonist would take practical action within their society to address the wrong.

The Pyrrhonist's particular experience of being stolen from, however, is where suspension of judgement is applied. While something evident may seem bad to us, we are unable to take all perspectives on it, or to have complete knowledge about it. We are unable to accurately predict the outcome. Perhaps this event will allow us to become closely involved in catching the thief. Not only might our property be restored, we might be considered a hero. Thus the theft might be to us a good thing. Or perhaps we learn that the thief was driven by great desperation. We take pity on the thief and extend compassion. So, while for ourselves while we would suspend judgment as to whether the theft for us was good or bad, as there is no criterion of truth. There is a criterion of action. We look at the appearances and make a decision about what to do, such as to report the theft to the police.

This is an easy example because there is general agreement about what constitutes theft and whether theft is wrong. The current political issues of any era or place operate at the cutting edge of disputed matters. This is where things get tricky. In dealing with this trickiness, it is helpful for Pyrrhonists to give deeper consideration to what moral customs have widespread agreement.

In 1993, a hundred years after the renowned World Parliament of Religions met in Chicago a second parliament was convened. That parliament issued a document declaring that there were "four broad, ancient guidelines for human behavior which are found in most of the religions of the world." The document was signed by two hundred religious leaders representing, if not officially, pretty much all the world's religions. These guidelines are:

1. A commitment to a culture of non-violence and respect for life;
2. A commitment to a culture of solidarity and a just economic order ;
3. A commitment to a culture of tolerance and a life of truthfulness;
4. A commitment to a culture of equal rights and partnership between men and women.

Of course, various people and various cultures interpret these ideas in wildly different ways (ask a communist and a capitalist about their ideas on what is a just economic order, or a vegan and an omnivore what constitutes respect for life, for example), but it's a start.

Another good place to start is through investigating how ethical decisions turned out for other people. A good example of this is Plutarch's *Parallel Lives*. In this book Plutarch gives a biographical essay of a famous Roman, followed by one of a famous Greek whose circumstances were similar. Afterward he gives a short essay comparing the individuals' ethical decisions and their results. It's a good illustration of a non-dogmatic approach to ethical analysis.

Ritchie further criticizes Pyrrhonism, saying: "As a response to the world around us today, let alone that of Nazi Germany, it is surely found wanting." Here Ritchie goes down the rabbit hole of Godwin's Law – conflating anything you don't like with Hitler and the Nazis – showing that he doesn't grasp the absurdity of the idea that Pyrrhonists would be complicit in one of the most dogmatic political philosophies ever devised.

So, let's go down that rabbit hole with Ritchie. What would the Nazis have thought of Pyrrhonists? We have a good answer to that question from the Nazi psychologist, Erik Jaentsch. In his 1938 book, *Der Gengentypus* ("The Antitype") Jaentsch describes dogmatic certainty as a characteristic of a healthy personality and a tolerance for ambiguity as a sign of mental illness.[133] This line of thinking, though, is not confined to Nazis. Any rabid dogmatist is likely to divide the world into three groups: the virtuous who accept the dogma, the evil ones who accept a contrary dogma, and the insane people who do neither. But really, it is the other way around. It is those who are free of dogma who are sane. Those who have succumbed to dogma have taken on parasites that disease the mind.

What would a Pyrrhonist have done in Nazi Germany? First, it would depend on the circumstances of the Pyrrhonist. A Jewish, Gypsy, or homosexual Pyrrhonist would pay attention to the appearances, reasonably conclude that the Nazis were dangerous, and would try to escape, as it is natural to prefer life over death.

An Aryan German Pyrrhonist would avoid getting caught up in all of the non-evident beliefs that Nazism entailed. They would likely question these beliefs and advocate for adhering to Germany's traditional laws and customs and avoiding rash changes. However, in the face of the Nazi's willingness to use violence, this would all be done cautiously and diplomatically. A good example of how this might be done can be seen in the actions of the Pyrrhonist philosopher Montaigne. Montaigne's life spanned a period of intense violence between French Catholics and Protestants. Montaigne not only managed to stay out of the conflict, but also

---

133 Jamie Holmes, *Nonsense: The Power of Not Knowing*, 2015, p 12.

managed to be both respected by both sides, as he was always on the side of common sense and peace.

In the political realm, moderation, conservatism (in the traditional usage of that term, not as a synonym for right-wing, but a preference for preserving the status quo and making change incrementally), and inaction have not historically been the great sources of suffering. The greatest sources of suffering have come from dogmatic utopians, such as the Nazis, Bolsheviks, Maoists, and the Pol Pot regime. These dogmatists were convinced that they had seen the light outside of Plato's cave and that they were morally right in rapidly and radically transforming their societies. They believed that their dogmatic utopian ends justified their means, and the means were violence and coercion.

Although following custom is an imperfect guide, customs have been tested by time; they have achieved consensus, at least in the past, and they can incorporate elements of practical wisdom that people may be unaware of, but which have been attained unconsciously, via social evolution. Customs change over time, and they can change without the rash precipitancy of the dogmatists, and without the coercion and violence that dogmatic change tends to entail.

Of course, the extent to which a Pyrrhonist might have resisted Nazism would vary from person to person, and these efforts would almost certainly have been unsatisfactory to those committed to ideologies opposed to Nazism. But is it realistic to expect heroic resistance? We know from Milgram's famous Obedience to Authority Experiment that under pressure to conform, people will oblige. It is absurd to criticize hypothetical Pyrrhonists for failing to perform better than actual humans in historical cases.

Reverend Doctor Ritchie, rather than dismissing hypothetical Pyrrhonists as being unable to react appropriately to Nazis, why don't you tell us how effective your Christianity was in resisting the Nazis in Germany? Wasn't Germany an overwhelmingly Christian country then? How well did Christianity do in Italy in resisting Mussolini? Wasn't Italy a universally Catholic country then? How about in Spain, where it was against the law not to be Christian? Did that stop the Fascist dictator Generalissimo Francisco Franco from waging civil war? How does one explain the Catholic Church's active support of Franco in that war? And, while we're at it, what about the horror show of awful things that have been endorsed or enabled by Christian dogmatism throughout history, even in our lifetimes? I'm personally glad that I wasn't exposed to the risk of being a Catholic altar boy in the 1970s under the supervision of a pedophile priest. Why should anyone believe you when you take Pyrrhonists to task about – snort – enabling Nazis?!

Pyrrho was fond of quoting anything that bore on the uncertainty, emptiness, and fickleness of the affairs of man. We are all swept up in the great tide of history. In Nazi Germany there passed a point where arguments calling dogmatism into question would no longer work. What any one individual can do in the face of all of this is limited. It is the custom to support one's community and to follow its laws. Once the Nazis were in power, active resistance from the inside was futile. The practical thing to do would be not to get caught up in the dogma and engage in a kind of passive resistance. It takes time, but this kind of resistance has been shown to work. Consider the fall of the Soviet Union. Despite dictatorial control, and an educational and propaganda system centered on instilling adherence to Soviet Marxist dogma, after a few generations of experience with the Soviet system, the appearances of it convinced Soviet citizens that the system was morally, intellectually, and economically bankrupt. Mass apathy set in. People mouthed the dogmas, but few believed in them. Eventually a tipping point came where allegiance to the dogmas was so thin that the system collapsed. All of the sacrifices to build the Soviet state turned to naught. The millions killed and imprisoned as a result of the revolution, and by Stalin – it was all for nothing.

Another example can be seen by comparing the origins of Canada and the United States. The two countries are highly similar. The Americans obtained and preserved their independence from the British through two wars: the American Revolution and the War of 1812. The Canadians suffered no such turmoil, achieving by peaceful means their independence from the British about 75 years later, without all of the suffering the Americans caused.

Social change is entirely possible via Pyrrhonist approaches. While it would be reasonable to describe the Pyrrhonist approach to social and political change as "pragmatic," or "conservative" or "moderate" in as much as these terms are antonyms to terms such as "radical" and "dogmatic," it would not be appropriate to use those terms in as much as they may be used in the context of describing particular political directions. The Pyrrhonist approach allows evolutionary change and avoids revolutionary change.

How does evolutionary social change come about via Pyrrhonist approaches? Consider how the Pyrrhonist technique of setting one argument against another would be applied to the arena of customs and laws, and historical cases of how that turned out.

In the United States, the controversy over gay marriage proceeded quickly and smoothly – by the standards of a major societal change in customs. A war wasn't needed. There were no riots. How did this happen?

The custom of heterosexual couples who loved each other being allowed to marry was set against the custom of homosexual couples who loved each other being prohibited from marrying. This produced the issue that if the former was customary, then why shouldn't the latter also be customary? Inquiry into this demonstrated that the answers to that question were contrary to existing customs about fairness and equality under the law. This process of setting custom against custom convinced the majority of people, over time, that the custom of prohibiting homosexuals to marry was incompatible with other customs and the most rational thing to do to resolve the incompatibility was to allow homosexuals to marry.

This is hardly the first time that customs about who and who may not marry have been changed. Plutarch tells us that in ancient Greece there was an upper age for marriage, as marriage was for the purpose of producing children.[134] At some point that custom got changed too, peacefully and non-dogmatically. An exploration of the history of marriage customs in Western societies shows many customs that would now be considered abhorrent but were in the past customary, such as child betrothal and the purchase of brides. Pyrrhonism recognizes that customs are in some sense arbitrary, that circumstances change, and that customs need to change with them.

Similarly, the women's rights movement went smoothly (again, as a relative term, as these sorts of changes go). It first began with the right to vote. If men can vote, then why not women? It became increasingly difficult for men to claim on the basis of the appearances that their mothers, wives, and daughters were so inferior to them that they should not be allowed to vote. In this case, custom was set against appearances, and the appearances led the way to changing the custom.

The American Civil Rights Movement provides another positive example. The brilliant leadership of Martin Luther King enabled the movement to achieve many of its objectives. King kept focused on the argument that it was the aspiration and custom of the United States to treat everyone equally under the law, yet it was evident that this was not the case for Black citizens. The appearances needed to be harmonized with the customs. While the Civil Rights Movement was marred by riots and killings, of not only King but of many others, the movement achieved great change in less than a generation. Again, the technique was to set custom against appearances.

While certainly dogma was a driving force for actors on both sides in these examples of successful social change, the important thing to notice is how success can come from setting the custom to be changed against

---

134 Plutarch, *Solon*, Chapter 20.

either other customs or against the appearances. For example, I remember arguing about gay marriage with my stepfather, Tom Miller. Tom was an award-winning and famous political journalist. He was also a devout Christian who believed marriage was only to be between a woman and a man. So he argued that gay marriage was against his religion. My counter-argument was that it wasn't against mine, and that the issue wasn't about requiring the church to perform gay marriages but about requiring the government to recognize gay marriages. Tom's dogma gave him no counter-argument to this that was acceptable by American customs. All over America people started thinking through these issues. They found that to keep their customs consistent, something had to change. This moved public sentiment from gay marriage being unthinkable to being unremarkable.

Let's now look at what causes the process of social change to go badly. A good example of a change that went badly is the American Civil War. Over 150 years have passed since that war, and it seems that Americans are still fighting it. Go to the site of Pickett's Charge at the Gettysburg battlefield, retrospectively considered the turning point in the war, and to this day one can commonly see Southerners with tears in their eyes, grieving for the lost cause of their now-distant ancestors. Any substantive analysis of the ongoing political divisions in the United States cannot avoid pointing out the still-lingering effects of the Civil War. I suggest that our thinking about that war is laden with dogmatism and an investigation of the history of that war is instructive about how, as Timon pointed out, dogmatic conflicts lead to disaster.

While tensions had been building for a couple of decades in the United States, that the country should be plunged into war was a surprise, not only to Americans, but to the entire world. The institution of slavery was historically ubiquitous, yet nowhere else in the world did the abolition of slavery entail a savage civil war. For example, in 1861 Russia freed its 30 million serfs, at a time when Russia's total population was 74 million. In the US there were only about 4 million slaves in a population of 31.4 million. Why was Russia able to free such a large portion of its population peacefully whereas America fell into war over a much smaller portion? That America had to have a war is even more perplexing when one considers that a resolution Thomas Jefferson proposed to Congress in 1784 to end slavery in 1800 lost by a mere one vote, a vote that it would have passed if a delegate from New Jersey not been absent.[135]

Thereafter it became the custom in the US to keep the ratio of slave to free states at 50/50. This custom started to break down in the years leading

---

135 Rodriguez, Junius P. (1997). *The Historical Encyclopedia of World Slavery*, Volume 1; Volume 7. Santa Barbara, California: ABC-CLIO, Inc., p. 380.

to the war, as the increasingly more populous North increasingly wished to end this custom both for economic and moral reasons. In the North there was a growing militant abolition movement, so dogmatically assured of its moral superiority that it was willing to break norms of custom and law and to advocate violence. Talk turned to action with John Brown's raid on the federal armory at Harpers Ferry in 1859 to steal weapons for a slave rebellion. While the raid was quickly put down, terror spread in the South about abolitionist dogmatists who disregarded custom, who disregarded the law, and who were now disregarding lives.

The initiation of violence indicates dogmatism just as smoke indicates fire. It was with good reason Timon called dogmatism "murderous."

The year after the Harpers Ferry raid, Abraham Lincoln was elected president on a platform of ending the spread of slavery into new US states. He got 39.8% of the vote. This was not only one of the smallest percentage of votes for a winning presidential candidate ever, but also, in many states Lincoln did not have enough supporters to even be on the ballot. As a consequence, the deep South decided, based not only on the precedent of the American Revolution but the fact that Virginia and Rhode Island explicitly stipulated that they were joining the United States while reserving the right to secede from it, that they were entitled to self-determination. They decided to secede, with immense approval from their electorates. Lincoln, however, opposed secession based on the dogmatic belief that individual States had no right to leave the Union. He then enticed the South into armed conflict to justify preventing secession by persuading people to view it as an insurrection. The enticement worked, because of the dogmatic belief of the Confederate government that they had to violently resist the Union occupation of an island in Charleston harbor. While the war did result in ending slavery, that wasn't Lincoln's objective. Indeed he adamantly denied that freeing the slaves was his objective. His objective was always about preventing secession, as Lincoln said:

> My paramount object in this struggle is to save the Union, and is not either to save or to destroy slavery. If I could save the Union without freeing any slave I would do it, and if I could save it by freeing all the slaves I would do it; and if I could save it by freeing some and leaving others alone I would also do that. What I do about slavery, and the colored race, I do because I believe it helps to save the Union; and what I forbear, I forbear because I do not believe it would help to save the Union. I shall do less whenever I shall believe what I am doing

> hurts the cause, and I shall do more whenever I shall believe doing more will help the cause.[136]

So, instead of custom being contrasted with either custom or the appearances, the country fell into a dogmatic strife. The result was estimated casualties of 620,000 dead, 476,000 wounded,[137] impoverishment of the South that still lingers in parts of it today, the creation of a century-long apartheid system that was not much better for Blacks than the slavery from which they had been freed, and even 150 years later racial discrimination is still a problem.

The South did not want war. They wanted independence. A large portion of the North didn't want war, either. In 1864 Lincoln got only 55 percent of the vote in an election that included only the North. The opposition party's platform was for ending the war. As about two thirds of the population of the United States was in the North, this implies that 63 percent of the people in the country did not want the war, yet they got sucked into a horrible war all due to the dogmatism of a minority. As Cicero, an Academic Skeptic, said: "an unjust peace is better than a just war."

It seems evident that changing oneself is difficult and time-consuming, but changing society is even more so. It may be the case that societal change operates similarly to how paradigm shifts happen in science. When a new cultural paradigm is proposed, young people will choose between the competing paradigms whereas older people, due to the propensity for confirmation bias, will adhere to the existing paradigm. Eventually the adherents of the old cultural paradigm will die off and the new cultural paradigm will take over as the dominant paradigm. The key difference in how this process works in science versus in politics is that in politics one side sometimes resorts to violence in order to speed the process. This is not to deny that scientists don't ever adopt dirty tactics to achieve their ends, but the magnitude of the dirtiness is far greater in politics.

Pyrrhonists should feel free to ask questions of the political dogmatists. Pyrrhonists should give the benefit of the doubt to the status quo, encourage gradual changes that seem reasonable, through the process of contrasting custom with custom or with the appearances. Pyrrhonists should work to discourage dramatic changes, most especially when such changes involve the use of violence or force, as there is widespread agreement that violence is bad.

---

136 *The Collected Works of Abraham Lincoln*, edited by Roy P. Basler, Volume V, "Letter to Horace Greeley" (August 22, 1862), p. 388.

137 http://www.civilwar.org/education/civil-war-casualties.html

Beyond this, engagement with politics seems to draw people into dogmatism – a particularly ugly dogmatism that uses the threat of violence and the coercive powers of the state for enforcing dogmatic ideologies. Politics seems to promote black-and-white thinking, tribal feuds, selfishness, and rage while discouraging reason, respect, and an appreciation of the dignity of others, especially those who hold different opinions. It encourages extreme reactions instead of careful seeking of measured responses that are in accordance with the appearances. Politics distances decisions from local knowledge of the appearances in preference to adherence to non-evident propositions. In doing so it limits moral wisdom by making it harder to achieve virtuous outcomes even when motivated by virtuous impulses.

The virtuousness of those "virtuous impulses" is questionable. With regard to politics, many people have come to see anger as a virtue. Almost none of the ancient Greek philosophers would have agreed with that idea. Anger is one of the disturbing emotions that Pyrrhonism is designed to eradicate. Only Aristotle came close to endorsing anger as a virtue, and he thought what was most appropriate was for anger to be greatly moderated and only for appropriate situations. Many people now endorse the idea that "If you aren't outraged, then you just aren't paying attention." This makes anger synonymous with political and cultural awareness, and lack of anger synonymous with ignorance and perhaps stupidity, allowing the angry to shame those enjoying ataraxia. Because of this association, anger serves as a sign to many individuals that their lives are meaningful.

In the *Kathavatthu Sutta*, the Buddha gives advice on what topics of conversation should be avoided. His list included conversation about kings, robbers, and ministers of state. These were the topics of ancient politics. The advice applies equally well to the topics of modern politics. This practical advice seems suitable for Pyrrhonists, too.

Political opinions are nothing to be proud of. We shouldn't believe in them, and we should avoid getting excited about them. We shouldn't believe they are noble. We should question whether our political opinions are just there to make us feel superior to others at no real expense to us.

It appears that for the most part following politics is at best a form of amusement and at worst an addiction. Politics absorbs huge amounts of time and mental energy. We should question whether those resources could be better used. Is the time you spend on politics actually producing any apparent positive results? That's not to say that one should endeavor to be uninformed and to not vote. Look at the appearances and ask yourself, what is your investment in politics doing for you or anyone else?

....

43
Tips on Pyrrhonist Practice

If you are going to up-end all human understanding, you've got to go back to the beginning. And our Western understanding does really start with the Ancient Greeks. God knows why.... God doesn't know how they got started on that particular questioning which led to their love of reason and their ability to organize things.... it was lost.... The Romans never really picked up on it. But I asked [Sarah Vinke] the question: 'Did the Greeks, the Ancient Greeks, think that Quality was part of their thought?' And she said, 'It was every part of their thought!'
Robert M. Pirsig,
Zen and the Art of
Motorcycle Maintenance

Virtue's the chiefest beauty of the mind,
the noblest ornament of humankind.
Virtue's our safeguard, and our guiding star,
that stirs up reason when our senses err.
Anonymous, 1813, stitched on a
sampler, Twillingate Museum

Is something bothering you? This is a question that is probably constantly in the back of your mind. When the answer is yes, it's a sign you should engage your Pyrrhonism skills. Engage in self-argumentation. What you will likely find is that you have some belief that something is right or wrong, good or bad. That belief has hit against something contrary to it. Your first job is to identify the belief. Your second job is to dethrone it as a belief.

If the belief is not strongly held, you may be able to dispel it through reciting one or more of the Pyrrhonist maxims to yourself. As your get more experience with Pyrrhonism, these maxims become more effective as they help you recall your past experiences with dethroning beliefs.

The maxims, however, are not going to be sufficient for entrenched beliefs, beliefs with deep emotional roots. In these cases, there's no short-cut. You need to start constructing arguments against your belief. If you have trouble coming up with arguments, review the modes. Contemplate each mode to come up with arguments. Avoid investing time and effort into coming up with arguments for why your belief is correct. Focus on coming up with counter-arguments. Kee doing this to wear away the belief. Remember, you only need to get yourself to the point of suspending judgement. You do not have to convince yourself that your prior belief was false. You just have to get to the point where you are no longer convinced that it is true.

The most vexing beliefs usually have to do with moral judgments. Keep reminding yourself that nothing is inherently good or bad. Good and bad exist relative to something. You may judge something that happened to you as bad, but how can you be certain? Expand your perception of time. For example, because something is happening to you that may seem bad at the moment, perhaps later something good will come of it. That good thing may be far better than the bad thing, so much that you'd prefer having the bad thing happen to you so as to get the good thing. Expand your perception of those affected. While it may seem bad to you, who might it seem good for? How can you tell that their good does not outweigh the bad that befell you?

Did you lose something or someone you were attached to? Is it not evident to you that life is change? Remember, at some point you lose everything. Why is now worse than some other point? Maybe you are losing this now to save you some even more painful loss later.

For those familiar with Buddhist practices about disturbing thoughts, the cure by argument is strikingly different. If the thought is based on a belief, one does not let the thought pass, or to see it as just a thought, or do anything that one might call "letting go" of the thought. Instead, one grabs onto the thought and subjects it to rational assault – the Pyrrhonist cure by argument. This is not a process of getting rid of the thought or letting the thought go. This is a process of disempowering the thought. The power the thought has is because it got you to believe it. Get rid of the belief, and the thought is powerless. It becomes just another piece of speculation floating in the mind.

Self-argumentation is a form of cognitive distancing. It doesn't really matter what arguments you come up with. It doesn't matter whether they are good. It matters that you argue. It matters that you put distance between your feeling and your action. The Stoics recited the alphabet to do this.[138] The Pyrrhonists engage their maxims and modes to do this.

One thing one may observe in practicing Pyrrhonism is that one is likely to become a bit more optimistic about things. Martin Seligman, the psychologist who is famous in the field of positive psychology and is

---

138 http://donaldrobertson.name/an-ancient-stoic-meditation-technique/

particularly noted for his research on learned helplessness and on optimism, says that optimists tend to be happier and have better life outcomes relative to non-optimists, even though they have a distorted view of reality. Adopting the Pyrrhonist view, that there is nothing inherently good or bad, and the only things that one should make decisions about are issues about which one needs to take an action, appears to be an antidote for pessimism. The only reason we act is because we think acting will be better for ourselves and others than non-acting. This turns one's view away from how bad things might be, to what actions can be made that will make things better.

I have found it useful in my Pyrrhonist practice to pay careful attention to how I word things that involve the verb "to be." I try to think about whether anybody is likely to view an issue differently from how I view it. If so, rather than saying something like "X is Y" I try to say that "X appears to be Y" or such to remind myself that this is just an appearance to me. I determine nothing. What appears and what is the truth are not the same things.

This approach is not unique to Pyrrhonism. David Bourland devised a writing and speaking style based on Alfred Korzybski's General Semantics called "E-Prime," which may be defined as "English without the use of 'is.'" Here is Robert Anton Wilson's summary of E-Prime, which is remarkably Pyrrhonist in sentiment.

> You'll find that by dispensing with "is", and trying to reformulate without "is", you just naturally fall into the kind of expression which is considered acceptable in modern science. And also, it's the type of consciousness that Zen Buddhism tries to induce. Using E-Prime, you will understand modern science and Zen Buddhism both a lot better than you've ever understood them before. Martin Gardner has written a long essay proving that to think like this will destroy your mind. I think it adds tremendously to clarity. I am removing the "is" from my writing more and more. Removing it from your speech is even harder.
>
> Instead of thinking, "The grass is green," think that "the grass appears green to me." And this saved me a lot of time. By the way, I don't get embroiled in arguments like Beethoven is better than Mozart, or rock is better than soul. I define such things as meaningless. And so when people get into arguments like that I just

say, "Well, Beethoven seems better to me than Mozart most of the time." I don't say, "Beethoven is better than Mozart."

I return to E-Prime in my thinking whenever I find myself getting angry with somebody, or feeling depressed or hopeless, or having negative emotional states in general. Once you take out all of the "ises" out of all of your negative statements, you find out they are all relative to how you feel at the moment.

People, by and large, would act a hell of a lot more sanely, especially when they got rid of "is" they put "maybe" in more sentences. I think if everybody used "maybe" more often, the increase in general sanity would seem absolutely astonishing and completely flabbergast everybody. What the hell, suddenly we have a planet full of sane people? When did that start to happen? I didn't even notice it. You just listen to the craziest people on the news and on television, or the craziest columnists in the newspaper. You notice they never say maybe, they are always quite sure. There is no "is." They never say "seems," they always say "is."

I am continually astonished at all of the people in the world who think they know the answer to everything. None of them ever suspect they might be cosmic schmucks and have the wrong answer. And I find that any explanation that makes sense to me is in Korzybski's Science and Sanity. These people don't know how to use language properly. They are using language in an overly-dogmatic way which sets their brain in totally dogmatic modes. So they think dogmatically, they perceive dogmatically, they even smell dogmatically, they hear dogmatically. They are locked in a trap of fixed neuro-semantic circuits in their brains. Whereas, knowing I'm a cosmic schmuck, I always think of at least five alternatives.[139]

The first professional editor who worked on my manuscript expressed strong concerns about this aspect of my writing. They insisted that I must follow their editorial dogma, and admonished me as follows:

---

139 https://antilogicalism.com/tag/robert-anton-wilson/

> Avoid weak and editorializing words such as "seems," "probably," "I suppose," "I think," "I believe," "I suspect," "it seems to me." (In particular, the word "seems" can often be replaced by "is" or "can be.") In writing, the constant use of such language weakens a message and can become tiresome to the reader.

If I ever get around to writing a modernized version of Sextus' book *Against the Grammarians*, I know what I'll start with. The dogma of our modern grammarians is to push writers into making their statements dogmatically. Instead, writers need to be encouraged to use these kinds of weak and editorializing words so that they and their readers can better understand where the limits to knowledge actually reside. Their messages need to be weakened. They need to display more intellectual humility. Yes, I suppose this can become tiresome to readers because it pushes them to pay attention to the differences between knowledge of the appearances and dogmas about the non-evident. For those unaccustomed to it, it's work.

Montaigne also noted this problem.

> I can see why the Pyrrhonian philosophers cannot express their general conception in any manner of speaking; for they would need a new language. Ours is wholly formed of affirmative propositions, which to them are utterly repugnant; so that when they say "I doubt," immediately you have them by the throat, to make them admit that at least they know and are sure of this fact, that they doubt. Thus they have been constrained to take refuge in this comparison from medicine, without which their attitude would be inexplicable: when they declare "I do not know" or "I doubt," they say that this proposition carries itself away with the rest, no more nor less than rhubarb, which expels evil humors and carries itself off with them. This idea is more firmly grasped in the form of interrogation: "What do I know?" – the words I bear as a motto, inscribed over a pair of scales.[140]

I find it useful to note that to quote is not to assert. Quoting someone else is a way of availing oneself to an idea without committing to it, without putting it forward as if oneself said it. Quoting something that employs metaphors bordering on the obscure and that allows for multiple

---

140 Montaigne, *Apology for Raymond Sebond.*

interpretations may be an even more intricate way of not affirming anything.

Perhaps people do not acquire their views through active belief formation, coming to think that something is so-and-so based on consideration of evidence or reasons. Instead, perhaps, beliefs grow on us like a fungus does, allowing the first spores we come in contact with to colonize us. We come to think of the world in ways that are non-transparent to us, caused by non-rational means such as conventions and custom. Perhaps forces far beyond us decide for us, and our actions issue from elaborate chains of causation regarding what is to happen next. This is an idea that Diogenes Laertius says the Pyrrhonists invoked. It may be hubris to conceive of oneself as a deliberator, who takes action based on self-determination. Several of the quotes Pyrrho was fond of undermine our self-conception as reasoners who convey information when we speak, who act based on our own choices, and who arrive at conclusions based on our own thoughts.

It seems to me that Sextus made a mistake in writing an introduction to Pyrrhonism that was full of complicated arguments that are difficult to follow. But, maybe that's why his book was preserved and we should all be thankful for it. Maybe there were simpler books that did not survive, and Sextus did not make a mistake. It seems to me that any idea that is going to help large numbers of people cannot be long and complicated. It cannot be out of the grasp of ordinary people leading ordinary lives. Pyrrhonism is about how to live an ordinary life following the rules of ordinary life. Pyrrhonism is not a doctrine: it is a system and an ability. Not much needs to be learned. Its core is the practice of suspending belief about anything non-evident, doing so through opposing arguments. Pyrrhonism is something you do.

Before one studies Pyrrhonism one assumes that things like mountains and rivers really are mountains and rivers. In studying Pyrrhonism one learns that these are mental constructs. They are beliefs about the definitions about mountains and rivers. How big must a mountain need to be to be a mountain and not a hill? How big must a river be to be a river and not a brook? Then, after recognizing the fundamental baselessness of our intellectual categorizations, one goes back to the normal course of life, where we routinely deal with things such as mountains and rivers, but this time understanding the baselessness underneath all of our concepts.

Pyrrhonist indeterminacy is a way of looking at experience. It adds nothing to and takes nothing away from the raw data of physical and mental appearances. You look at appearances without concern whether there's truth to them. I call it "indeterminacy" because it is indeterminate about the nature of reality. It lacks the dogmas we usually add to the appearances in our process of making sense out of them. These are the theories and opinions we create and borrow to explain things. Although theories may have some utility in making predictions about future appearances, Pyrrho found that going beyond that, and using them to make truth claims, makes people anxious and disturbed.

Pyrrhonism requires attending to one's mind. It takes effort. I periodically find myself slipping, particularly if I'm tired and I am dealing with a disturbing topic. There's a Russian proverb: "The morning is wiser than the evening."

It is helpful to avoid making assertions. Remember aphasia (non-assertion). Try to make your points using questions.

Eudaimonia for Pyrrhonists is not what you may think. Ordinary life is the same for Pyrrhonists as it is for anyone. We experience pleasure and pain. There are things we want to have and things we want to avoid, just like everyone else experiences, but the feelings about pain and the not-getting are muted as there's no belief that these are by nature bad.

44
Pyrrhonism as a Path to Buddhism

No form, no words, no object of taste, or smell, or touch,
no other object of perception has any distinctive character.
*Anonymous ancient Pyrrhonist
or Academic Skeptic commentary
on the* Theaetetus[141]

Therefore in emptiness there is no form; no sensation,
perception, mental reaction, consciousness; no eye, ear,
nose, tongue, body, mind; no color, sound, smell, taste,
touch, object of thought; no seeing and so on to no
thinking....   *Maha Prajnaparamita Heart Sutra*

Just as Aenesidemus suggested that Pyrrhonism was a path to Heraclitean philosophy, Pyrrhonism can also be a path to understanding Buddhist philosophy. Understanding Pyrrhonism has greatly improved my understanding of Buddhism. People I've taught Pyrrhonism to have told me that Buddhism started making much more sense to them after they understood Pyrrhonism. While I don't expect Buddhist teachers to adopt Pyrrhonism, I do hope that they will find the ideas and techniques of Pyrrhonism to be useful in teaching Buddhism and helping their students. I attest that the cure by argument has worked better for me than meditation did. I know of no doctrinal reasons the cure by argument cannot fit comfortably in the Buddhist toolkit. Nagarjuna's probably-Pyrrhonist-inspired Madhyamaka philosophy is extremely similar to Pyrrhonism. Pyrrhonism can be viewed as just a useful formulation of that philosophy for working with Western-thinking minds. I already know of one Buddhist teacher, Vira Avalokita, who explicitly teaches Pyrrhonist techniques as Buddhist practices.

Towards helping people see Pyrrhonism as a path to understanding and practicing Buddhism, I've created Pyrrhonist adaptations of three famous Zen Buddhist texts, replacing the Buddhist terms with Pyrrhonist terms as demonstrations of this idea. These adaptations mostly emphasize the similarities between the Buddhist and Pyrrhonist perspectives, but in some cases, they point out differences between the Pyrrhonist

---

141 Thomas McEvilley, *The Shape of Ancient Thought*, p 419, also https://www.academia.edu/6394469/Anonymous_commentary_on_Platos_Theaetetus

and Buddhist approaches. The principle differences revolve around truth claims, mysticism, and paradox versus rationalism.

The Encounter with the Emperor

The Zen lineage considers its founder to be Bodhidharma, an Indian monk who traveled to China. Given the descriptions we have of Bodhidharma – blue eyes and red beard – it seems unlikely that he was ethnically Indian. Perhaps he descended from the Bactrian Greeks who converted to Buddhism after the Greeks lost control of western India. According to legend, the pivotal moment in which Bodhidharma started the Zen lineage was when he met Emperor Wu, which is recounted as an origination story of Zen. The Buddhist content of this story can easily be swapped out with Pyrrhonist content to say the same thing.

> Emperor Claudius once visited Alexandria, where he sought out Aenesidemus to ask him questions, having heard he was a sage.
>
> The Emperor asked Aenesidemus, "Since I came to the throne, I have built many temples and public works, written several learned treatises, and supported many philosophers. How great is the merit in all these?"
>
> Aenesidemus replied, "There's no evident merit."
>
> Claudius was surprised by this, but went on to ask his next question, "What is the essence of philosophy?"
>
> Aenesidemus replied, "It's acataleptic."
>
> Claudius, now annoyed, asked, "Who is it who is giving me such answers?"
>
> Aenesidemus replied, "I don't know."

A Pyrrhonist Xinxin Ming

At the beginning of this book we looked at the *Xinxin Ming*. It is among one of the most beloved and earliest Zen Buddhist texts. As an early Chinese expression of Zen Buddhism, it adapts Taoist terminology to the Buddhist concept of awakening, and it is said to be an expression of the essential unity of opposites and the basic nature of emptiness. You may recall from the chapter on Heraclitean philosophy that Heraclitus pointed out the unity of opposites and that Pyrrhonists think this is an observation anyone could make. You may also recall that Heraclitus used paradoxical statements much like one can find in Buddhism. So, like how Aenesidemus said that Pyrrhonism could be used as a path to understanding Heraclitean philosophy, in the same way we can see from looking at the

Xinxin Ming as a Pyrrhonist text that we can see Pyrrhonism as a path to understanding Buddhism. Remember all of those translations of the title?

- Inscribed on the Believing Mind
- Verses on the Faith Mind
- Inscription on Faith in Mind
- Inscription on Trust in the Mind
- Have Faith in Your Mind
- The Mind of Absolute Trust
- Trusting in Mind
- Affirming Faith in Mind
- Faith in Mind
- Trust in Mind
- Faith in Heart-and-Mind
- Faith Mind Sutra

Those all seem at best misleading and at worst blatantly wrong regarding what the poem is about. The poem is not about encouraging faith or trust as in belief; it is about trusting that one can think without dogma. The poem is medicine for curing minds of dogma. Do you suffer? Here, I have some verses for you. Take these verses repeatedly until you figure out that the cause of your suffering is dogma, and that what you need to do is to stop dogmatizing.

Here's the *Xinxin Ming* rendered using the language of Pyrrhonism and without the magical and religious wordings that were persuasive in the medieval era but are now off-putting.

Verses for the Dogmatic Mind

The Great Way is not complicated
For those who suspend judgment.
When inclinations are set aside
The Way stands clear and undisguised.

But even a slight inclination
Sets earth and heaven far apart.
If you wish to have ataraxia,
Discard opinions pro and con.

To founder in dislike and like
Is nothing but the mind's disease.
Not seeing how this comes about
Disturbs the mind's natural peace.

The Way feels perfect, like vast space,
Where there's no lack and no excess.
Our choice to assent to the non-evident
Prevents our eudaimonia.

Striving for dogmatic goals
In both the inner and outer worlds
Condemns us to psychological entanglements.
Just apply the cure by argument,
And all dogmas will depart.

The more you dogmatize,
The more you sever your link with the appearances.
When you give up dogmatizing
You will no longer encounter mental obstructions.

Focus on the evident and you will see the point.
Focus on the non-evident and you will miss it.
The moment you follow the non-evident
Ataraxia becomes far away.

Do not dwell in dogmatism.
Make sure you do not purse the non-evident.
The moment you judge good and bad,
Is the moment you lose your ataraxia.

Dogmatic views arise through indicative signs
Do not be stuck in dogmatism.
When to non-evident ideas one no longer inclines,
Everything will be just fine.

If there's a trace of dogmatism,
Equipollence is lost.
When dogmas are driven out,
Nothing in the world offends.

And when no pragmata can give offense,
Then all obstructions cease to be.
Once your dogmas disappear,
You no longer get in your own way.

For diaphora are diaphora because of mind,
As mind is mind because of diaphora.
These things are merely relative,
And both are acataleptic.

In acatalepsia these things are not two,
Yet in each are contained all appearances.
Once coarse and fine are seen no more,
Then how can there be inclinations?

The Great Way is unconstrained
By ideas of easy and hard.
But those who hold to dogmas
Are anxious and inflexible;
Their rash precipitancy just slows them down.

If you hold to dogmas,
You surely will go astray.
Both gain and loss, and right and wrong –
Once and for all get rid of them.

When you have ataraxia
You will be your natural self.
If you get caught up in thoughts of the non-evident,
You slip into a dream world.

To stick just with the appearances
Frees us from mental entanglements.
When all is seen with equipollence
To our natural selves we return.

This state of mind goes beyond
All dogmatic rationalizations.
Pyrrho's Path doesn't require any mystical experience:
No great truth, no ultimate finality, no mysterious source.

With natural mind one naturally finds the Way,
All dogmatic props to the ego fall away.
Perturbance and anxiety disappear,
And so ataraxia pervades our lives.

There is no dogma that clings to us,
Yet nothing is left behind.
Remaining in dogmatism,
You'll never know ataraxia.

And not to know equipollence
Lets conflict lead you far astray.
When you assert that appearances are the truth
You mistake ideas for reality.

But to assert that truth is inapprehensible,
Also misses the mark.
Cut off all useless theorizing
And the world opens up to you.

If you reify appearances
You overlook their source.
Do not go searching for some ultimate truth
Just let those fond opinions go.

Abide not in dogmatism,
Refrain from all pursuit of it.
Let go now of your beliefs,
And the appearances return to being appearances.

See that dogmatism clouds the way,
And you are in step with the Great Way.
But live in bondage to your beliefs,
And you will be confused and unclear.

This heavy burden weighs you down –
Why keep judging good and bad?
They do not exist by nature.

If you would walk the highest Way,
Do not deprecate the appearances.
For as it is, whole and complete,
Living with the appearances is eudaimonia.

The wise do not strive for dogmatic objectives,
But fools put themselves into such bondage.

The Great Way doesn't have those kinds of differences,
The foolish are inclined one way or another.

To seek ataraxia through theorizing about the non-evident
Has been shown to be a grave mistake.
From dogmatic mind comes rest and unrest,
But non-dogmatic mind transcends both.

Delusions spawn dogmas –
Theories are just castles in the sky –
Why work so hard at holding onto them?
The appearances are self-revealing, indeterminate, yet clear,
Without overlaying non-evident theories onto them.

Theorizing cannot reach this state,
Here the pathé are of no avail.
In this world of acatalepsia
Sharp definitions are no more.

In adiaphora all definitions blur into one
With nothing clearly separate from another thing.
This Way requires no mystic epiphany,
No paradoxical claims.

The appearances are right before your very eyes.
Nothing is more this than that.
If this in not yet clear to you,
You're still far from eudaimonia.

When doubt and mind are not separate,
And not separate are mind and doubt,
This is beyond all verbal constructs and theories.

The Heart of the Great Wisdom of Epoché Sutra

The best known and most popular text in Zen and all of Mahayana Buddhism is the *Maha Prajnaparamita Heart Sutra*. Its Sanskrit title, *Prajnaparamitahridaya*, can be translated as "The Heart of the Perfection of Wisdom." This text, too, can be converted to Pyrrhonist terms. One particularly interesting thing to note is how one of the most difficult to grasp Buddhist concepts, sunyata (emptiness), can be substituted with the Pyrrhonist concept of "epoché." This substitution is not novel.

In his translation of Nagarjuna's *Fundamental Wisdom of the Middle Way*, Nishijima Roshi renders "sunyata" as "balanced state" as he felt this was the best way to render the concept into English.

Pyrrho of Elis,
While practicing equipollence,
Looked upon pragmata
And seeing that they were adiaphora, astathmeta, and anepikrita
Said, "Here Timon,
Pragmata are all acataleptic.

"Our thoughts and sensations
Neither tell the truth, nor do they lie.
Here, Timon, all pragmata have no firm definitions.
They are not definable by creation or destruction,
By purity or defilement,
Completeness or deficiency.
Therefore, Timon, in epoché, we do not know form,
Perception, memory, nor consciousness.

"No sight, no sound, no smell, no taste, no touch, and
    no thought;
No theory, no causal chain
Has any characteristic we can be certain of.
Therefore, Timon, without dogmatizing about anything,
The wise ones take refuge in epoché
And live without walls of the mind
Without walls of the mind, and thus without fears,
They see through dogmas and find ataraxia.

"All skeptikoi past, present, and future
Also take refuge in epoché
And realize eudaimonia.
You should therefore know the procedure for epoché,
The procedure of great effectiveness,
The unexcelled procedure,
The procedure which heals all pathé.

"This is apparent to all who sincerely try it.
Therefore set forth the cure by argument.
Set forth this cure and say:

it no more is than it is not,
or it both is and is not,
or it neither is nor is not."

45

Pyrrhonism and the Art
of Motorcycle Maintenance

Great doubt, great awakening. Little doubt, little awakening. No doubt, no awakening.   *Zen proverb*

I went to Tiresias,[142] explained my case fully, and im-
plored him to give me his views upon the best life. He is
a blind little old man, pale and weak-voiced. He smiled
and said: "My son, the cause of your perplexity, I know,
is the fact that doctors differ; but I may not enlighten
you; Rhadamanthus[143] forbids." "Ah, say not so, father,"
I exclaimed; "speak out, and leave me not to wander
through life in a blindness worse than yours." So he drew
me apart to a considerable distance, and whispered in
my ear: "The life of the ordinary man is the best and
most prudent choice; cease from the folly of metaphysical speculation and inquiry into origins and ends, utterly
reject their clever logic, count all these things idle talk,
and pursue one end alone – how you may do what your
hand finds to do, and go your way with ever a smile and
never a troubling emotion."   *Lucian of Samosata,*
                                       Book of Necromancy

Robert M. Pirsig begins his famous book, *Zen and the Art of Motorcycle
Maintenance* with the following statement:

And what is good, Phaedrus,
And what is not good...
Need we ask anyone to tell us these things?

Deep in *Zen and the Art of Motorcycle Maintenance* Pirsig attempts to answer that question, starting with a discussion of *arete. Arete* is usually translated into English as "virtue" and occasionally as "excellence." These terms

---

142 A blind prophet of Apollo, famous for accurate clairvoyance and for being transformed
   into a woman for seven years.

143 One of the judges of the dead. The conversation takes place in Hades.

fail to reflect the full meaning of this term, which was central to the ancient Greek ethos. Homer describes *arete* in both the Greek and Trojan heroes and in female figures. In the Homeric poems, *arete* is frequently associated with bravery, but it more often is associated with effectiveness. The man or woman of *arete* is a person of the highest effectiveness. They use all their faculties – strength, bravery and wit – to achieve results. Arete involves all of the abilities and potentialities available to humans.

Pirsig describes how Plato demoted *arete* from its position of highest honor in Greek thinking to being in second place, after Truth, which Plato combined with the Good. That which is true is good; that which is good is true. Subordinating *arete* to the True and the Good set the stage for other philosophers to come up with arguments that *arete* should be demoted further within a "true" order of things. That's what Aristotle did. As Pirsig put it:

> Aristotle felt that the mortal horse of Appearance which ate grass and took people places and gave birth to little horses deserved far more attention than Plato was giving it. He said that the horse is not mere Appearance. The Appearances cling to something which is independent of them and which, like Ideas, is unchanging. The "something" that Appearances cling to he named "substance." And at that moment, and not until that moment, our modern scientific understanding of reality was born.

It is this part of Aristotle's philosophy that Pyrrho seems to have been reacting to in developing his own philosophy. Aristotle subordinated the appearances to a non-evident idea he named "substance" which was independent of the appearances. It is this "substance" that Pyrrho was likely most keen to point out was *adiaphora*, *astathmeta*, and *anepikrita* in order to return the appearances to their rightful status.

- *Adiaphora* (not differentiable by logical differentia, in other words, the use of logical categories for classifying the "substances" doesn't work. There are no clear ways of consistently classifying the elements of the "substances." Hence, undefinable, unclassifiable, uncategorizable, non-different, without distinguishing characteristics)
- *Astathmeta* (unstable, unbalanced, unmeasurable)
- *Anepikrita* (undecidable, unfixed, unjudged)

In other words, Aristotle said that behind the appearances there was some stable, unchanging, definable essence, which he called "substance." It is these substances that allow for things to be differentiated from each other. Pyrrho said Aristotle was wrong. Things cannot be differentiated on the basis of these "substances" because nothing has essence. Nothing is stable. We cannot accurately make the kinds of judgments that Aristotle claims we can make.

It was likely this idea of "substance" that Timon was reacting to in saying, "appearance is strong in every way, everywhere." Aristotle would have you believe the opposite, that it was the "substances" that were strong, in every way, everywhere, and that the appearances were just flimsy things that clung to the "substances."

Aristotle rearranged the hierarchy of philosophy to put "substances" into second place, after the True. Reason, logic, and knowledge became the primary concerns. He demoted the Good to a minor branch of knowledge called "ethics." This became the new Western worldview, and it survives to this day. *Arete* wasn't exactly "killed" as Pirsig claimed, but it was conspicuously absent from Aristotle's thinking and appears only as a minor topic in ethics. Replacing *arete* was a new goal: to create an endless proliferation of information about the "substances" and to call this "knowledge."

Pirsig, a former professor of rhetoric, particularly lamented the status of rhetoric in Aristotle's new hierarchy. Rhetoric, which was once the very essence of learning, was reduced by Aristotle to the teaching of mannerisms and forms. What Pirsig saw as the result was that the front-row students who were good at mimicking got their Aristotelian A's, whereas the students with real *arete* wondered what was wrong with themselves because they found that they could not like this so-called "rhetoric."

Writing in 1974, Pirsig notes that:

> …those few Universities that bother to teach classic ethics anymore, students, following the lead of Aristotle and Plato, endlessly play around with the question that in ancient Greece never needed to be asked: "What is the Good?" And how do we define it? Since different people have defined it differently, how can we know there is any good? Some say the good is found in happiness, but how do we know what happiness is? And how can happiness be defined? Happiness and good are not objective terms. We cannot deal with them scientifically. And since they aren't objective they just exist in your mind. So if you want to be happy just change your mind. Ha-ha, ha-ha.

"Change your mind." You may have heard that before. It has become a Buddhist slogan one can find on t-shirts and bumper stickers. Laughter aside, we seem to have two things we can change. One is our circumstances; the other is our minds. Both have limitations. Most people's knowledge and skill about changing their circumstances seems to be greater than their knowledge and skill about changing their minds, but our potential ability to change our minds greatly exceeds our potential ability to change our circumstances.

Not only does Buddhism aim to change minds, so too do the Hellenistic philosophies of life. Perhaps that's why, starting about a generation after the publication of *Zen and the Art of Motorcycle Maintenance,* a popular revival of the Hellenistic philosophies would arise – outside the universities, which in the twentieth century somehow mostly lost their ability to teach classical ethics, into which the Hellenistic philosophies had been subsumed. It seems no surprise that among the various Hellenistic philosophies that are being revived, it is the highly virtue-centric Stoicism that has by far achieved the greatest interest. Stoicism is perhaps second only to its philosophical forebear, Cynicism, in its focus on virtue. Cynicism, however, places extraordinary ascetic demands on its adherents, which limits its appeal.

Sextus said that the practice of Pyrrhonism makes it "…possible to seem to live rightly ('rightly' being taken, not as referring only to *arete*, but in a more ordinary sense)…." Pyrrhonism puts *arete* back into its original place, no longer subordinate to that unsupportable Aristotelian idea of Truth. It uses rhetoric – the art of argument – as its principal tool for achieving this end. It does so without falling into the relativism of the Sophists (or the Post-Modernists), the nihilism of the negative dogmatists, or the rash conceit of the dogmatists. As no criterion of truth can be demonstrated, there's no firm ground for truth to stand on. Truth with a capital T is disempowered of its ability to subordinate anything. Pyrrhonism allows us to pursue arete and eudaimonia, free from the tyranny of the hobgoblins of dogma.

Pyrrhonism changes your mind.

Pirsig seemed to get close to what Pyrrho saw as what was fundamentally wrong with Aristotle's philosophy, identifying many of the same problems that Pyrrhonism does.

In another section of *Zen and the Art of Motorcycle Maintenance* Pirsig notes how yes or no, this or that, zero or one represent the discrimination upon which all of knowledge is built. Then he reports his glimpse into the philosophical space where Pyrrhonism resides:

Because we're unaccustomed to it, we don't usually see that there's a third possible logical term equal to yes and no which is capable of expanding our understanding in an unrecognized direction. We don't even have a term for it, so I'll have to use the Japanese mu.

Mu means "no thing." Like "Quality" it points outside the process of dualistic discrimination. Mu simply says, "No class; not one, not zero, not yes, not no.'" It states that the context of the question is such that a yes or no answer is in error and should not be given....

Pirsig's use of "mu" here comes from his experience working on the Zen koan "Joshu's Mu." A koan is something like a case study that the koan student is given by their Zen teacher. There are thousands of recorded koans. The koan is designed to help trigger an insight for the student. The answer the student gives is the insight they have on the koan. Joshu's Mu is commonly the first koan given to a beginning Zen koan student. The koan is:

A monk asked Joshu, "Does a dog have Buddha-nature or not?"
Joshu replied, "Mu."

This is the "mu" to which Pirsig is referring. It is indeed a word in Japanese, and it comes from a similar word in Chinese. But Pirsig's understanding of it was not correct from a Zen perspective. Early in working on the mu koan with my Zen teacher, James Ishmael Ford (Zeno Myoun, Roshi) – co-author with Melissa Myozen Blacker, Roshi of *The Book of Mu: Essential Writings on Zen's Most Important Koan* – I once brought up Pirsig's discussion of mu. He immediately swept it aside, saying that Pirsig did not know what he was talking about.

Eventually I gave an answer to the mu koan that my teacher accepted. And, yes, what Pirsig says about mu isn't relevant to the koan. It's not as Pirsig wrote, that Buddha nature cannot be captured by yes or no questions. That's not what Joshu was talking about.

The "great secret" about koans, according to James Ford Roshi is:

...that they point to the twin truths of our lives, that we are at once unique, if temporary, and completely bound up in a great play of things that can be named one or empty, but which is something that cannot ever be fully captured; well, then it is possible to think one's way to the answers. Despite what some who haven't engaged them might think, or, write, they are the essence of logical.[144]

Pyrrhonism is also the essence of logical. While it is not cloaked in mystery like koans are, it has unfortunately been cloaked in disinformation. Pyrrhonism also points to the twin aspects of our lives. Within the realm of the appearances we have the experience of being unique, albeit transient, yet all that we experience takes place within an acataleptic reality.

Mu and koans aside, Pirsig was however hot on the trail of something important. It's something that has turned out to be far more important to me than the mu koan, and it is something relevant to understanding the importance of Pyrrhonism.

Pirsig goes on to say:

> That mu exists in the natural world investigated by science is evident. It's just that, as usual, we're trained not to see it by our heritage. For example, it's stated over and over again that computer circuits exhibit only two states, a voltage for "one'" and a voltage for "zero.'" That's silly!
>
> Any computer-electronics technician knows otherwise. Try to find a voltage representing one or zero when the power is off! The circuits are in a mu state. They aren't at one, they aren't at zero, they're in an indeterminate state that has no meaning in terms of ones or zeros.

Mu is evident. It is an indeterminate state. This way of seeing things should now sound familiar.

Pirsig continues:

> The dualistic mind tends to think of mu occurrences in nature as a kind of contextual cheating, or irrelevance, but mu is found throughout all scientific investigation, and nature doesn't cheat, and nature's answers are never irrelevant.

The dualistic mind is the mind attached to dogmas. It believes things must be one way or the other. It has great difficulty when the appearances don't conform to the dogmas.

---

144 http://www.patheos.com/blogs/monkeymind/2017/08/great-way-not-difficult-zens-koans-way-broken-heart.html#Ek21A6z6fTRA1is1.99

Pirsig seems to lose the scent for a while in his discussion, focusing on the relevance to mu to scientific inquiry, then he picks up the scent again.

> Mu is the "phenomenon'" that inspires scientific enquiry in the first place! There's nothing mysterious or esoteric about it. It's just that our culture has warped us to make a low value judgment of it.

That "phenomenon" – and the scare quotes are Pirsig's – derives from the same Greek word the ancient Greek Pyrrhonists used for the appearances. While the phenomenon may seem mysterious or esoteric to the mind full of delusions, full of dogma, it is not actually so. It's right here, before one's very eyes.

When we stick closely to the appearances, we do pretty well using binary discrimination. We're generally accurate about what we know and don't know about the appearances. We make some mistakes, but our minds are seldom troubled in these things. If one mistakes a rope for a snake and is startled by it, one is not upset about this the next day. We accumulate know-how that makes us effective. Our problems are when we venture into the non-evident. Our minds want to continue to use the binary discrimination that works so well for us with what is evident and apply it to the non-evident. It's a good hammer. The nails go in well. Let's use it on the screws!

But the non-evident properly belongs to the third logical term that Pirsig calls "mu." Pirsig claims it is "no class; not one, not zero, not yes, not no." Remember what Pyrrho said: "it no more is than it is not, or it both is and is not, or it neither is nor is not." The logical term is properly identified as indeterminacy. The ancient Pyrrhonist term for it is "acata-lepsia," which means that which cannot be intellectually grasped. Each of us appears to be a metaphorical voltmeter reading into the non-evident and wanting to project onto it a binary reading. Human minds do not seem to like indeterminacy, so they reflexively sweep it under a dogmatic rug of binary, dualistic thinking.

Pirsig saw that there was something foundationally wrong in Plato and Aristotle. He saw that it involved the appearances, dogma, indeter-minacy, *arete*, rhetoric, and the evident and the non-evident. I wonder if he had read Sextus at the right time whether he might have had the same epiphany I had.

Pirsig did, however, write about having read Poincaré. What Pirsig relates about Poincaré indicates that Poincaré was getting close to the same insight that Pyrrho had. As Pirsig said about him:

Poincare's contemporaries refused to acknowledge that facts are preselected because they thought that to do so would destroy the validity of scientific method. They presumed that "preselected facts" meant that truth is "whatever you like" and called his ideas conventionalism. They vigorously ignored the truth that their own "principle of objectivity" is not itself an observable fact…and therefore by their own criteria should be put in a state of suspended animation.

They felt they had to do this because if they didn't, the entire philosophic underpinning of science would collapse. Poincare didn't offer any resolutions of this quandary. He didn't go far enough into the metaphysical implications of what he was saying to arrive at the solution. What he neglected to say was that the selection of facts before you "observe" them is "whatever you like" only in a dualistic, subject-object metaphysical system!

Note the fear that "truth" might be "whatever you like;" the discomfort with accepting convention; the state of denial that that the principle of objectivity is non-evident, and that by their own criteria judgment should be suspended. Again, Pirsig hones in on the relevant parts of the problem. He sensed that the entire philosophic underpinning of the dogma accepted by the modern world was ready to collapse.

He was right. His alter ego, Phaedrus, found himself drawn towards Plato's old nemeses, the Sophists. It's important to note that it was Plato who created the category of "philosophers" to differentiate them from the "sophists." As far as others were concerned at the time, Plato and Socrates were sophists and it was only Plato making this distinction. Some sophists then were hacks, just as some people calling themselves "philosophers" these days are also hacks. Plato's key distinction between the terms seemed to be about the degree to which one was connected to Socrates or agreed with Plato. In Pirsig's telling, the Aristotelians staffing what Phaedrus describes as the "Church of Reason" had never seen a real live Sophist such as Phaedrus – i.e., someone who profoundly disagreed with Plato and Aristotle. Pirsig identified the heart of the disagreement as deriving from his anti-Platonic stance:

I have never seen a fatal argument against the Metaphysics of Quality. Most academic philosophers ignore it, or badmouth it quietly and I wondered why that was.

I suspect it may have something to do with my insistence that Quality not be defined. I was asked recently to write a preface to a book on Plato. I remembered a quote from Alfred North Whitehead which read: "The first thing you can learn about western philosophy is that it is all footnotes to Plato." MoQ was not that. Plato and Socrates insisted on all terms being defined. If you start with a term that is undefined, like quality, it is no longer a footnote to Plato.[145]

In his 1984 afterword, Pirsig said that what made *Zen and the Art of Motorcycle Maintenance* so unique could be described by the Swedish concept of *kulturbärare*, which he translated as "culture bearer" – a concept or person who upholds or moves a culture forward. Pirsig did not think that the success of his book hinged on literary merit, nor did he think that the ideas in it changed society. Rather, the book arrived at the exact moment where cultural attitudes had started shifting and the ideas in the book helped to crystalize the shift.

His book was indeed a culture bearer. It heralded that the foundations of the West's Aristotelian worldview were vulnerable to erosion from below, and that they were subject to giving way. In the early twenty-first century, we are experiencing that happen. The news used to carry Aristotelian knowledge. Now the media seem to be mostly about conveying opinions.

One of the seeming paradoxes of Pyrrhonist "inquiryism" is its devotion to continual inquiry along with its simultaneous expectation that it is unlikely to find truth. Some people argue that this is ridiculous. Why should anyone continue to inquire if the inquiry is pointless? But isn't this conclusion that it is pointless just a projection from the human voltmeter? That's looking at it as if the only thing worthwhile was Truth. But Pyrrhonism dethrones truth, putting *arete* back into its rightful place. It is through non-dogmatic inquiry that *arete* is achieved: living rightly, excellence, eudaimonia, and ataraxia. To live rightly, to enjoy ataraxia and eudaimonia, means to live effectively. What is getting in the way of these things is dogmatism. Rather than forcing the world into a procrustean bed of true and false, we must embrace the indeterminacy of our experience if we want to live well.

The early twenty-first century finds *arete* under attack. In the West, the values of the ancient Greeks have waxed and waned over the centuries. In this early part of the twenty-first century they seem to be waning, with

---

145 "Zen and the art of Robert Pirsig", *The Guardian*, 18 Nov 2006. https://www.theguardian.com/theobserver/2006/nov/19/features.review87

attitudes towards *arete* being a major fault line in the culture war going on in the West. A few generations ago, almost every educated Westerner would have read Homer. Many would have known by heart this famous line from the *Iliad*, spoken by Glaucus:

> Hippolochus begat me, and I claim to be his son. He sent me to Troy, and often gave me this command, to strive always for the highest arete, and to excel all others.

These days thoughts like this are alien to many Westerners. They do not see *arete* as the principle thing to strive for. Instead, they think of other things, such as equality and diversity. Those are contrary to *arete*. If everyone is equal, excellence cannot exist. *Arete* cannot exist. If diversity is defined as the good, then *arete* can no longer define what is excellent.

Pirsig was right that the problems were in the foundations created by Aristotle and Plato. He was right that they were vulnerable to assault. Our societal problem is about how to fix those foundation stones.

46

The Stoics

But if Epictetus[146] combats indolence, he leads to pride,
so that he may be very injurious....   *Pascal*

'Tis pride, rank pride, and haughtiness of soul; I think
the Romans call it "Stoicism."   *Joseph Addison*

Most of the people I've encountered who have become Pyrrhonists have tried either Buddhism or Stoicism first – and often both. Because of Pyrrhonism's philosophical similarities with Buddhism, Pyrrhonism fits comfortably with Buddhism, with many people seeing it as an alternative form of Buddhist practice. The opposite is the case with Stoicism. The two philosophies are fundamentally antithetical. Indeed, at the time Sextus was writing he described the Stoics as being currently the Pyrrhonists' chief opponents.[147]

Most of the Pyrrhonist arguments we have from antiquity against specific dogmas are against Stoic dogmas. Some of these Pyrrhonist arguments against the Stoics point out things the early Stoics upheld that were embarrassing to the later Stoics, such as arguments from Zeno and Chrysippus in favor of incest and cannibalism, or that it was okay for a man to cohabit with a prostitute and to live off of her earnings, or that the women of a city should be held as communal property by the men.[148]

Ancient Stoicism contained extensive dogmas about how the physical world works, what we would today call "science." Because most of these dogmas are now obviously and sometimes laughably erroneous, modern Stoicism has largely jettisoned nearly everything from Stoic philosophy except for its ethical dogmas and its spiritual practices – practices some people call "life hacks." While these spiritual practices are today commonly assumed to be unique to Stoicism, this was not the case in antiquity. For example, one of the famous Stoic practices, the *premeditatio malorum* ("the pre-meditation of evils"), was developed by the Cyrenaics prior to the advent of Stoicism.[149] The Stoics simply adopted this hedonist practice

---

146 The teacher of Stoic philosophy whose works are one of our best surviving accounts of ancient Stoicism.

147 Sextus Empiricus, *Outlines of Pyrrhonism*, Book I, section 65.

148 Sextus Empiricus, *Outlines of Pyrrhonism*, Book III section 205.

149 Cicero, *Tusculan Disputations*, Book III, 13-14.

because it works. It's unknown how many other spiritual practices now considered "Stoic" were just practices that were found to be useful, without any inherent connection to Stoic philosophy.[150] What is important to note is that these practices are not dogmas; they are techniques. These practices can be useful for anybody, regardless of their philosophy or religion, as they require no beliefs. They're just things that people have found to be helpful.

Here are a few of the Stoic dogmas that modern Stoics find embarrassing:

- All physical objects are made up of earth, air, fire, and water.[151]
- The gods have foreknowledge that is revealed to humans by oracles.[152]
- The sun is fed by the sea. The moon is fed by fresh waters. The stars are fed by the earth.[153]
- The earth is immovable.[154]
- The seed of the female is unproductive because it is devoid of tone, small in quantity, and watery.[155]
- The universe is deterministic. Everything happens according to fate.[156]

These days nearly everyone thinks these dogmas are either false or impossible to substantiate – which is what the ancient Pyrrhonists said about them. Unfortunately, modern Stoicism clings to ancient Stoic ethical dogmas that the Pyrrhonists also long ago refuted. These dogmas include:

- The only good is moral good, and the only evil is moral evil.
- Pleasure is not a good and pain is not an evil.
- Faults committed against us cannot touch us.
- He who commits a fault hurts only himself.
- We can suffer no harm whatsoever from the actions of anyone else.
- People are the authors of their own problems.[157]

Presently one can find many people who are firmly committed to the belief that all of these are true. Although a thorough refutation of Stoic ethical dogmas is beyond the scope of this book, some examples of refutations are worth illustrating. Whole books could be written refuting Stoic dogma.

---

150 For more on this see John Seller's discussion of "Stoic" first-aid at https://modern-stoicism.com/two-types-of-stoic-therapy-by-john-sellars/

151 Diogenes Laertius, *Life of Zeno*, 136.

152 Cicero, *On Divination*, II.63.

153 Diogenes Laertius, *Life of Zeno*, 71.

154 Diogenes Laertius, *Life of Zeno*, 71.

155 Diogenes Laertius, *Life of Zeno*, 85.

156 Aulus Gellius, *Attic Nights*, Book 7 section 2.

157 Pierre Hadot, *The Inner Citadel: The Meditations of Marcus Aurelius*, pp. 36-43.

Indeed, that would largely describe several of the books written by Sextus Empiricus. Perhaps someday this shall be done again, as Zen Buddhists vow: "Delusions are inexhaustible. I vow to end them."

One Stoic dogma that is still held, but seldom spoken of, is the dogma of *katalepsis*. According to the Stoics, the mind is constantly being bombarded with impressions. Some of these are true and some false. Impressions are true when they are truly affirmed, false if they are wrongly affirmed, such as when one believes an oar dipped in the water to be broken because it appears so. Believing that the mind instinctively discriminates between real and false impressions, the Stoics say that one ought not to give credit to everything which is perceived, but only to those perceptions which contain some special mark of those things which appeared. Such a perception is called a *kataleptic phantasia*. The *kataleptic phantasia* is that which is impressed by an object which exists, which is a copy of that object, and can be produced by no other object.

A famous refutation of *katalepsis* was made by King Ptolemy Philopator of Egypt, who employed the Stoic philosopher Sphaerus as a court philosopher. Sphaerus had studied Stoicism under both Zeno and Cleanthes. During a discussion of the question of whether a wise man would allow himself to be guided by opinion, the king arranged for his servants to offer Sphaerus some fake pomegranates made of wax. Sphaerus fell for the ploy and bit into a wax pomegranate, upon which the king shouted, "ah ha, you've given in to a false impression!"[158]

As was discussed at length in this book's chapter on the criterion of truth, one simply cannot make the kinds of truth claims the Stoics assert to, based on their dogma of *katalepsis*. The Stoics' rash conclusions that they know the truth cause them to make all sorts of mistakes – mistakes far worse than biting into wax pomegranates. Stoic dogmas cause errors of moral judgment. According to Stoic dogma, virtue is the only good. Wealth, health, pleasure, and anything else are indifferent. Another king demonstrated the flaw in this dogma by playing another trick on another Stoic philosopher. King Antigonus II Gonatas, who was so widely known as a great patron of philosophy that the Indian King Ashoka once sent a contingent of Buddhist philosophers to his court – a contingent we have no record of arriving at their destination[159] – once invited Zeno, the founder of Stoicism, to come to his court in Macedon. Zeno was too old and frail to make the journey, so he sent his favorite and most eminent student, Persaeus, author of a dozen books on Stoicism. Persaeus subsequently became an important figure at the court. One day

158 Diogenes Laertius, *Life of Sphaerus*.

159 *Edicts of Ashoka*, 13th Rock Edict, S. Dhammika.

Antigonus tested Persaeus by having a messenger deliver false news to the court that Persaeus' estate had been ravaged by the enemy. Upon hearing the news, Persaeus was visibly saddened. The king, pointing out Persaeus' gloominess, remarked, "you see that wealth is not a matter of indifference."[160] Sometime after this incident Persaeus stopped working as a philosopher. He went into government, with the king making him the ruler of Corinth. Apparently, the king successfully persuaded Persaeus that wealth and power were not matters of indifference.

Before this, Persaeus had been Zeno's most eminent student.[161] Like most of Zeno's other students, he appears to have been unwilling to continue with Stoicism. Consequently, Zeno ended up having to choose his notoriously dull-witted student Cleanthes as his successor.[162] Zeno said that having him as a student was like writing upon a tablet of hard wax: it's done with difficulty, but it retains what is written upon it. Indeed, it appears that Cleanthes was the only one of Zeno's students who wanted to carry on the school as Zeno envisioned it. Not only does it appear that Persaeus left, but most of Zeno's other eminent disciples disagreed with Zeno about virtue being the only good. His disciple Herillus considered knowledge to be the chief good. Zeno's disciple Dionysius completely deserted the Stoa and declared that pleasure was good.[163] Zeno's disciple Aristo thought that the chief good was to live in perfect indifference to all those things which are of an intermediate character between virtue and vice. He also thought that natural philosophy was beyond current understanding and that the wise man would hold no opinions – a position Persaeus argued against. We know that Timon praised Aristo,[164] presumably for eschewing dogmatizing, and this is probably why Cicero thought that Pyrrho and Aristo held similar philosophies.

Just as most of Zeno's original disciples ended up disagreeing with Zeno, one can observe wide-spread disagreement among Stoics today. One major disagreement is about whether Stoic theology should be retained or discarded. Another major disagreement is about what the Stoic virtue of justice is in practice, with the lines of disagreement reflecting current political ideas of justice. As the Stoics wildly disagree among themselves over fundamental issues of, as Sextus Empiricus put it, "their so-called 'philosophy,'" why should anyone believe in the remaining dogmas they don't happen to be disagreeing about at this time?

---

160 Diogenes Laertius, *Life of Zeno*, 31.

161 Diogenes Laertius, *Life of Zeno*, 36.

162 Diogenes Laertius, *Life of Cleanthes*, 3.

163 Diogenes Laertius, *Life of Zeno*, 36.

164 Diogenes Laertius, *Life of Aristo*.

Contemplate for a moment what affect there might be on temperament or personality due to believing in and acting upon both *katalepsis* and the dogma of virtue being the only good. If hubris or arrogance come to mind, that would concur with what people have pointed out about Stoicism from the very beginning. Timon, who was a contemporary of Zeno, criticized Zeno for his pride.[165] The biography we have of Zeno describes him as having a morose and bitter countenance, with a constantly frowning expression.[166] The biography we have of Chrysippus – arguably the most influential and important philosopher among all of the ancient heads of the Stoic school – says he was a man of exceeding arrogance.[167]

Hubris and arrogance would seem to be a predictable result of combining the beliefs that one can have certain knowledge, that one can be certain about virtue, and that one can focus on virtue as the only good. This is not to say that it is a necessary result. For example, modern practitioners of what is known as "Traditional" Stoicism, which preserves the pantheistic dogmas of ancient Stoicism, in contrast to the atheism of "Modern" Stoicism, use this element of the philosophy – that the entire universe is divine, conscious, and rational – to curb tendencies toward pride, although even this is not without problems. It's all too easy for people to justify their beliefs and actions as being the divine will of Zeus, or the will of the *logos*.

Regardless, Stoicism has much worth investigating. Their spiritual practices are useful. Even some of the dogmas, when reinterpreted to be heuristics for making decisions, can have some practical utility. The same can be said for Epicureanism, Platonism, Peripateticism, Cyrenaicism, Academic Skepticism, and other Hellenistic philosophies. It is particularly useful in investigating these philosophies to see how their dogmas contradict one another, as this leads to epoché, and epoché leads to ataraxia.

---

165 Diogenes Laertius, *Life of Zeno*, 14.

166 Diogenes Laertius, *Life of Zeno*, 16.

167 Diogenes Laertius, *Life of Chrysippus*, 8.

....

47
Are We There Yet?

And now I will be off to metamorphose myself. When
we next meet, there will be no long, shaggy beard, no
artificial composure;[168] I shall be natural, as a gentleman
should. I may go as far as a fashionable coat, by way
of publishing my renunciation of nonsense. I only wish
there were an emetic that would purge out every doctrine they have instilled into me; I assure you, if I could
reverse Chrysippus's plan with the hellebore,[169] and drink
forgetfulness, not of the world but of Stoicism, I would
not think twice about it. Well, Lycinus, I owe you a debt
indeed; I was being swept along in a rough turbid tor-
rent, unresisting, drifting with the stream; when lo, you
stood there and fished me out, a true *deus ex machina*.[170]

Lucian of Samosata,
Hermotimus

Just as cathartic drugs flush themselves out along with
the various materials in the body, so these arguments
apply to themselves .... *Sextus Empiricus,*
Outlines of Pyrrhonism

Regarding that search for eudaimonia we began with, has it occurred to
you yet that eudaimonia is a non-evident idea?

The past exists only as memories. The future exists only as thoughts.
The appearances at the present moment are the closest thing we have to
reality. The motorcycle that you are aware of is just a mnemonic sign in
your head. That's where all those indicative signs are, too. The appearances
precede the intellectualization used to turn appearances into signs. Everything we think we know comes from the appearances. Because modern
education trains people to focus on abstractions, this simple fact is easy to

---

168 Philosophers in the Greco-Roman world had a characteristic appearance that included
a beard and a plain toga, much like how Buddhist monks distinguish themselves with
a robe and a shaved head.

169 An ancient drug.

170 Literally "machine of the gods." Equipment used in the theater to allow gods to
swoop in and save people.

overlook and to forget in our reflexive urge to quickly turn everything into an intellectual form. This is perhaps why dogmatism is such a widespread disease among intellectuals, why it turns them into idiots, and why the inability to perceive the cause of this disease is so pervasive. The appearances end up being considered to be an unimportant and uneventful step on the path from reality to that stuff we think of as reality – what is in our minds. We then get so attached to what is in our minds that we stop considering whether the appearances are in any way different from our intellectual conceptions of them.

Above the tree line, near the summit, the Pyrrhonist path meets the Zen path. All intellectualizations are set aside so that the appearances can be appreciated in their pure form. However that happens, the trance of the signs is broken, and one sees that all the stories we tell ourselves – our dogmas – aren't really what's there.

Those who are familiar with the Zen literature will notice that in the opening lines of this book I took a famous phrase from Dogen and recast it to be Pyrrhonist. I'll close by doing that again here with another one of Dogen's famous phrases summarizing his experience studying the Buddhadharma.

> Before I started studying philosophy, mountains were mountains and rivers were rivers.
>
> After I started studying philosophy, mountains were no longer mountains and rivers were no longer rivers. They were atoms and void; manifestations of a rational, universal logos; form and emptiness; and something I could not step into twice.
>
> After I came to study Pyrrho's Way, mountains were again mountains, and rivers were again rivers.

Book VI
The Emperor and the Pyrrhonist

48
Sextus Empiricus of Chaeronea

Everything we hear is an opinion, not a fact. Everything
we see is a perspective, not the truth. *Marcus Aurelius*[171]

Seldom, very seldom, does complete truth belong to any
human disclosure; seldom can it happen that something
is not a little disguised, or a little mistaken. *Jane Austen*

The Marcus Aurelius quote that begins this chapter is wildly popular
and frequently repeated, much to the consternation of present-day
Stoics, because not only is it not authentic, it represents a view that's contrary to Stoicism – a Pyrrhonist view. The quote appears to have originated in a paraphrase of the *Meditations* done by Dan Joseph and published
on SpiritSite.com.[172] So, while this quote is not in the *Meditations*, the
paraphraser felt it was, and the many readers of the *Meditations* who have
cited the quote seem to feel it's there, too. Not in those exact words, but in
sentiment. This chapter explores how that may have come about through
Marcus having been substantially influenced by Sextus Empiricus.[173]

First, it's useful to reflect on whether Marcus Aurelius can be either
confidently or thoroughly considered a Stoic. Brad Inwood, in *Stoicism:
A Very Short Introduction*, says this about the philosophy of Marcus
Aurelius:

> The emperor was not a professional philosopher and
> sometimes expresses views that conflict with what we
> know about the school from other sources. Some schol-
> ars even question whether it is right to count him as a
> Stoic at all; after all, he credits philosophers from others'
> schools with inspiring his thought and even refers to
> Stoics in the third person (Stoics are "they" not "we")....

---

171 It is perhaps a meaningful coincidence that this quote itself is not a fact. It's just an
     opinion about what Marcus said. See the first paragraph of this chapter for a full
     explanation.

172 http://www.spiritsite.com/writing/maraur/part1.shtml

173 I dedicate this chapter the late Matthew Neale Ph.D., who introduced me to the ar-
     gument that Sextus Empiricus and Sextus of Chaeronea were the same person based
     on Sextus' biography in the *Suda*, which inspired me to investigate further.

For Marcus, Stoic philosophy is often held at arm's
length, as it is by many of us.[174]

Cassius Dio, the Roman historian and contemporary of Marcus Aurelius,
said this about Marcus' philosophy:

> Marcus Antoninus, the philosopher, upon obtaining the
> throne at the death of Antoninus, his adoptive father,
> had immediately taken to share his power [with] Lucius
> Verus, the son of Lucius Commodus. For he was frail in
> body himself and devoted the greater part of his time to
> letters. Indeed it is reported that even when he was em-
> peror he showed no shame or hesitation about resorting
> to a teacher, but became a pupil of Sextus, the Boeotian
> philosopher, and did not hesitate to attend the lectures
> of Hermogenes on rhetoric; but he was most inclined to
> the doctrines of the Stoic school.

Note "most inclined." That's indeed what one sees in the *Meditations*: a
writer with a broad interest in philosophy who is simply most inclined
to Stoicism. The idea that Marcus might not have been fully Stoic an-
noys some present-day Stoics. They want to paint him to be as thor-
oughgoing of a Stoic as Epictetus and Musonius Rufus. But those two
writers were teachers. Men such as Marcus and Seneca had to deal with
a variety of different people and to be effective in society. They could not
afford to be as dismissive and abusive of other philosophies as Epictetus was. They needed be respectful in dealing with people who thought
differently. This respect is visible in their philosophical writings, which
treat ideas from other philosophies charitably. Indeed, in the *Meditations*, Marcus approvingly cites more non-Stoic philosophers than he
does Stoic philosophers.

Marcus tells us a little about his philosophy teachers in the first book
of the *Meditations*. Several of these teachers are known not to be Stoics.
Marcus himself tells us that he appreciates philosophies other than Stoicism and is grateful to philosophers who are not Stoics. Marcus had a
keen interest in philosophy, and the resources of the empire at his disposal.
Surely, he had access to and considered Pyrrhonist perspectives. I not only
think that this happened, but that the "Sextus" of whom Marcus was a pu-
pil is the same Sextus as Sextus Empiricus, and that Pyrrhonist influences
appear in the *Meditations*.

---

174 Chapter 2.

Part of our current uncertainty about whether these two Sextuses are the same person is due to how names were used in ancient Rome. In that naming system, each man had a name composed of three and sometimes four parts. One part is what we would call a first name, which was given to them at birth by their parents. This was the person's "praenomen." Unfortunately, only a couple of dozen praenomen were in common use, so praenomen were not good ways of identifying anyone. Another part of the naming convention was the "nomen," which designated one's clan or family. Unfortunately these too tended to be common. Therefore, many people shared the same combination of praenomen and nomen, especially over time, as families tended to repeatedly use the same praenomen over generations. The third part was the "cognomen." The cognomen was a nickname, usually reflecting some distinguishing characteristic of the person. Some people also had a fourth name, an "agnomen," which was an additional nickname which reflected the holder's personality, physique, or achievements. This resulted in a messy naming convention in which the same person could be referred to by one name by one writer and another name by another writer. Already in this chapter you've seen an example of this. Marcus Aurelius and Marcus Antoninus (which is the name Cassius Dio used in the quote above) are the same person, but if one didn't know better one would think that they were two different people. This messiness produces many problems in understanding ancient Roman history because of uncertainties about whether two similar names refer to two different people or to the same person because of the different naming conventions different writers used.

We know almost nothing about Sextus Empiricus, except for his philosophy. We know that "Sextus" was his praenomen and "Empiricus" was a cognomen indicating that he was a physician practicing in the Empiric school of medicine. Pyrrhonism was closely aligned with the Empiric school. Many teachers in the Empiric school were also Pyrrhonist teachers. So the cognomen "Empiricus" adds some useful information in the context of teaching Pyrrhonism. We know that Sextus was at one time the head of the Pyrrhonist school. We don't know where he lived, but based on a reference he made to Athens it appears that he had once been there, but was not writing from there. And if he was not in Athens, then it seems likely he was in one of the other two main centers of Roman intellectual life in that era: Rome or Alexandria. We know that Sextus was Greek because of statements he makes comparing the morals of ethnic groups in which he uses "we" to mean the Greeks.

We know quite a bit about Sextus of Chaeronea, except for his philosophy. We know who he was related to, that he lived in Rome, and that his cognomen or adnomen was a reference to where he was born, as few residents of Rome would have been born in the small town of Chaeronea, in Boeotia, a region of Greece.

The question is whether these are two different philosophers who share a common praenomen, or one philosopher named Sextus who was distinguished by both a cognomen and an agnomen – one for his unusual profession and one for his unusual place of birth.

The *Suda*, a 10th-century Byzantine encyclopedia of the ancient Mediterranean world that drew upon ancient sources now lost to us gives a clear answer to this question. Sextus Empiricus and Sextus of Chaeronea are the same person.

> A Chaeroneian, a nephew of Plutarch, born in the time of Caesar Marcus Antoninus; a philosopher, and a student of Herodotus of Philadelphia [a teacher of both Pyrrhonism and Empiric medicine]. He adhered to the teachings of Pyrrho and was so esteemed by the emperor that he sat in judgement with him. He wrote *Ethica* and ten books.
>
> [Marcus Antoninus]…emperor of [the] Romans, the philosopher admirable in every respect. He attended the lectures of many different [instructors], but ultimately ended up as a student of Sextus, a philosopher from Boeotia, in Rome itself, seeking him out and going to [his] house. A certain rhetorician named Lucius, an associate of the rhetorician Herodes Atticus, asked him, as he was going out, where he was going and why. And Marcus responded, "[It is] good even for an aging man to learn. I am on my way to Sextus the philosopher to learn things I do not yet know." And Lucius lifted up his hand to heaven and said "o Helios, the emperor of Rome in his old age is still taking up his slate and going to his teacher's house. But my king Alexander died at thirty-two."[175]

The *Suda* has many errors in it, and many scholars believe that this is an error. Yet in my research I've yet to encounter an explanation about why it should be considered an error. For example in the otherwise apparently carefully-researched book, *Sextus Empiricus: The Transmission and Recovery of Pyrrhonism*, Luciano Floridi states, completely without any substantiation, that identifying Sextus Empiricus with Sextus of Chaeronea

---

175 See *Suda Online* for a searchable online version of the entire text here: https://www.cs.uky.edu/~raphael/sol/sol-html/

"is almost certainly erroneous."[176] I not only don't agree, I think the identification is probably correct, which I demonstrate in the remainder of this chapter. For some readers, this demonstration may be tedious and uninteresting. Readers who are willing to accept this conclusion and who are uninterested in such a demonstration may skip to the next chapter.

The first reason to suspect that the two are the same person is that while Sextus of Chaeronea is well attested as having been a famous philosopher, we have no details about what he taught, no books, no quotes. We know who he was but not what he did. Identifying him by his place of birth is about who he was. The opposite is the case for Sextus Empiricus. We know almost nothing about his identity, but he left us many books. We know what he did, but we don't know who he was. Identifying him by his profession is about what he did. The names the authors chose to identify Sextus appear to fit with what they want to say about Sextus and not necessarily any firm way in which Sextus was known by.

We know that the two Sextuses lived at about the same time, with enough variability in the estimates that they could have been the same person. Since we know when Marcus Aurelius ruled, we can be confident that Sextus of Chaeronea was teaching towards the end of his rule, which was from 161 to 180 CE.

Figuring out when Sextus Empiricus lived is more difficult. The last datable reference in the works of Sextus Empiricus is to Emperor Tiberius, 42 BCE to 38 CE. So, Sextus cannot have lived earlier than that. Diogenes Laertius refers to Sextus Empiricus as being a student of Herodotus of Tarsus (the *Suda* says Sextus Empiricus was a student of Herodotus of Philadelphia, so presumably the same Herodotus), who was the student of Menodotus of Nicomedia. Enough is known about Menodotus to estimate that he flourished around 80-100 CE. This would suggest that Sextus Empiricus was born circa 140-160 CE and died circa 220-230 CE.[177] We also have reference to Sextus Empiricus in the works of Pseudo-Galen[178] that suggests that Sextus Empiricus may have flourished between 150 and 170.

The biography of Marcus Aurelius in the *Historia Augusta* has a passage in it that many people think identifies Sextus of Chaeronea as a Stoic philosopher, which would rule out his being the same person as Sextus Empiricus. While the *Historia Augusta* is so full of errors it is considered to be unreliable – and this can be considered reason enough to dismiss this

---

176 Luciano Floridi, *Sextus Empiricus: The Transmission and Recovery of Pyrrhonism*, 2002, p 6 .

177 For a thorough analysis, see Luciano Floridi, *Sextus Empiricus: The Transmission and Recovery of Pyrrhonism*, 2002, pp 3-7.

178 Pseudo-Galen, *Introductio*, 14.683 K.

evidence – it can be demonstrated that the passage actually indicates that Sextus was not a Stoic. Here's what that passage says:

> Furthermore, his zeal for philosophy was so great that, even after he joined the imperial family, he still used to go to Apollonius' house for instruction. He also attended the lectures of Sextus of Chaeronea, the nephew of Plutarch, Junius Rusticus, Claudius Maximus and Cinna Catulus, Stoics. He went to lectures by Claudius Severus too, as he was attracted to the Peripatetic School. But it was chiefly Junius Rusticus, whom he admired and followed – a man acclaimed in both private and public life and extremely well practiced in the Stoic discipline.

The above is not the translation commonly used to support the idea that Sextus of Chaeronea was a Stoic. What is given in that translation is "Sextus of Chaeronea, the nephew of Plutarch, Junius Rusticus, Claudius Maximus and Cinna Catulus, *all* Stoics." I don't include "all" in my translation because in the original Latin there's no "all" in the text.[179] It's just "Stoics."

I see four possible ways to interpret this sentence.
1. All four philosophers were Stoics.
2. Marcus attended the lectures of these four philosophers, and some Stoics whose names were not recorded.
3. Sextus of Chaeronea was Plutarch's nephew and therefore not a Stoic while the other three philosophers were Stoics.
4. Sextus of Chaeronea was Plutarch's nephew and therefore not a Stoic. Marcus also attended the lectures of these other three philosophers, and some Stoics whose names were not recorded.

The first and third interpretations could be ruled out if we were to know that one of the other three philosophers was not a Stoic. Of the four philosophers in this list, we only know that one of them was a Stoic: Junius Rusticus. We don't know whether Cinna Catulus and Claudius Maximus were, but there is reason to suspect that Claudius Maximus was not a Stoic. Apuleius mentions Claudius Maximus in regard to defending himself against a charge of magic in a case being judged by Claudius Maximus. According to Apuleius, Maximus was a pious man who shunned ostentatious displays of wealth and was intimately familiar with the works

---

179 tantum autem studium in eo philosophiae fuit ut adscitus iam in imperatoriam tamen ad domum Apollonii discendi causa veniret. audivit et Sextum Chaeronensem Plutarchi nepotem, Iunium Rusticum, Claudium Maximum et Cinnam Catulum, Stoicos.

of Plato and Aristotle. Why not Stoic authors, such as Zeno, or Chrysippus, or Epictetus? In his defense Apuleius mentions the sternness of his judge's philosophy. This might be considered to imply that the judge was a Stoic, as Stoicism is notable for its sternness. On the other hand, Apuleius was clearly trying to flatter his judge. Sternness would seem to be a virtue in a judge, and neither the Platonists nor the Peripatetics were typically accused of being lacking in sternness. Although we cannot be certain, based on what Apuleius tells us Claudius Maximus was more likely a Peripatetic or a Platonist than he was a Stoic.

What's most notable in the passage is that Sextus gets described as an individual – the "nephew of Plutarch." The next three names do not get such additional individual descriptions. The author may have intended "Stoics" to apply to just those following three names and not Sextus, as he'd already said something else about Sextus: that he was Plutarch's nephew, implying that Sextus taught in his uncle's tradition – which was not Stoicism. Indeed, Plutarch was highly critical of Stoicism.

We have another mention of Sextus connecting him to Plutarch that further informs why this connection is so important. In the introduction to Apuleius' novel, *The Golden Ass,* the protagonist says he was:

> ...descended of the line of that most excellent person Plutarch, and of Sextus the philosopher his nephew, which is to us a great honor....

That the author would have his protagonist be kin to Plutarch and Sextus and have him state this at the beginning of the tale implies that there's something distinctive about the protagonist's family and that this foreshadows the story. *The Golden Ass* happens to be the oldest surviving example of a novel employing magical realism. It whimsically plays on making things we normally think of as being false as being true. Since we know that Plutarch was a Platonist who defended Academic Skepticism, and we know that Academic Skeptics and Pyrrhonists were routinely criticized by the philosophers of other schools as being disconnected from reality, the protagonist's kinship reads as an inside joke to the philosophical cognoscenti.[180] Plutarch and Sextus see uncertainty between what is real and what is imaginary; hence, the reader can expect the same to be true about the protagonist, being a member of that family. This signals to the philosophically knowledgeable reader that what is going to follow in the novel is a highly sophisticated, outlandish tale that reads like it is real, but

---

180 This has been previously noted by others, but attributed to being about Platonism, not Pyrrhonism/Academic Skepticism. See S.J. Harrison, *Apuleius: A Latin Sophist,* p 217.

is it is imaginary – which is precisely what happens.

It's a clever joke, assuming, of course that Sextus was a Pyrrhonist. If Sextus had been a Stoic the joke wouldn't work and therefore it wouldn't make sense to mention Sextus.

Apuleius, coincidentally, is our source for the proverb that "familiarity breeds contempt; rarity brings admiration." In *Apuleius: A Latin Sophist*, scholar S.J. Harrison says that this proverb is "very likely to derive from a previous source … though in fact I can find no earlier source."[181] Although not stated as a proverb, there is an earlier source. The proverb concisely states the ninth mode of Aenesidemus, which is about how things are perceived as a function of occurrence.

Connecting Sextus with Plutarch implies that Sextus taught in his uncle's tradition. We know that Plutarch strongly criticized Stoicism,[182] and we know that he defended Arcesilaus and Academic Skepticism, despite the fact that the Academy was no longer inquiryist. We know that Plutarch wrote three now-lost books with titles suggesting an affinity with Pyrrhonism: *Whether One Who Suspends Judgment on Everything Is Condemned to Inaction, On Pyrrho's Ten Modes*, and *On the Difference between the Pyrrhonians and the Academics*. We know that Plutarch was careful to show arguments on both sides of each issue. Like a Pyrrhonist, he attached little importance to theoretical questions and doubted the possibility of ever solving them.

A perhaps meaningful coincidence is that one of Plutarch's two brothers was named Timon. Perhaps this was in honor of the most famous person to have ever held that name, Timon the Pyrrhonist philosopher. And if not, it at least suggests the family was not repelled by such a connection. According to Plutarch, his brother Timon was particularly likeable. This likeability may have positively disposed young Sextus towards the philosopher who shared the name of his own father or uncle.

Plutarch may have been even more supportive of Academic Skepticism than his surviving works suggest, as most of his Academic Skeptic works did not survive. Plutarch's student, Favorinus, self-identified as an Academic Skeptic,[183] despite the fact that the Academy was long-since

---

181 S.J. Harrison, *Apuleius: A Latin Sophist*, p 149.

182 Plutarch wrote three books criticizing Stoicism: *On Stoic Self-Contradictions*; *The Stoics Speak More Paradoxically than the Poets*; and *Against the Stoics, on Common Conceptions*.

183 The observations here about Plutarch, Favorinus, and Epictetus come from Jan Opsome, "Favorinus versus Epictetus on the Philosophical Heritage of Plutarch. A Debate on Epistemology", in Judith Mossman (ed.), *Plutarch and His Intellectual World*, 1997, p. 17-39. Opsome, however, does not connect these arguments to the identity of Sextus Empiricus.

no longer inquiryist. Favorinus – and perhaps his teacher, too – saw little difference between Academic Skepticism and Pyrrhonism. Aulus Gellius, a student of Favorinus, wrote:

> ...although the Pyrrhonists and the Academics express themselves very much alike about these matters, yet they are thought to differ from each other both in certain other respects and especially for this reason – because the Academics do, as it were, "comprehend" the very fact that nothing can be comprehended, and, as it were, decide that nothing can be decided, while the Pyrrhonists assert that not even that can by any means be regarded as true, because nothing is regarded as true.[184]

Galen, in his critique of Favorinus, speaks of the Academics and Pyrrhonists as if they are interchangeable.[185] Favorinus wrote two now-lost books, the *Pyrrhonist Ten Modes* and *Against Epictetus*, indicating his interest in Pyrrhonism and his antipathy to Stoicism.

In the *Discourses* Epictetus gives the following argument against the Academic Skeptics that alludes to Plutarch, who was a priest of the Pythia – the oracle of Apollo at Delphi – and who served as an interpreter of the oracle's cryptic messages.

> "That there are no gods, and, if there are, they take no care of men, nor is there any fellowship between us and them; and that this piety and sanctity which is talked of among most men is the lying of boasters and sophists, or certainly of legislators for the purpose of terrifying and checking wrong-doers." Well done, philosopher, you have done something for our citizens, you have brought back all the young men to contempt of things divine. "What then, does not this satisfy you? Learn now, that justice is nothing, that modesty is folly, that a father is nothing, a son nothing." Well done, philosopher, persist, persuade the young men, that we may have more with the same opinions as you who say the same as you. From such principles as these have grown our well-constituted states; by these was Sparta founded: Lycurgus fixed these opinions in the Spartans by his laws and education,

---

184 Aulus Gellius, *Attic Nights*, Book 11, Section 5.

185 Galen, *De optima doctrina*, 1,40-52 K.; Fav. frg. 28.

that neither is the servile condition more base than honorable, nor the condition of free men more honorable than base, and that those who died at Thermopylae died from these opinions; and through what other opinions did the Athenians leave their city? Then those who talk thus, marry and beget children, and employ themselves in public affairs and make themselves priests and interpreters. Of whom? Of gods who do not exist; and they consult the Pythian priestess that they may hear lies, and they repeat the oracles to others. Monstrous impudence and imposture.[186]

Favorinus struck back for Plutarch in his now-lost book, *Against Epictetus*, which was an imagined dialogue between Epictetus and one of Plutarch's slaves, cleverly implying that it was beneath Plutarch's dignity to rebut the former slave Epictetus, and that the task was appropriately delegated to his slave. To this, we appear to have Epictetus' retort:

If I were slave to one of these men, even if I had to be soundly flogged by him every day, I would torment him. "Boy, throw a little oil into the bath." I would have thrown a little fish sauce in, and as I left would pour it down on his head. "What does this mean?" "I had an external impression that could not be distinguished from olive oil; indeed, it was altogether like it. I swear by your fortune." "Here, give me the gruel." I would have filled a side dish with vinegar and fish sauce and brought it to him. "Did I not ask for the gruel?" "Yes, master; this is gruel." "Is not this vinegar and fish sauce?" "How so, any more than gruel." "Take and smell it, take and taste it." "Well, how do you know, if the senses deceive us?" If I had three or four fellow-slaves who felt as I did, I would have made him burst with rage and hang himself, or else change his opinion. But as it is, such men are toying with us; they use all the gifts of nature, while in theory doing away with them.[187]

This is Epictetus, author of the famous slogan, "bear and forbear." This is Epictetus, who says in *The Enchiridion:* "Remember that it is not he who

---

186 Epictetus, *Discourses*, Book 2, Section 20.

187 Epictetus, *Discourses*, Book 2, Section 20.

gives abuse or blows who affronts, but the view we take of these things as insulting. When, therefore, anyone provokes you, be assured that it is your own opinion which provokes you."[188] This is Epictetus totally losing his highly proclaimed Stoic self-control and *apatheia* to go out of his way to torment someone merely because that person holds a different opinion.

Given that:

1. Plutarch and the Stoics were publicly and bitterly at odds with each other;
2. The differences between Academic Skepticism and Pyrrhonism were generally considered to be minor;
3. Plutarch probably viewed Pyrrhonism favorably; and
4. Support of Academic Skepticism was dying out in the Academy.

It would seem to be both unremarkable and congruent with his family's philosophical tradition for Plutarch's nephew to situate himself with the Pyrrhonists; whereas joining the Stoics would have been a remarkable defection to the enemy – a remarkable defection about which we suspiciously have no remarks! Wouldn't it seem that the mentions we have of Sextus of Chaeronea being Plutarch's nephew would include something about his shocking repudiation of his famous uncle? The situation would be like Karl Marx having a famous nephew who was a proponent of capitalism. How could all of those mentions we have of Sextus of Chaeronea being Plutarch's nephew resist adding such scandalous tidbit that Sextus had devoted his life to repudiating his uncle's philosophy? It seems just too juicy to omit. Surely some Stoic would want to gloat about this.

There's also a peculiarity in the works of Sextus Empiricus that suggests Sextus is Plutarch's nephew. Jonathan Barnes mentions this peculiarity in the introduction to his and Julia Annas' translation of *Outlines of Pyrrhonism*.

> ... in the second century one of the major Dogmatic traditions was Platonism; and in Sextus Platonism plays a very minor role. Where Sextus does not speak promiscuously of "the Dogmatists," his chief adversaries are always the Stoics.[189]

The explanation Barnes supposes for this is that Sextus was a mere copyist who assembled the works of others into a new form, and it just so

188 Epictetus, *Enchiridion*, Section 20.

189 Sextus Empiricus, *Outlines of Skepticism*, edited by Julia Annas and Jonathan Barnes, 2000, p xvi.

happened that those older works were produced when Stoicism was the dominant philosophy. This is plausible, but unconvincing. The explanation appears more to be just another expression of the contempt in which Barnes holds Sextus. What Barnes did not appear to consider is that if Sextus Empiricus were Plutarch's nephew, his avoidance of criticizing the Platonists would make complete sense. Sextus would be most inclined to attack the school that attacked his uncle and least inclined to criticize the school his uncle belonged to. This is exactly what Sextus does.

49
Marcus Aurelius on Sextus Empiricus

Fables should be taught as fables, myths as myths, and miracles as poetic fancies. To teach superstitions as truths is a most terrible thing. The child-mind accepts and believes them, and only through great pain and perhaps tragedy can he be after-years relieved of them. In fact men will fight for a superstition quite as quickly as for a living truth – often more so, since a superstition is so intangible you cannot get at it to refute it, but truth is a point of view, and so is changeable.

Attributed to *Hypatia of Alexandria*[190]

I feel safer with a Pyrrho than with a Saint Paul, for a jesting wisdom is gentler than an unbridled sanctity.

Emil Cioran,
A Short History of Decay

As we can now have some confidence that it is Sextus Empiricus that Marcus Aurelius wrote about in the introduction to his *Meditations*, we now know something about Sextus' character. Marcus speaks of him in glowing terms as a master of Pyrrhonist practice. Sextus was a shining example of living his philosophy.

The *Meditations* was a notebook Marcus wrote for himself. It does not appear that he intended it for publication. It is poorly organized and not carefully written. As is common with notes to one's self, Marcus occasionally leaves out words and writes ambiguously. He's writing to remind himself of things, not to be clear to others or precise with his wording. The *Meditations* is available in several different translations, and because of the ambiguities in the text, the translations vary substantially, sometimes so much they seem to give contrary meanings.

When a translator encounters an ambiguity in a text the translator must fill in that ambiguity or explain the ambiguity parenthetically. Most translators of the *Meditations* appear to assume that Sextus must have been a Stoic. Pierre Hadot even claims Sextus as a Stoic in his book about the *Meditations, The Inner Citadel.* Knowing that Marcus was referring to a Pyrrhonist and not a Stoic sheds new light on this passage and renders

---

190 http://wisdomofhypatia.com/blog.php?s=quotations-from-hypatia

some interpretations of the text, such as Hadot's, erroneous.

Here is my rendering of what Marcus said about Sextus. Appendix 1 gives more detail with regard to how this passage can be interpreted.

> From Sextus, a benevolent disposition, and the example of a family governed in a fatherly manner and the mind of one according to nature; and venerable natural character, and to look carefully after the interests of friends, and to tolerate ignorant persons and those who form suppositions without consideration: he had the power of readily accommodating himself to all, so that conversation with him was more agreeable than any flattery; and at the same time he was most highly venerated and those who were with him prized the time; and the intellectual grasp and the ingenious discovering and ordering of lessons for necessities for life; and he never showed anger or any other disturbing emotion, but was free from disturbing emotions, and also most affectionate; and he could express approbation unobtrusively and he possessed various, great knowledge without ostentation.

Based on what we know about Sextus Empiricus, what Marcus Aurelius says here seems to fit him, and nothing he says would allow us to conclude he was talking about someone else. We know from the works of Sextus Empiricus that he was a methodical systematizer, and uniquely possessed of various, great knowledge. These are two remarkable things about him. Marcus remarks about both.

We would also expect, based on Sextus' being a master of Pyrrhonism, that he would never display any sign of anger or disturbing emotions, to be entirely imperturbable while at the same time being full of kindly affection, and to be focused on essential decisions of life – i.e., following the criterion of action – rather than being distracted with non-essential ideas of the non-evident. Marcus mentions these notable characteristics, too.

Marcus said that Sextus was patient with those who made suppositions without consideration. The making of suppositions, particularly those without consideration, is what Pyrrhonism is a treatment for. One would expect a master of Pyrrhonism to be adept at handling such people.

Some people think the comment about Sextus having a mind in accord with nature indicates that Sextus was a Stoic because Stoicism advocates that one should live according to nature. But having a mind in accord with nature also fits with Pyrrhonist teachings about following the guidance of nature, as part of the criterion of action.[191] So, such a comment would apply equally as well to a Pyrrhonist as to a Stoic. Besides, at that time, and still today, saying that someone behaves in a natural manner is a compliment, regardless of whatever philosophy that person may hold.

We are fortunate to have this passage from Marcus, as it gives us insight into the behavior of a practicing master of Pyrrhonism.

---

191 Contrary to Pierre Hadot's conclusion that this line confirms that Sextus of Chaeronea was a Stoic. *The Inner Citadel*, 1998, p 14.

50

Pyrrhonist Influences on Marcus Aurelius

So many schools of philosophy pass away without a successor.... Who is there to hand on the teachings of Pyrrho? *Seneca the Younger*[192]

Are you dead Pyrrho?
I doubt it. *Stobaeus*[193]

As it seems that Marcus studied under Sextus Empiricus, the question arises about whether a Pyrrhonist influence appears in the *Meditations*. While in the *Meditations* Marcus is primarily focused on Stoic practice, he seems to be less dogmatic than other surviving Stoic writers. Twice he approvingly quotes Epicurus and at points expresses suspension of judgment between the Epicurean view that everything in the universe is made of atoms and the Stoic view that divine providence guides the universe. While he doesn't cite any Pyrrhonists, the *Meditations* has many comments that could easily have been made by a Pyrrhonist, and a few comments that may be considered Pyrrhonist views contrary to Stoicism.

Sextus may not have been the only influence on Marcus in this regard. Alexander Peloplaton, also known as Alexander of Seleucia, also taught Marcus. Like Sextus, one version of Alexander's name refers to what Alexander was known for: "Peloplaton" means "clay Plato" – Alexander was a disciple of Favorinus – and the other version refers to where he was from. Marcus mentions Alexander in the *Meditations* shortly after his mention of Sextus, saying:

> From Alexander the Platonic, not frequently nor without necessity to say to anyone, or to write in a letter, that I have no leisure; nor continually to excuse the neglect of duties required by our relation to those with whom we live, by alleging urgent occupations.[194]

---

192 Seneca, *Natural Questions*, 7.32.2.

193 *Anthology*, Volume 2, Section 576.

194 Marcus Aurelius, *Meditations*, 1.12.

A search for Pyrrhonist influences in the *Meditations* turns up several passages.

> 2.15 "Everything is what you suppose it to be." For the words that were addressed to the Cynic Monimus are clear enough, and clear too, the value of that saying, if one accepts its inner meaning, so far as it is true.[195]

To demonstrate how difficult the *Meditations* is to translate, here's an alternative translation by George Long of this same section. This version appears to mean something different.

> Remember that all is but opinion. For what the Cynic Monimus said is obvious: and obvious too is the use of what he said, if a man accepts what may be got out of it only as far as it is true.

This is an easily misinterpreted passage in the *Meditations,* as proper understanding of it requires background information that Marcus doesn't mention. Monimus was a Cynic philosopher who lived in the 4th Century BCE. He was a student of Diogenes the Cynic and was acquainted with Crates the Cynic, who was the teacher of Zeno of Citium, the founder of Stoicism.

What Monimus actually said was that "everything is *tuphos.*" Translating *tuphos* is tricky. Literally it means "mist" or "smoke." Figuratively it means "vanity" or "delusion." In the first translation above it is rendered "as what you suppose it to be" and in the second as "opinion." Neither of these seems to properly convey this Cynic idea. Instead it is rendered to read more like some similar Stoic ideas.

Further, the second translation misses an important point which the first translation captures, and in capturing this it changes the meaning of the final few words, "as far as it is true." The words that were addressed to Monimus were his own words, which were used to point out that his statement was self-refuting, i.e., the statement applies to itself and is therefore a delusion, too. This doesn't appear in the second translation. Marcus acknowledges that the statement is paradoxical, and points to the inner meaning of the paradox, which he accepts. To go on to the point where the statement refutes itself is to go beyond where the statement is true. That's what is meant by "as far as it is true."

Sextus discussed the same saying Marcus mentions, saying:

---

195 Robin Hard's translation, 2016.

Xeniades of Cornith, as we pointed out earlier, says that nothing is true, and perhaps also Monimus the Cynic when he says that "everything is tuphos" – which is thinking of things that are not as if they are.[196]

Sextus also noted two other ideas from Monimus. One was that Monimus thought that no criterion of truth had been demonstrated. The other was that Monimus "compared existing things to a scene-painting and supposed them to resemble the impressions experienced in sleep or madness."[197]

As Stoicism was derived from Cynicism, the views of the Cynics, particularly those who predated Stoicism, were influential with Stoics. Monimus' views, however, do not sit comfortably with Stoicism. They're nearly Pyrrhonist. Marcus cites only a few philosophers by name in his *Meditations*. Why should he approvingly cite Monimus, who was not particularly influential and whose philosophy is contrary to Stoicism? Perhaps it was because Sextus repeatedly reminded Marcus of this Cynic philosopher whose positions were nearly Pyrrhonist.

4.3 The world is nothing but change. Our life is only perception.[198]

The Pyrrhonists argued that the only thing that was accessible to us were the appearances, i.e., what we perceive. The Stoics argued that our life was more than just perception, that knowledge was attainable.

5.10 Things are wrapped in such a veil of mystery that many good philosophers have found it impossible to make sense of them. Even the Stoics have trouble. Any assessment we make is subject to alteration – just as we are ourselves. Look closely at them – how impermanent they are, how meaningless. Things that a pervert can own, a whore, a thief. Then look at the way the people around you behave. Even the best of them are hard to put up with—not to mention putting up with yourself. In such deep darkness, such a sewer – in the flux of material, of time, of motion and things moved – I don't know what there is to value or to work for.[199]

---

196 Sextus Empiricus, *Against the Logicians*, Book 2, Section 5.

197 Sextus Empiricus, *Against the Logicians*, Book 1, Section 88.

198 George Long's translation, 1945.

199 George Long's translation, 1945.

This passage is the only one where Marcus mentions Stoicism. Note how he refers to "the" Stoics, not "we" Stoics. Who would be those philosophers Marcus declares to be "good?" Logically they would be Pyrrhonists and Academic Skeptics, philosophers who say that reality is acataleptic. Marcus concedes that the Stoics have trouble making sense of things, and concludes that any assessment – including those of the Stoics – is subject to being found wrong. This is what the Pyrrhonists claim. Marcus concludes with his own doubts about what to value or work for, contrary to the clear dogma of the Stoics: one should value and work for virtue.

> 5.23 Keep in mind how fast things pass by and are gone – those that are now, and those to come. Existence flows past us like a river: the "what" is in constant flux, the "why" has a thousand variations. Nothing is stable, not even what's right here. The infinity of past and future gapes before us – a chasm whose depths we cannot see. So it would take an idiot to feel self-importance or distress. Or any indignation, either. As if the things that irritate us lasted.[200]

Marcus points out that the "why" has a thousand variations. That's a Pyrrhonist observation – that there is a multiplicity of explanations of the non-evident – and one that is contrary to the Stoics who, on many matters, narrowed the why down to a single dogma. Marcus also here agrees with what Pyrrho said: nothing is stable, not even what's right here.

> 5.26 Let the leading and ruling part of your soul stand unmoved by the stirrings of the flesh, whether gentle or rude. Let it not commingle with them, but keep itself apart, and confine these passions to their proper bodily parts; and if they rise into the soul by any sympathy with the body to which it is united, then we must not attempt to resist the sensation, seeing that it is of our nature; but let not the soul, for its part, add thereto the conception that the sensation is good or bad.[201]

That things are inherently neither good nor bad is a Pyrrhonist teaching.

> 6.52 You have it in your power to form no opinion about this or that, and so to have peace of mind. Things

---

200 George Long's translation, 1945.

201 George Chrystal's translation, 1902.

material have no power to form our opinions for us.[202]

Pyrrhonism and Stoicism have in common this idea of forming no opinion as a means of producing peace of mind. This is but one of the many mentions of this idea in the *Meditations*.

> 6.57 Honey tastes bitter to a man with jaundice. People with rabies are terrified of water. And a child's idea of beauty is a ball. Why does that upset you? Do you think falsehood is less powerful than bile or a rabid dog?[203]

Sextus uses this honey example twice in *Outlines of Pyrrhonism*[204] among many examples of differencing preferences. One of the objectives of Pyrrhonist practice is to eliminate false opinions from one's mind, doing so via the questioning and arguing that Marcus is doing here.

> 7.16 The mind doesn't get in its own way. It doesn't frighten itself into desires. If other things can scare or hurt it, let them; it won't go down that road on the basis of its own perceptions. Let the body avoid discomfort (if it can), and if it feels it, say so. But the soul is what feels fear and pain, and what conceives of them in the first place, and it suffers nothing. Because it will never conclude that it has. The mind in itself has no needs, except for those it creates itself. Is undisturbed, except for its own disturbances. Knows no obstructions, except those from within.[205]

Marcus notes here that mental suffering is due to making conclusions about non-evident matters, and the elimination of suffering is through eliminating the conclusions. Epoché eliminates conclusions. Like the Pyrrhonists, he accepts that physical pain exists and it is natural to wish to avoid it.

> 8.49 Pronounce no more to yourself than what appearances directly declare. It is told you that so-and-so has spoken ill of you. This alone is told you, and not that you are hurt by it. I see my child is sick; this only I see. I do not see that he is in danger. Dwell thus upon first

---

202 George Chrystal's translation, 1902.

203 George Long's translation, 1945.

204 Sextus Empiricus, *Outlines of Pyrrhonism*, Book 1, Sections 102 and 211.

205 George Long's translation, 1945.

appearances; add nothing to them from within, and no harm befalls you: or rather add the recognition that all is part of the world's lot.

8.50. Is the gourd bitter? Put it from you. Are there thorns in the way? Walk aside. That is enough. Do not add, "Why were such things brought into the world?" The naturalist would laugh at you, just as would a carpenter or a shoemaker, if you began fault-finding because you saw shavings and parings from their work strewn about the workshop. These craftsmen have places where they can throw away this rubbish, but universal Nature has no such place outside her sphere. Yet the wonder of her art is that, having confined herself within certain bounds, she transforms into herself all things within her scope which seem to be corrupting, or waxing old and useless; and out of them she makes other new forms; so that she neither needs matter from without nor a place where to cast out her refuse. She is satisfied with her own space, her own material, and her own art.[206]

This is typical Pyrrhonist advice to stick with the appearances and not add non-evident speculation to them. The gourd is bitter to you. The thorns are in your way. Such appearances and judgments are relative to you, but good and bad do not exist in nature. Whatever we might think of as bad, nature puts to good use. We cannot judge nature.

11.11 It's the pursuit of these things, and your attempts to avoid them, that leave you in such turmoil. And yet they aren't seeking you out; you are the one seeking them. Suspend judgment about them. And at once they will lie still, and you will be freed from fleeing and pursuing.[207]

Suspension of judgment is at the core of Pyrrhonist teachings. Pyrrhonism points out that the source of mental turmoil is the pursuit of things that are thought to be good by nature, and the avoidance of things that are thought to be bad by nature. Epoché lets the soul lie still, ending the pursuing and fleeing.

---

206 George Chrystal's translation, 1902.
207 Gregory Hays' translation, 2002.

....

Appendix

Appendix 1
Translation of the *Meditations*

I have no expertise in translating ancient Greek, but the *Meditations* is often used in teaching ancient Greek; in addition to that, study aids for the complicated terms in the text are readily available. I give here what Marcus said about Sextus, noting all of the key terms in the text and alternative meanings from the ones I propose. This is a clunky way of reading, but nuances in what Marcus says here matter. As the various Hellenistic schools of philosophy widely agreed about the behaviors and dispositions of wise people, it's difficult to assess a person's philosophy based on their behavior. What they argued about was how one became wise.

From Sextus, a benevolent disposition,
> [*eumenes*: beneficial, well-disposed, favorable, gracious, kindly]

and the example
> [*paradeigma*: pattern, example, sample]

of a family
> [*oikos*: household]

governed in a fatherly manner
> [*patronomizo: pater + nomizo*, to use customarily, like a father's ruling]

and the mind
> [*ennoia*: the act of thinking, consideration, meditation; a thought, notion, conception, mind, understanding, will, manner of feeling, and thinking]

of one according to nature;
> [*phusis*: with kata, according to nature]

and venerable natural character,
> [*semnos*: august, venerable, to be venerated for character, honorable]
> [*aplastos*, adverb: literally as not molded; in a natural state]

and to look carefully after the interests
> [*kedemonikos*, adverb: providential; verb as one who is in charge in the sense of being a guardian]

of friends, and to tolerate
> [*anektos*: from *anechomai*, to endure]

ignorant persons
> [*idiotes*: a private person, common man, unskilled],

and those who form suppositions
> [*oiomai*: to suppose, to think, to mean]

319

without consideration:
    [*atheoretos*: lacking in *theoreo* (*theoria*) – contemplation, looking at]
he had the power of readily accommodating
    [*euarmostos*: to be well harmonized (*harmozo*)]
himself to
    [*pros*: in the direction towards which]
all, so that conversation
    [*homilia*: association, converse]
with him was more agreeable
    [*prosenes*: soft, gentle]
than any flattery; and at the same time
    [*kairos*: occasion, opposed to *kronos*]
he was most highly venerated
    [*aidesimos*: exciting shame; connotes fear and respect]
and those who were with him prized the time; and the intellectual grasp
    [*katakeptos*: intelligent, methodical, able to keep in check: from *kata-lambano*, to seize, apprehend]
and the ingenious discovering and ordering
    [*taktikos*: pertains for ordering of soldiers]
of lessons
    [*dogmata*, teachings, principles, lessons, dogmas]
for necessities for
    [*eis*: into]
life; and he never showed
    [*parecho*: to exhibit, hold in readiness; with para, beside]
anger
    [*orge*: wrath, anger]
or any other disturbing emotion,
    [*pathé*: emotion, affection, feeling]
but was free from disturbing emotions,
    [*apathes*: not to have *pathé* or unmoved]
and also most affectionate;
    [*philostorgos*: *philos* (dear, loving) + *orge* (wrath, anger) forming a negation of anger]
and he could express approbation
    [*euphemos*: uttering sounds of good omen]
unobtrusively
    [*apsopheti*, adverb: without noise or sound],
and he possessed various, great knowledge
    [*polumathes*, having learned much, polymathic]
without ostentation.
    [*anepiphantos*, adverb: without *phaneros* or making manifest or evident]

Acknowledgments

I'd like to thank Stephen Batchelor for his particularly helpful contributions to this manuscript regarding skeptical interpretations of Buddhism and how these might relate to Pyrrhonism, and also how to best understand Montaigne's approach to Pyrrhonism.

This book is indebted to Christopher Beckwith, both because of the clear demonstration he achieved in his book, *Greek Buddha*, connecting the origins of Pyrrhonism with Pyrrho's interpretation of the Buddha's Three Marks of Existence, but also his many helpful comments on this manuscript.

Not only was Pyrrhonism partially dependent on Buddhist thought in its origins, but there's good reason to suspect that later Buddhist thought was partially dependent upon Pyrrhonist thought. As this book is about how to practice Pyrrhonism, that subject is outside the scope of this book. However, the works on this subject by Thomas McEvilley, Matthew Neale, and Adrian Kuzminski have been influential to my understanding of Pyrrhonism and have helped me leverage my understanding of Buddhism to reverse engineer from Buddhism to fill in some gaps in what we know about Pyrrhonist practice.

I'd also like to thank my Zen teacher, James Ishmael Ford Roshi, for his encouragement in following this rather unorthodox path. There are certain coincidences in life that must be recognized. Somehow, I ended up as the Zen student of the only Zen teacher in the world who not only worked as a Unitarian Universalist minister, but in the past had been a Gnostic priest and a practitioner of Sufism. That I wanted to go off and do Pyrrhonism did not seem so strange as it might have to some other teacher. One should not, however, extrapolate from this that he endorses Pyrrhonism.

Many of the participants in the Facebook Pyrrhonism discussion group have been particularly helpful in clarify my thoughts on Pyrrhonism, most particularly John Douglas.

I began writing this book shortly before my mother's death. Sadly, I couldn't even tell her about it because a stroke had destroyed her mind. In my 30s she confided to me that when she was pregnant with me, she prayed fervently that I should become wise. That's a matter for other people to judge. With the publication of this book, it would seem that I have now contributed something meaningful to the wisdom literature, and I am honored to have at least in this small way contributed to my mother's wishes, as she gave more to me than I was ever able to repay her for.

Printed in the USA
CPSIA information can be obtained
at www.ICGtesting.com
CBHW032345120824
13112CB00004B/52